EAST ANGLIA

With Best Wishes to the Brighton family
of Achany where the writing of the book
was finished in June 1978.

Peter and Barbara Steggall.

The Regions of Britain

EAST
ANGLIA

PETER STEGGALL

Robert Hale Limited · London

ISBN 0 7091 7398 9

Robert Hale Limited
Clerkenwell House
Clerkenwell Green
London EC1

PRINTED IN GREAT BRITAIN BY
EBENEZER BAYLIS AND SON LIMITED
THE TRINITY PRESS, WORCESTER, AND LONDON
AND BOUND BY REDWOOD BURN LIMITED

Contents

Contents

Illustrations

Suffolk Punch and Red Polls at Benacre (*Peter Steggall*)
Cottages at Lavenham (*Peter Steggall*)
Flatford Mill and Willy Lott's Cottage (*Peter Steggall*)
Wood Walton Fen—Great Raveley Drain (*Peter Steggall*)

between pages 144 and 145

Terrington St. Clement Church (*Peter Steggall*)
Wisbech—Ely Place, Library and Church
(*Cambridgeshire County Council*)
River Nene—East Lighthouse and Wisbech Pilot (*Peter Steggall*)
Denver Sluice and New Bedford River (*Peter Steggall*)
Mullicourt Aqueduct, Outwell (*Peter Steggall*)
Ouse Washes looking north-east from Coveney
(*Cambridge University Collection*)
Whitemoor Up Yard, March, from Control Tower (*Peter Steggall*)
Ely Maltings and Cathedral (*East Cambridgeshire District Council*)
Little Ouse joining Great Ouse, Brandon Creek (*Peter Steggall*)
Wicken Fen Windpump (*Trevor James*)
Kings Lynn Custom House (*Peter Steggall*)
Santon Downham forestry village (*Trevor James*)
Forest Walk, Santon Downham (*Trevor James*)

between pages 192 and 193

Thetford Church and Thomas Paine (*Trevor James*)
Helmingham Hall (*Trevor James*)
Anglesey Abbey (*Peter Steggall*)
Snape Maltings—Music School, Concert Hall and old maltings
(*Trevor James*)
Helmingham Estate Cottages (*Trevor James*)
Lode Mill, Cambridgeshire (*Trevor James*)
A.B.M. Maltings and B.S.C. Sugar Factory, Bury St Edmunds
(*Peter Steggall*)
Gough's Maltings, Bury St Edmunds (*J. Gough & Sons Ltd*)
Snape Maltings—roadside buildings (*Trevor James*)

The author wishes to thank those who gave permission for the use of their copyright photographs

(The maps were drawn by J. V. Todd, and were based upon Ordnance Survey Maps with the permission of the Controller of Her Majesty's Stationery Office—Crown Copyright Reserved)

Acknowledgements

This is by far the most difficult part of the book to write. So many people have given their time answering my letters, taking me round buildings, and guiding me to sources of information. I cannot name them all, but I hope they will realize from what appears in the book that their help has been both useful and appreciated. Friends and colleagues have stimulated me by their interest and encouragement, and I am particularly grateful to John Todd for drawing the maps and to Trevor James for many of the photographs. Staffs of local and other authorities, county libraries and the Suffolk Records Office, agents for the Elveden and Helmingham Estates, and the managers of Easton Farm Park and Letheringham Farms, have all been most co-operative. As the book finishes with Snape, as a sort of climax and epitome, I hope I may, without offence to others, mention especially Mr William Servaes and Mr John Trew, respectively general manager and secretary of the Aldeburgh Festival—Snape Maltings Foundation, and Mr Robert Ling, caretaker of the Maltings Concert Hall.

Mr Chesterfield, for the publishers, has patiently and promptly responded to all my pleas for advice on the inevitable problems I have encountered.

Some of the books and reports which I consulted are listed in the bibliography, but this is by no means comprehensive, and does not include Ordnance Survey Maps which were, of course, invaluable.

Finally, I must record that, but for the encouragement and constructive comments of my wife, Barbara, and her company on journeys all over East Anglia, and above all her typing of the whole book, it would never have been completed.

Introduction and Theme

East Anglia by conventional standards is flat and dull, but when looked at closely its landscape reveals a fascinating and unexpected variety. Its history and character are different from those of the rest of the country. It exists in comparative isolation from the rest of Britain, by its position clear of the main national routes and its shape as a large peninsula more than half surrounded by sea and estuaries. It is near the Continent and has always been subject to invasions and influences from across the North Sea.

Our fellow Britons in the rest of the kingdom seem to know very little of the region; most of them know it only as a rounded bulge on the map and they condemn it as flat and uninteresting. As a native, I cannot agree with them and I offer no apology for thinking East Anglia is different and special.

When I first thought of writing a book, it was to be a straight, descriptive book but a labour of love and nostalgia. In the early nineteen hundreds, and indeed up to 1939, before the great surge of tourists and growth reached the quieter regions, many delightful books on all parts of Britain were written by topographical explorers. I still enjoy Donald Maxwell's *Unknown Suffolk* and *Unknown Norfolk*, and H. Alker Tripp's *Suffolk Sea Borders*, all written in the 1920s; and W. A. Dutt's *Highways and Byways in East Anglia*, published in 1901. They were wonderfully illustrated by evocative water colours and pen-and-ink drawings. A later book is perhaps the best, and probably the last in the romantic style. Julian Tennyson's *Suffolk Scene* was published in 1939, just before the world was changed by one of its greatest disasters; Tennyson himself died fighting the Japanese in Burma. It is a book full of love and enthusiasm for his native county. Books such as these inspired me and stimulated my interest in East Anglia, and no doubt sowed the seeds which now germinate in this book, which alas cannot claim to possess any quality approaching theirs.

Since the war topographical writers have acknowledged that it has become unrealistic merely to describe rural beauty and urban charm, and to ignore modern trends in building, agriculture and social conditions. They now elaborate on geological and social history and other influences that have shaped the land and the people, but I think a little space should still be given to personal and subjective appreciation.

My earliest recollections are of infancy and school days in Ipswich and of visits to my grandmother in Bury St Edmunds where I had been born in her house on Angel Hill. Of Ipswich in those days, I remember mostly the docks and the sailing barges, the railway station and the steam trains, the last of the trams and the first of the trolley-buses, and the beauty of the Orwell estuary seen from the paddle steamer sailing down to Harwich and Felixstowe. Of Bury I recall the inside and outside of the old timber-framed, plaster-fronted house facing up Northgate Street, the ducks and swans and the old walls and ruins in the Abbey Gardens, the spaciousness of the Angel Hill and the narrowness of the old streets in the centre of the town. I remember very little of the countryside except the heaths beside the railway between Ipswich and Felixstowe. On my ninth birthday I was destined to leave Suffolk of which I had become passionately fond even at such an early age. I was then in exile for over thirty years, four of them spent overseas in wartime. During all those years, East Anglia, and Suffolk in particular, seemed like the promised land.

At last, in 1962, came the opportunity to return to Suffolk, indeed to Ipswich, with work that enabled me to see and learn more of the county and the region. My exile had ended and I could now explore and enjoy East Anglia in fact rather than in fancy. Time indeed began again to "fetch good [East Anglian] minutes for me, instead of carrying them aimlessly away", to use the remarkably apt words of Miss E. Arnot Robertson in *Ordinary Families*, a novel set on the shores and waters of the Orwell. Had I not returned, I would have been tempted to write nostalgically of my early days in Suffolk and of my all too rare visits between 1930 and 1960. I trust I can now write more objectively on what I have discovered and rediscovered. This book will not be a sentimental journey, although it will include some personal views and a few relevant reminiscences. I have not tried to be comprehensive or erudite on the geology, archaeology and history of the region; those aspects have been very well covered by experts and their works are there for those who require specialized information. Neither have I written a guide book (such have been published in plenty, though they vary greatly in quality) and I have concentrated on the coast and countryside rather than on the towns.

My long absence gave my imagination a good deal of exercise and I became accustomed to visualizing the region in a panoramic way, which helped me and helps me still, to see it whole. It is after all a large and distinctive part of England with strong characteristics in its shape and its landscape, its people and its towns and villages. I suppose I must declare the boundaries I have used in my study. Some experts limit East Anglia to Norfolk and Suffolk; some add the old Cambridgeshire, others take in all between the Thames estuary and the Wash. The government's East Anglia Economic Planning Region leaves out Essex, but extends west to include the whole of the new Cambridgeshire which consists of the old counties of Cambridgeshire, the Isle of Ely, Huntingdon and Peterborough. The area I have covered corresponds mainly with that of the official region, but I have wandered a little over the boundaries where the nature of the country demanded it, and have left out parts which seem to belong elsewhere.

After writing on the Origins and Evolution of the region, I have divided it into parts based on the five main types of country, but the difficulties of defining their boundaries are all too apparent. The chapters on the coast include the Broads, the heaths and woodlands of north Norfolk and east Suffolk, and the Naze at Walton in north-east Essex. For the East Anglian Heights I have taken an area with strong characteristics deriving from the presence of the chalk, and have included the northern tip of Hertfordshire, southern Cambridgeshire, north-west Essex and parts of west Suffolk and north-west Norfolk. It was almost impossible to draw a boundary for Farming Country, but it is broadly 'High Suffolk' and mid-Norfolk. For the Fens I had to restrain myself from straying far into Lincolnshire. Departing from honourable precedents, I have made the Breckland subordinate to the Forest as that is now the dominant feature of the stony lands between Bury St Edmunds and Swaffham, with the few remaining heathland areas widely scattered between the new pine forests and the reclaimed agricultural land of the great estates.

East Anglia is very rich in interest for the naturalist, and it is in the nature reserves and other protected lands that we can see more clearly the natural changes that are still going on. This is particularly true on the coast, but there are several remarkable reserves in the Fens and the Breckland where former 'natural' conditions can be maintained and studied. We can learn a great deal of what has been happening for centuries over larger tracts of country, and we can still enjoy and study natural habitats and flora and fauna, all of which were much more widespread before being transformed or destroyed by man as farmer, landowner and builder. I have written quite a lot on this topic in various chapters, as it is very significant and seems to be of interest to an increasing number of people.

I had insufficient space to describe the many splendid houses and parks, and the varied industries related especially to an agricultural region, but I hope the selection of *Mansions and Maltings* in the last chapter gives some indication of their importance.

My exploration of East Anglia has impressed me with the scale and speed of change, and this theme has become almost an obsession. Because of its geological nature and its nearness to London and Europe, the region has always changed faster than most, in natural and unnatural ways. Physiographical changes continue apace, especially on the coast and in the Fens. Ecological changes are spectacular and often alarming with new farming methods, drainage and afforestation. Man is making great changes with the effects of the growth of population and resultant increases in recreation, traffic, port development, Continental trade and tourism. All this has led to the existence side by side of traces of primitive, early civilization and startling modern developments. We have the site of the Sutton Hoo burial ship not far from large military air bases; on the coast Orford Castle and Aldeburgh Moot Hall contrast with radar establishments and a nuclear power station; near Cambridge, one looks from the Iron Age hill fort at Wandlebury towards the radio astronomy telescope at Lord's Bridge.

East Anglia was, until about 1962, one of the quietest and most sparsely populated parts of southern Britain. It has retained much of its peace and remoteness and charm, but in the 'sixties and 'seventies its population, industry and traffic have grown faster than the national average. The Continental connection, over 2000 years old, is in the late twentieth century being strengthened in new and dramatic ways. I have therefore taken the theme of the changing landscape of a region I have always loved and have come to know better in the past sixteen years. I have tried to describe in a broad, but I hope reasonably accurate and objective way, the natural and human shaping of the coast and countryside from earliest times, what it looks like now (as a general rule I have not described what I have not seen) how and why it is still changing, and what may happen to it in the future. The reader is left to judge whether this theme emerges satisfactorily from the various chapters. If it does, he may be stimulated to go out and explore East Anglia and to make good in his own way whatever I have not described adequately.

Finally, I hope that my analysis of change is relieved and warmed by some evidence of the beauty and loneliness of the coast and heath and marsh, and the richness of their wildlife.

I

Origins and Evolution

"EAST ANGLIA, that countryside so largely founded on glacial deposits almost as young as man." Thus Jacquetta Hawkes epitomizes the evolution of the region, and gives the vital clue to the reasons for the continuing rapid changes in the landscape. A land so young, and clothed with glacial sands and gravels and clays, and alluvial soils, is inevitably subject to erosion by weather, water and sea; and its fertility—and even its barrenness in parts—ensure intense activity by man especially as farmer and forester.

There are three main zones, a clay belt flanked by areas of lighter soils, but each of the three contains a variety of soils, and reveals to a greater or lesser degree how it has come about and what lies beneath it. The chalk, a tremendously deep stratum, underlies the whole of East Anglia, but is near the surface only in a belt across south Cambridgeshire and west Suffolk to Bury St Edmunds, emerging again on the sides of the Gipping valley north-west of Ipswich, and the 'downs' and cliffs of the extreme north-west corner of Norfolk.

The Fens are part of a vast, low-lying, flat area that reaches from Cambridge to the Wash, westwards to Peterborough, and northwards up to Lincoln between the chalk and limestone ridges, and along the Lincolnshire coast. The main, central area is of black peat, much of it below sea level, but the northern part is of brown silt from about the latitude of March to the Wash. Bordering the north-eastern Fens and running up the east side of the Wash is a belt of greensand, with sandy soils, heaths and birch woods, notably on the royal estate of Sandringham. Here and there pockets of clay formerly supported more dense woodland and must indeed have helped the growth of the splendid trees in parts of the royal gardens and parkland.

East and north-east of the greensand is the 'Good Sand' region, so named by Arthur Young in the late eighteenth century. It was in the main anything but good until after the tremendous agricultural improvements in the previous hundred years by those great Norfolk landowners, Coke of Holkham and Townshend of Raynham. It is mostly an 'upland' area, behind the coastal dunes and marshes, and even now is far from being uniformly fertile. The remaining poorer, sandy, gravelly areas, as at Weybourne and Salthouse, carry heathland, which though infertile is beautiful particularly in its closeness to the sea.

Mid-Norfolk, covered with boulder clay once thickly wooded, is fertile farmland, but still bears some oakwoods. South Norfolk, mostly lower in elevation, has even heavier soils and was also covered with thick woodland. High Suffolk has probably the heaviest boulder clay soils, and in the flatter parts, in spite of modern agricultural methods, drainage is still a problem in a wet season. Here too were dense forests and a few old woods remain, but here I think there has been the greatest transformation effected by man in recent years and it continues apace. These parts of Norfolk and Suffolk will be described in my chapter on Farming Country.

To the north of Norwich, between mid-Norfolk and the Broads, is an area of glacial loams, with sandy stretches which were once heathland but are now either cultivated or afforested. Broadland, unique in Britain and probably in the world, consists of alluvial valleys with winding rivers linking the numerous 'lakes' or broads, bordered by wide flat grazing marshes, and overlooked by peninsulas and islands of higher, fertile land.

East of the Fens and straddling the Norfolk–Suffolk border, is the Breckland, an area of about 400 square miles most of which a hundred years ago was barren heathland. Since then thousands of acres have been ploughed and cultivated or grazed, and nearly 50,000 acres have been afforested. But, for reasons which I shall explore later, a considerable part of Breckland still keeps a measure of the primitive beauty and remoteness of wild heathland. The other sandy part of the region is known as the Sandlings, and stretches along the Suffolk coast from the River Stour to Lowestoft. Its soils are mainly glacial sands and gravels, improved to moderate fertility at the northern and southern extremities, but still mainly poor between the Deben and the Blyth. In that section much heathland remains, but conversion to arable continues and about 8,000 acres have been afforested since 1920.

The coast of East Anglia is in a sense a separate geological part of the region. The dunes and marshes and shingle banks are peculiarly distinct and separate from the immediate hinterland, but the nature of much of the coast depends on the soils and structure of what lies behind it, and there is a belt of variable width, including estuaries, heaths and woods, that shares the feel and atmosphere and climate of the sea.

Having thus set the general scene, I must try to compress the region's geological history into a few pages, explaining the origins of form and soils and rocks, and the way in which the landscape has developed.

There seem to have been three eras. The first ran from earliest geological times millions of years ago, up to the end of the Ice Age, and was almost entirely the work of nature. The second began as the ice receded and man returned about ten thousand years ago, and continued until the eighteenth century; it was very much a saga of his colonization and taming of the landscape, though until late Saxon times much of the region was still uncultivated and was still evolving naturally by the effects of wind, weather and water. The third period started at about the time of the Industrial Revolution, since when man has had increasing power to modify the landscape more swiftly and drastically than in earlier centuries during which changes had proceeded by traditional methods to meet inevitable but natural needs as population grew. This is the period in which we now live, and has a future on which I comment in my Epilogue. In this first chapter, however, I intend to discuss the general developments since the eighteenth century only briefly, leaving the details of accelerated and continuing change to the middle chapters which deal with the various parts of the region.

Although south-east England, including East Anglia, is the youngest part of Britain, and very young indeed by comparison with the highlands, the chalk was laid down in the seas of the Cretaceous Period, a very long period even in geological history, running it is thought from about 140 million years ago to 75 million years ago. During this long, slow era, the sea rose gradually, leaving only the higher parts of Wales and Scotland above water; over the south-east the chalk was deposited layer by layer on the sea bed. The deposits included small marine creatures which became fossilized; and sponges, the silica in whose skeletons became concentrated into nodules of flint. All this happened under the sea, long before man appeared, but, when the sea receded, chalk and flint were to be vital factors in the pattern of man's activities; and were to have profound effects on the look of much of the East Anglian countryside and of many of its buildings.

But I am running ahead too fast. The deposit of the chalk was followed by shelly red crag and coralline crag. The level of the sea fell, leaving these crags, now seen particularly in eastern Norfolk and Suffolk, where the lower reaches of the great Rhine river ran from Europe on a winding course to meet the sea at the coast which was then at about the latitude of the Dogger Bank. Britain was thus once again connected to the Continent. The rivers deposited beds of peat in

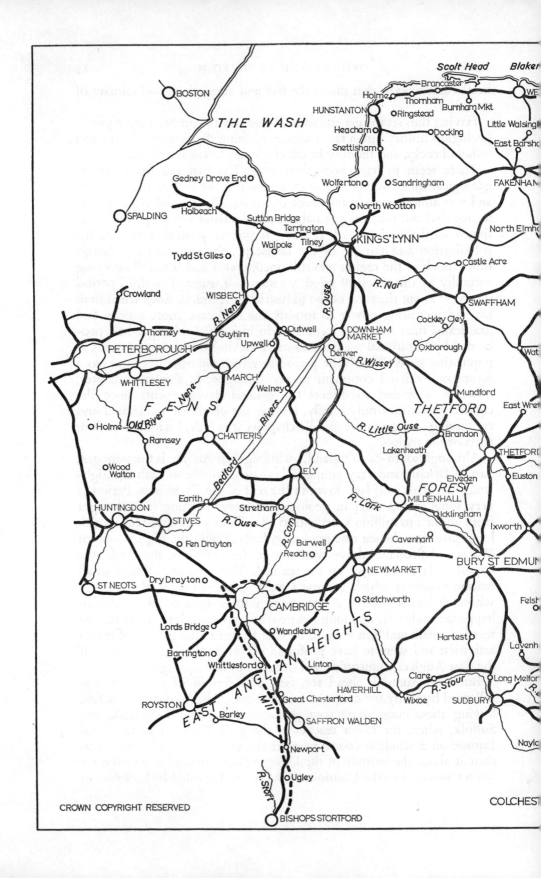

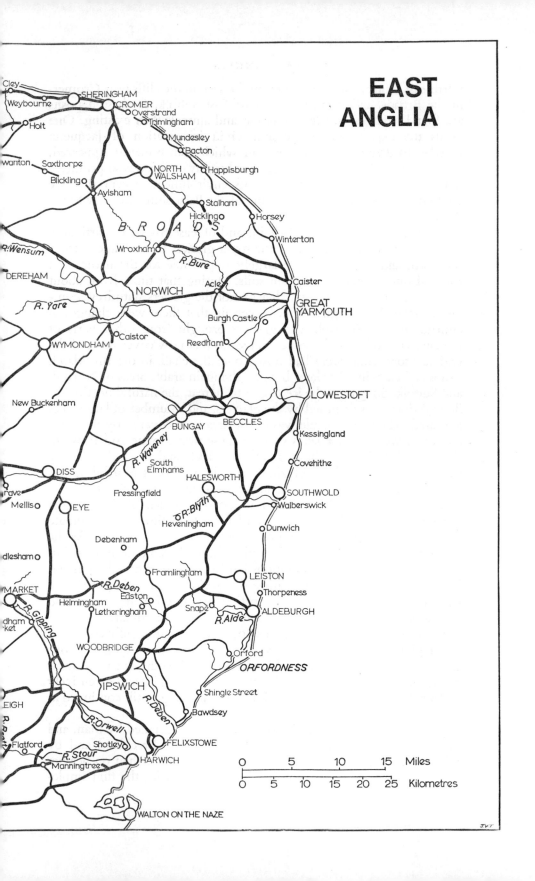

EAST ANGLIA

Cley
Weybourne
SHERINGHAM
CROMER
Overstrand
Trimingham
Holt
Mundesley
Bacton
wanton
Saxthorpe
NORTH
WALSHAM
Happisburgh
Blickling
Aylsham
Stalham
Hickling
Horsey
R.Wensum
Wroxham
Winterton
DEREHAM
R.Bure
Caister
NORWICH
Acle
R.Yare
GREAT
YARMOUTH
Burgh Castle
WYMONDHAM
Caistor
Reedham
LOWESTOFT
New Buckenham
BUNGAY
BECCLES
Kessingland
R.Waveney
South
Elmhams
Covehithe
DISS
HALESWORTH
rave
Fressingfield
SOUTHWOLD
Mellis
EYE
R.Blyth
Walberswick
Heveningham
Dunwich
Debenham
dlesham
Framlingham
LEISTON
R.Deben
Thorpeness
MARKET
Helmingham
Easton
Snape
ALDEBURGH
Letheringham
R.Alde
R.Gipping
dham
ket
WOODBRIDGE
Orford
ORFORDNESS
IPSWICH
Shingle Street
EIGH
R.Deben
Bawdsey
R.Orwell
Flatford
Shotley
FELIXSTOWE
R.Stour
HARWICH
Manningtree

0   5   10   15   Miles
0   5   10   15   20   25 Kilometres

WALTON ON THE NAZE

JVT

north-east Norfolk where it can now be seen in the cliffs near Cromer, in the Broads, and along the coast of East Suffolk. In these deposits are found evidence of the vegetation and animals then existing. One needs the expert knowledge and vivid imagination of Jacquetta Hawkes to describe the landscape in which man presently appeared, apparently just before the Ice Age. But his way of life was so primitive that it had little lasting effect on his environment, except that we continue to find the flint implements of the Palaeolithic or early Stone Age.

The landscape of most of Britain, and of East Anglia in particular, was to be drastically altered by the great glaciers that advanced from the north and west, and were largely responsible for the nature and form of our present scenery and soils. During that time, from about 500,000 B.C. to 8000 B.C., whether or not the glaciers withdrew completely from East Anglia, it seems certain that there were changes in climate and in sea level. The glaciers brought from other parts of Britain many of the soils, stones and sands that now cover most of the region. Stony sands were laid down over the chalk in the Breckland, loams and clays in what later became the main arable areas of Norfolk and Suffolk. Soon after the ice began to retreat, the natural northward flow of rivers was dammed by the glaciers, and a number of large lakes appeared. The most notable was in the area now covered by the Fens, and there were smaller lakes such as those near Hoxne and Ipswich. Peat was deposited on the beds of these lakes and lies today on the surface of fertile arable or grazing lands; in north-east Norfolk it was later to be excavated in peat cuttings thus forming the Broads.

When the ice finally retreated it left over much of East Anglia spreads of clay, sand and gravel, and for a long time a cold climate supporting a tundra vegetation of birch and pine and willow. As the climate gradually turned warmer, pine forests became dominant, but these were superseded by deciduous hardwood forests of oak, elm and lime; beech came later still. During this period, the melting of the ice caused the sea level to rise again, cutting Britain off from Europe and giving us the beginnings of our maritime, temperate climate.

After the retreat of the ice, about 8000 B.C., man gradually colonized our region, and from about 6000 B.C., the greatest changes in our landscape were to be made by his activities. While this is true of most of lowland Britain, it probably happened more rapidly and extensively in East Anglia, and here too, I think, natural changes still continued at a faster rate than elsewhere.

At first the spread of the forests could not be curtailed by man, and he lived on the lighter, sandy areas such as the Breckland and by rivers and estuaries where the tree cover was thinner than on heavier lands. Evidence of occupation has been provided by the flint implements, though their extremely durable nature and the movement of surface materials by glaciers have made it difficult to be sure of the age of the relics, or of man's movements and settlements. Those early men lived mainly by hunting in the areas where the forests were not too thick, and the remains of trees and animals are found in the sands and crags of east Suffolk, the Fens and north Norfolk. For centuries, indeed up to Neolithic times, from 2500 B.C. to 1500 B.C., the population was so small, and its way of life and lack of need and power to clear the forests were such that only small inroads were made, and the landscape was modified more by nature than by man. The wetter and milder climate before and during the Neolithic and Bronze Ages favoured the deciduous forests which took the place gradually of the pine and hazel of drier times. The countryside was affected too by variations in sea level. Before Neolithic times a fall in level had deposited the lower peat in the Fens and left them habitable and cultivable. But a rise later caused the deposit of clay in Neolithic times. The upper peat was laid down in the Bronze Age when the sea level fell again. Thus were the bases laid of the fertility of the Fens, and thus is illustrated the complexity of the processes of nature. They were in many ways more complex and certainly more swift than the evolution of the hard highland regions, and East Anglia's present geological characteristics are that much more difficult to see, to understand and to describe.

Apart from the alternating settlement and abandonment of the Fens because of fluctuations in sea level, human settlement was concentrated for a very long time in two main areas of light land with access to the sea and rivers for communication. These were in the Breckland and in the Sandlings especially around Ipswich. While Stone Age man has left few extensive traces and we know relatively little of the pattern of farming and land use, flint mines and a couple of henge monuments have been found, and a great quantity of flint tools and some pottery. It seems that in the latter part of the Neolithic Age more settled farming methods were developed and some of the easier forest fringes were cleared with flint axes. This continued into the Bronze Age, whose people left clues to their way of life—and death—in the shape of metal tools and burial mounds. These mounds, or barrows, must have been, and indeed still are in places such as Martlesham and the Breckland, significant features in the scene. Many of the barrows of the Bronze Age and later times have been obliterated by development and ploughing, but more and more is being learnt about their form and distribution when they show up as crop marks seen and photographed from the air. The fact that cremation became normal practice, especially from about 1400 B.C., must have resulted in considerable felling of trees for fuel.

The development of farming and the consequent acceleration of forest clearance were helped in the later years of the Bronze Age by the introduction of the light plough, a much more effective implement than the hoe. The effect of early Iron Age farming on the landscape is not easy to assess, but the exploration of a site at West Harling on the eastern edge of the Breck revealed details of a farmstead in circular form. The archaeologists deduced that these farmers kept livestock, cultivated cereals and hunted wild animals. Flint tools were still made and used and many remains of pottery have been found.

The Iron Age people, themselves settlers from the Continent, suffered invasion in the third century B.C. by people from France. This led to the creation of hill forts such as Wandlebury, south-east of Cambridge. These, in our comparatively low East Anglian landscape, are not as spectacular as the Iron Age forts of Wessex, but Wandlebury by its size and position must have been a very prominent feature before it became shrouded in woodland 2,000 years later. The Ipswich people were left in peace until about 100 B.C. when they were subjugated by the Belgae who had the advantages of heavier implements enabling them to clear more woodland and to cultivate the heavy loams. Increasing insecurity and strife led to the concealment of hoards of valuable ornaments of gold and bronze and of coins. Some of these came to light only in the nineteenth and twentieth centuries. We cannot help being thrilled as we look at the woods of Ken Hill, Snettisham, and think of the events of those far-off days, and of the treasures lying under the ground for so many centuries before their discovery in such a remarkable state of preservation.

At about the time of the Roman invasion of south-east England, the Iceni were constructing defences at Thetford, Warham, Holkham and Wighton in Norfolk, against threats by the Belgae, a pattern to be repeated many times through history as successive waves of invaders arrived from the Continent and as the dominant people of various times fought and suppressed uprisings.

The Roman Age lasted about 400 years and left a vast amount of archaeological evidence. It was the first period of really considerable economic and population growth, especially in East Anglia. It saw the creation of towns and ports in a countryside that previously existed on a purely rural economy. The region was opened up by the construction of roads which incidentally still form an important part of our modern road system, and by the drainage of the Fens and the clearance of forests for agriculture. North-east Essex and south-east Suffolk were governed from Colchester (Camulodunum) and Roman roads extended far to the north-east with settlements at places such as Coddenham and Caistor-by-Norwich, but for some time the barrier of forest in High Suffolk continued to separate the Romans from the

Iceni to the west. The Romans built the first large stone buildings to be seen in East Anglia, but their remains are mostly slight as later people used the materials to build for themselves; this practice continued well into the Middle Ages in a region with very little native building stone.

Even during their first century of occupation the Romans had been establishing local settlements and capitals. At Caistor-by-Norwich they set up a small cantonal capital, with huts based on a gridiron pattern of streets on a site of about fifty acres of gently sloping land overlooking the valley of the little River Tas. In the late second century the town grew in importance, and stone buildings were erected and a massive outer wall. That was presumably the area, now enclosed by ditches and banks, that we see today as we look across the valley from the main road or the railway, or from the medieval churchyard in the south-east corner; and from the air at certain seasons, crop marks reveal still the pattern of Roman streets.

Farming methods from the Iron Age survived into Roman times and developed slowly until more settled times arrived. Then a hierarchy evolved of villas, farmhouses, and workers' huts, evidenced by excavated remains, but in general little is known of the Roman field system over most of East Anglia. It seems that cereals were grown widely, including in the Fens where on the silt the pattern of Roman fields has been revealed in sharp and fascinating contrast with the modern pattern of fields and ditches.

Another cause of change must have been the greatly increased demand for cheap crockery, met by the establishment of many kilns in boulder-clay areas where the raw material was present and where the clearance of woodland provided the charcoal for fuel. Iron was extracted from the greensand of north-west Norfolk, where traces of smelting are still found. Buildings were required on a larger scale, and therefore flint, sandstone and hard chalk were quarried.

Through much of Roman history in Britain cremation was the general practice, and the remains were placed in barrows, some impressive examples surviving at Bartlow on the Essex–Cambridge-shire border and described in the chapter on the East Anglian Heights. During the third century A.D., East Anglian towns grew, stone build-ings replacing some of the less solid buildings of wattle and daub. It seems that sheep grazed the Breck and other areas of light land, and one wonders if these looked then rather like parts of the present Sandlings where the existence of sheep in past centuries is recorded in surviving heathland areas still called Sheep Walks.

In the late third century, the Saxons were harassing the coasts of the Channel, and the Romans built massive fortresses to guard harbours which they were using as 'naval bases'. These forts were spaced out from the Solent to the Wash, and even their remains in the twentieth century are both extensive and impressive in many cases. Brancaster guarded the approach to the Wash, but has disappeared, its walls presumably having been demolished for the building materials; its site is now separated from the sea by nearly a mile of marshes, creeks and dunes. Walton guarded the mouths of the Deben, Orwell and Stour, but disappeared under the sea as the southern coast of Suffolk was eroded in the late Middle Ages. Burgh Castle, which stood above the great estuary serving Caister-by-Yarmouth and Norwich, still has its massive walls and round bastions on three sides of a great six-acre rectangle in which corn now grows in a peaceful countryside just above the confluence of the Waveney and the Yare. The harbour has narrowed since the Romans left it, but can still be seen in the mind's eye as one looks across the broad flat miles of grazing marshland and the wide estuary of Breydon Water towards Caister on its low hill nearly five miles away.

After the middle of the fourth century, the growth of towns slowed down, and farming continued to flourish, except that periodic flooding with brackish water made the Fens untenable soon after A.D. 400. Not long after this many Romans were recalled to the Continent, and the evidence of buried hoards suggests insecurity and haste as their hold on England declined. Grass grew over the ruins of their towns, forts and villas, the Fen farms were abandoned because of flooding, and the countrymen reverted to a primitive way of life side by side with immigrant barbarians. The Dark Ages followed, seen but dimly and darkly from our own times because of the sparseness of informative relics.

During the Saxon Age, further invaders came from north-west Germany and Denmark, mainly to the Wash and up the rivers that flow into it, to settle round the edge of the Fens which were then a watery waste. The linear earthworks which lie across the main lines of communication and are still so impressive on the map and on the ground probably date from the fifth century. Most of them are on the chalk of eastern Cambridgeshire or the sands of the Breckland, and begin and end in natural obstacles. Some run from river to river, like the Fossditch from the Little Ouse to the Wissey. Some stretch from Fen to woodland, like the most famous and fascinating of them all, the Devil's Ditch which runs for seven miles from the village of Reach up to the woods of Stetchworth 350 feet higher.

It is difficult to discover what the farms and the landscape looked like, but more and more evidence is coming to light, not only in East Anglia but elsewhere, notably at Mucking in Essex, which should help us to imagine and understand the environment and life of those far-off days. At West Stow, close to the River Lark, archaeologists have built huts of timber, clay and thatch as part of the reconstruction of a Saxon village, and a similar project has been carried out on an Iceni site at Cockley Cley; both sites are on the fringe of Breckland.

In the sixth and early seventh centuries, the population was much increased by further immigrants, many of whom settled in south-east Suffolk and this area became the centre of the East Anglian kingdom. Some of them had originated in southern Sweden, a fact confirmed by the nature and contents of the now famous burial ship discovered in the summer of 1939 at Sutton Hoo near Woodbridge; a staggering discovery that was at the time eclipsed by the imminence of the Second World War.

Christianity began to spread through East Anglia in the early seventh century, an event of tremendous significance socially and in the landscape, with the founding of churches and monasteries. In the early days they were built of timber, and little survived into later ages, but the beliefs and the sites became established and more permanent buildings took their place in late Saxon times and after the Norman Conquest. Most of these churches, modified and restored or neglected, and the remains of some of the monasteries, survive to this day.

Agriculture continued to be the basis of the economy, but there were some townships, of which Ipswich was a considerable trading centre in what was still the dominant part of East Anglia. With all its activity, the early Saxon Age was not as significant as the Iron Age and the Roman Age that came before. Indeed it was a time of long, slow and fairly steady recovery after the rather sudden decline at the end of the Roman occupation. The late Saxon Age which followed, from A.D. 850 until the arrival of the Normans, really laid the foundations of medieval and modern East Anglia, despite, as R. Rainbird Clarke has said, "the cataclysm of the Danish invasions". He went on to record that "by 1066, Norfolk and Suffolk had developed into two of the wealthiest and most populous counties in England".

The sacking and burning of towns, villages and farms in those troubled years must have wrought profound changes on the appearance of town and country, and destroyed much evidence of the life and work of the people, but in spite of this there were remarkable advances in the creation and growth of settlements and towns and in the rural economy. Clearance of forests to extend arable and grazing and to secure fuel and timber, went ahead as never before, and by 1066 a pattern of roads and towns and villages existed that has largely survived to modern times. That is clearly an over-simplification, but it is borne out by the contents of Domesday Book with its records of the location and numbers of people, stock and 'taxable localities'.

Many late Saxon activities changed the landscape. Salt pans were created beside the Wash and other estuaries, to provide salt for the preservation of meat. Peat was cut in what were to become the Broads, and in the Fens, perhaps as an alternative fuel to wood in places where timber was already becoming more scarce. Towns grew in size and importance as trading and financial centres. Norwich, Thetford, Dunwich, Bury St Edmunds and Ipswich were the largest, and it is interesting to reflect on their respective histories and fortunes since then. These are separate, fascinating studies, each worthy of a book of its own. The Danish attacks on churches and monasteries in the late ninth century must have slowed down the spread of Christianity, and probably explain why only late Saxon ecclesiastical remains are found.

After 1066 the Normans quickly dominated East Anglia and consolidated their control by building castles and private fortresses which were then new and significant features of town and country, and indeed they remain prominent to this day in places such as Orford, Framlingham, Castle Rising and Thetford.

Many monasteries were built in the eleventh and twelfth centuries, contributing much to the life and appearance of the countryside, and leaving eventually some very extensive and picturesque ruins as at Castle Acre and Bury St Edmunds. The monasteries usually held large estates, and contributed much to the expanding agricultural economy, with incidental changes in the landscape, by ploughing heathland and clearing woodland. Many parish churches were built, to become and to remain through the centuries the spiritual, social and visual focus of the villages. Continental trade grew, and trade with other parts of Britain, as the growing population needed more food, wine, pottery and stone for building the larger churches, and the cathedrals and castles.

From Domesday Book onward there are many written and graphic sources of information to supplement the visual, material evidence in the countryside and in museums. Estate and monastic records and accounts, early pictures, tapestries and maps, the published tales of early travellers leading up to Joshua Kirby, Daniel Defoe, Celia Fiennes and William Cobbett, give us a panorama, with tantalizing blanks, of East Anglia through the centuries between the Norman Conquest and the Industrial Revolution. We have also the work of the agricultural writers beginning with Thomas Tusser in the 1500s, resuming with Arthur Young in Napoleonic times, to tell us of the successive agricultural revolutions.

This middle period of my general account of the changes in the landscape was a very eventful one, though in the slow growth of towns and industry and in the virtual absence of mining and quarrying, the effects were neither so dramatic, disturbing or damaging as in, for example, the Black Country or South Lancashire. Nevertheless the emphasis moved very much to man-made changes within a frame of natural change, especially on the coastal and fenland fringes of the region. In the early Middle Ages a rise in sea level again converted the Fens into a swampy waste that was not properly drained and reclaimed until the seventeenth century. The coast, particularly in northeast Norfolk and in Suffolk, suffered increasing erosion of which the most spectacular example was at Dunwich.

Farming flourished and languished in turn, but the overall trend was one of increasingly rapid growth under the manorial system, though in East Anglia there were more freemen than average for England and the open-field system was by no means as common as elsewhere. Woodlands were felled for timber, fuel, buildings and ships, and for arable cultivation. In places, as early as the eleventh and twelfth centuries, large areas were 'emparked' for hunting, and later for the establishment of stately homes. Some of the banks and ditches of medieval parks can still be traced, and the one at Staverton in Suffolk has been well studied and documented; its boundaries and characteristics are still there for all to see.

From Norman times and through the Middle Ages, vast numbers of sheep were grazed. This animal was a vital feature of medieval rural economy over much of England, but in such areas as the Cotswolds and East Anglia it was of much more than local importance. The chalk grassland was admirably suited for sheep, and the woollen industry flourished. The East Anglian Heights were more open and green than now, as the sheep prevented the growth of scrub, and maintained a short turfy sward. The towns and villages benefited from the prosperity brought by the production, and later the weaving, of wool, and the export of wool and cloth. Fine houses and many of the finest churches were built during the era of the 'golden fleece'. Lavenham is perhaps the best, and certainly the best-known, example, with its unrivalled streets of timber-framed houses and its splendid church. One of the most impressive of the old buildings, the Guildhall in the Market Place, is now owned by the National Trust and contains a small permanent exhibition devoted to the history and manifestations of the woollen industry. This exhibition reminds one of the open landscape of the Middle Ages, and the creation of so much beauty in the villages and small towns, in particular the magnificent church towers that are such a feature of the countryside.

While sheep grazed on the broad acres of the chalk hills, arable and dairy farming spread on the heavier land of High Suffolk and mid-Norfolk, with the steady clearance of the woodlands. Inevitably there developed a complex system of roads and lanes to serve the holdings and to connect them to the villages; and of ditches to drain the heavy, fertile land. These roads, lanes and ditches formed a network much more dense and involved than on the lighter lands of the Breckland and the Sandlings, and determined to a great extent the pattern of our present landscape. I use the word 'pattern' deliberately rather than 'appearance', because, while the framework of roads, lanes and tracks has remained, many of the hedges and ditches which divided the intervening spaces have gone, and in many ways the arable areas have become very different to behold.

The early medieval years also settled the pattern of the centres of towns and villages, and where modern redevelopment has not been sweeping and insensitive, we are fortunate still to have the human scale, interest and intimacy of the old streets. This is superbly illustrated in Bury St Edmunds, and can be abundantly seen and felt in walking round, and, incidentally, can be appreciated and understood in a comprehensive and instant way from the air. Though few of us have the opportunity to see the town from above, we cannot fail to be fascinated and instructed by the overall scheme and the detail revealed in superb modern aerial photographs.

By royal gift and favour, and upon the dissolution of the monasteries in the sixteenth century, large mansions and estates were established or disposed, as indeed they were elsewhere in England, but here, in the fifteenth and sixteenth centuries the art of building in brick was revived and perfected in a way that rivals the splendour and beauty of other regional styles in stone or 'black and white'. In Norfolk we still see, in a remarkable state of preservation, the splendid ornamentation in mellow, moulded red brick at East Barsham Hall, and the impressive moated Hall at Oxborough. Suffolk has equally fine brick houses at Helmingham and Long Melford, and just beyond the edge of my area, are Layer Marney Towers in Essex. Scattered throughout East Anglia are many fine but smaller examples of the highest achievement in design and brick-laying in the beautiful mellow colours special to the region. Smaller houses, farms and barns had to use materials more readily to hand, and thus we see many local variations from the pebble, brick and pantile of Blakeney and Stiffkey to the timber studwork and plaster of Lavenham, with other local specialities in, for example, the clunch of the Breckland barns and the carstone cottages of north-west Norfolk. All these materials have been used for centuries and have created distinctive styles some of which I have described in their settings in other chapters.

The big houses of Elizabethan days were set in large estates, but the layout of the parks was rather informal until the 1700s saw the start of the 'designed' landscape, the consciously 'natural' parks that must in their early years have looked rather formal, but which became less so as the trees grew and the vistas and avenues softened. The comparatively tame landscape of East Anglia could not produce the hilly splendours of Stourhead or Scotney, but very beautiful parks were created at Audley End and Shortgrove on the chalky sides of the Cam valley, and the enthusiasm and skill of Coke and Townshend were not confined to making the Norfolk deserts fertile, but included the creation of fine parkland scenery at Holkham and Raynham.

As I sketched out the framework for this chapter, there came to me the idea that there must have been a point in time—or a relatively short period in history—when the man-made changes in the landscape progressed from those resulting from the natural evolution of his activities, to more unnatural, sweeping and positively planned and executed changes. It may be only a question of degree and speed, but before this point or period in many parts of Britain, including East Anglia, man's activities had been mainly evolutionary, traditional and inevitable results of the growth of population and the consequent need for food and space and shelter. Forests were cleared and land cultivated; the felled timber was used for building homes and farms and boats, and provided fuel, tools and weapons. Later came radical alterations resulting from legal changes in the holding of land, for example the enclosure movement. But even until a later date, the clearance of woods and the cultivation of poor land was going on until it must have seemed that all the available land on this small island was under plough and grazing. This stage coincided, however, with the so-called Industrial Revolution which had various effects on the rural life and scene. People left the land for the towns, which had to grow to house their rapidly growing population, and to accommodate new factories and mills and mines. Thus the towns encroached physically on the countryside, and drained the farms of labour just at the time when a tremendous increase in food production was called for. The outward and visible effects in East Anglia were not so dramatic as in the industrial areas, but our region lost its farm workers, and indeed is still losing them in the twentieth century, and being an important arable area, struggled to maintain and increase its production of corn and root crops.

What has followed has been by no means a simple progression or trend towards greater efficiency and production on the farm. The ups and downs of agricultural prosperity, very much at the mercy of national and international economics and politics, made it very hard for any but the very wealthy to make and carry out any firm, long-term plans for improvement. But it is surely from the time of the Industrial Revolution that we can trace the history of the 'agricultural revolution' in farming method and science, towards the large-scale and often drastic exercises of the mid-twentieth century. It started with Coke and Townshend, scientific and mechanical innovators, achieving even then results on the grand scale; and continued at Elveden in the

twentieth century with the more sophisticated methods of Lord
Iveagh and his son, who were however still limited by the stages then
reached in the development of farm machinery and agricultural
chemicals.

Their efforts in the second quarter of this century were followed, or
rather overtaken and extended, by the era, largely initiated in the
desperate years of the Second World War, of wholesale reclamation of
marginal land by drainage, ploughing and artificial fertilizers, and the
accompanying transformation of the rural scene, nowhere more so
than in East Anglia, by the removal of hedges and trees, and the filling
of ditches, to create vastly larger fields for the easier and more
economic working of larger machines for cultivating and harvesting,
and the application of fertilizers, pesticides and weedkillers. It has been
a ruthless progress, though many will call it justifiable and inevitable,
towards greatly increased yields with fewer and fewer men. What it
has done to the landscape is plain to see to even the casual observer
with only a short memory. To the more keenly interested lover and
student of nature and the countryside, the less immediately obvious
results of monoculture are perhaps much worse and less easily mitigated
or reversed. Trees, hedges and ditches were features of interest and
delight to most of us (as were the wild flowers of the cornfields) but
they were also the homes of a great variety and number of animals,
birds, insects and plants, all interrelated and interdependent. I have
discussed elsewhere the effects on wild life, but in this chapter I am
more concerned with the evolution of the landscape in a general and
panoramic way, and there is no doubt that especially in East Anglia the
man-made changes of the last century and a half have been spectacular.

A parallel change has occurred in the decline and disappearance of
many rural industries associated with agriculture. The region's landscape, well into the twentieth century, contained many windmills and
watermills, still grinding corn, but they disappeared steadily as they
could no longer cope with the ever-increasing demand. So these
familiar landmarks, some of the most picturesque and romantic of
rural buildings, were either demolished or allowed to decay, and huge
concrete flour mills appeared in the larger towns and especially the
ports such as Ipswich, to make their stark and impressive contribution
to the 'townscape'. In the Fens and the Broads, the old windpumps,
either wooden smock mills or brick tower mills, with their fascinating
silhouettes in the marshy levels, were superseded by diesel engines or
electric pumps in crude sheds of cheap brick and corrugated iron.
Village and small town maltings similarly decayed or disappeared.
Blacksmiths' forges outlived their usefulness and gave way to petrol
filling stations and agricultural engineers' workshops.

Since the last war the community have taken a growing if belated interest in saving relics of rural industry. Some windmills have been restored complete with machinery, some as mere shells, some as houses. Though a very small proportion remains of the many hundreds that existed in the nineteenth century, East Anglia inevitably has more than any other region in view of its long-established importance as a corn-growing area. Windpumps and watermills similarly have been saved by private and public enterprise, and although they are admittedly few in number they continue to play an important and much appreciated part in our rural scene. Maltings in Ely and Beccles have been restored and converted to community uses, and the Snape Maltings Concert Hall is internationally famous, both architecturally and musically.

East Anglia still bears traces of military defence works from pre-Roman times to the late Middle Ages, in the form of forts, earthworks and castles. Napoleonic times added the prominent and unique landmarks of the Martello Towers along the coasts of Sussex, Kent, Essex and Suffolk. All these developments, from Roman to Napoleonic times, must have seemed quite startling when they were built and they have left impressive marks on our coast and countryside. The advent of aerial warfare in 1914–1918 introduced the need for vast, flat, areas for aircraft to take off from and return to. Even so long ago, East Anglia, being close to the Continent and to the enemy, received a large share of the new airfields that had to be constructed. Trees and hedges had to be cleared over hundreds of acres, and huge hangars and other buildings erected. In places modest airstrips of grass were created and it is still possible to see what the Royal Flying Corps and later the Royal Air Force did at Martlesham and Orfordness, though the traces are being obliterated by later developments. The war of 1939–1945 saw tremendous advances—if one can call them such—in the size, power and speed of aircraft and in the techniques of aerial bombing and fighting. Many more and much larger airfields were needed and once again the region's involvement was probably matched only by Kent and Lincolnshire. Enormous areas of farmland and even of new conifer forests were cleared, and miles of concrete runways and acres of hangars were constructed, with all the accompanying traffic, noise and drama of war in the air. The effects linger on into the 1970s. The largest of the air bases remain, and become larger and more hideous with noise and buildings and barbed wire fences, and masses of lights at night. Many of the smaller airfields have closed down, but not all have yet lost their concrete runways and Nissen huts and bomb stores and air raid shelters.

Until a few years ago it was uneconomic to break up the concrete runways and to recover the land for agriculture, but machinery has been developed which can do the job for worthwhile returns both in hardcore for building and in reclaiming increasingly valuable farm-land. Thus the old airfields are gradually disappearing, but for many years the countryside over wide areas will remain unnaturally open and bare of trees. However change runs with change, and modern agri-cultural methods in surrounding areas have reduced the contrast to a matter of mere degree. Here and there, runways have been kept and used as bases for enormous warehouses, or for buildings housing pigs, chickens and turkeys by thousands and mushrooms by the million. Some of the buildings, like the former mushroom 'farm' at the old Debach airfield, are a quarter of a mile long, and are prominent for miles around. Thus the airfields of two wars have left their subtle or blatant scars.

For nearly fifty years, up to about 1960, the Royal Air Force had a flying boat station on the east side of Harwich Harbour, where the giant hangars remain as warehouses for the enormously expanded port of Felixstowe. Behind them on Landguard Common, are many airmen's houses and some derelict military buildings, including the massive fort at Landguard Point. Army camps and military sidings were scattered about over much of the region, especially during the second war. Many have been cleared, but here and there traces remain as in the concrete roads on the Norfolk heaths overlooking the sea at Salthouse, and in parkland at Fornham and Holton in Suffolk. Large areas of forest and heath were used for tank training near Orford and in the Breckland. Most of them were abandoned after the war, and are now afforested or cultivated. These parts of the country were 'prohibited places' and those of us who never saw them can only imagine the dusty devastation that must have been caused. The Army have kept their battle training ground in the Stanford area north of Thetford, and despite the fact that a good deal of damage has been done to buildings and the countryside, this is the largest single area with some resemblance to the Breckland landscape of the days before large-scale afforestation and agricultural reclamation.

Turning now to transport during the last century and a half, we see the region, until well into the second half of the twentieth century, as a large cul-de-sac peninsula, not on the way to anywhere else and visited only by residents and holidaymakers. The road system, with its Roman and pre-Roman skeleton and its network of medieval country roads, was improved gradually as trade increased with the Industrial Revolution and the growth of population. But the coming of the railways in the nineteenth century caused a decline in road traffic, and affected the rural scene by the consequent neglect of road maintenance and the falling off of activity and trade in roadside villages. As in most parts of the country, the trend was reversed with the coming of the internal combustion engine, but 'progress' was slower and later here as the rural branch lines lingered on and road traffic increased less rapidly. Not until the 1950s and 1960s did most of the branch lines close, with the belated growth of car ownership in East Anglia (now, incidentally, above the national average in the 1970s), and the rapid increase in holiday and commercial road traffic. The dual carriageways and the motorways came late to the region, and have come now mainly because of the thousands of vast, articulated, container lorries going to and from Europe through East Anglian ports. Such roads are now cutting wide swathes through the quiet countryside, taking hundreds of acres of arable and pasture, but they are bringing blessed peace to the towns and villages on the old main roads and leaving them once again fit to live and work in.

Railways probably had less ultimate effect on the landscape than in more hilly counties, though the long cuttings and embankments must have seemed very raw during construction and for some time afterwards. They must have caused a strong feeling, which by now has become largely forgotten and unnoticed, of severance and created a barrier to communication between villages and parts of farms and estates, and a visual barrier across former open country. In many places the scars were camouflaged within a generation by man and nature planting trees and bushes and by the rich growth of wild flowers. The close network of lines opened new vistas by penetrating country formerly not seen by the general public, but the most profound effects were undoubtedly social and economic. In East Anglia, perhaps more than in most regions, the railway station, and its ancillary houses for the station master and staff, signal box, goods shed and railway inn, became a centre of new activity in the village, often accompanied by corn, seed and coal merchants and maltsters. In many quite small villages and towns, the railway created a new dimension as at Tivetshall, on the Ipswich to Norwich line, where large maltings were built. Some railways split villages by crossing the village greens. At Mellis the huge green remains in two parts separated by the railway, the level crossing and the buildings associated with the railway. To conclude this brief note on the rise and fall of the railways, it is worth drawing attention to the new and impressive style of buildings that were erected on some lines. Of particular note were the neo-Jacobean stations between Ipswich and Bury St Edmunds. These remain, but unfortunately the declining prosperity of the railway has led to neglect of the buildings and of their settings.

From earliest times the estuaries served the invaders and the traders, and ports were established at their mouths and their heads. Development stagnated somewhat as the era of sail slowly came to an end, and steam and oil-fired ships used mainly the larger ports elsewhere. But in East Anglia, sail, like the horse, survived longer than in most areas, and the traditional sailing barge, magnificent to see and unique in design and capabilities, continued to trade in large numbers between London and the ports of Essex, Suffolk and Norfolk, and into the remotest creeks, until the Second World War which saw many barges destroyed by enemy mines and aircraft. They were, at rest or under way, very beautiful and special features of our coast and estuaries. A few with full sail and auxiliary engines, and many pitifully cut down and motorized, carried on trading, with the last fully-rigged sailing barge giving up as late as 1971. Fortunately about a couple of dozen have been saved and restored and are sailed as yachts, and the wonderful, nostalgic sight of a fleet of barges under sail is seen in the annual Barge Matches on the Orwell and the Blackwater estuaries.

The real revival and transformation of our ports, from the old-fashioned quaintness that survived until about 1950, to modern, mechanized efficiency, did not come until the 1960s as international trade and especially trade with the Continent expanded rapidly, and ports like London were unable to adapt quickly enough or to maintain good enough labour relations. We then saw the tremendous development at Harwich, Ipswich and Felixstowe, and to a lesser degree at Kings Lynn and Great Yarmouth, which I have described in the chapters on the coast. Apart from the serious effects on wild-life habitats, all the new quays and buildings and cranes seem to have been absorbed into the landscape better than other forms of development. Perhaps the worst feature of port growth has been the effect of the heavy road traffic on the towns and villages and the country of the hinterland.

Except for the Fen rivers, the artificial navigations are few in number, neither long nor spectacular, and they have never been very busy or prosperous. The old navigable rivers, such as the Stour, the Lark, the Little Ouse and the Gipping, are pleasant relics of a bygone age, worthy of exploration on foot or by canoe, and are rewarding to the rambler, the naturalist, the angler and the artist. Recreation of other kinds has had a staggering effect on parts of the region, mostly on the coast and the Broads.

In this first chapter, I have tried to describe what I have called, for want of a better phrase, 'natural evolution', both geological and human, of the whole landscape up to the time when man's activities became markedly more dramatic, deliberate and unnatural. I have then summarized what happened from that time onwards, and have gone into more detail in the rest of the book on how these activities have affected the various parts of the region and are still working on them.

Some may think my demarcation artificial, but I maintain that there is something in it that bears examination and is comprehensible in its relation to the recent past, the present and the future. After writing this chapter, I was heartened by reading the following words of Jacquetta Hawkes in her book *A Land*:

Recalling in tranquillity the slow possession of Britain by its people, I cannot resist the conclusion that the relationship reached its greatest intimacy, its most sensitive pitch, about two hundred years ago. By the middle of the eighteenth century men had triumphed, the land was theirs, but had not yet been subjected and outraged. . . . Rich men and poor men knew how to use the stuff of their countryside to raise comely buildings and to group them with instinctive grace. Town and country having grown up together to serve one another's needs now enjoyed a moment of balance.

2

Coastal Panorama

ONE fine afternoon, a few years ago, we were returning on the Dutch ship from Holland to Harwich. The landfall was farther north than we had expected, and we found ourselves at about the latitude of Orfordness, but still ten miles or more from the Suffolk coast. Although we were heading into a declining autumn sun, the whole of the coast from Southwold to Walton-on-the-Naze could be seen with startling clarity. Every landmark and subtle rise and fall were visible and identifiable over a sweep of thirty miles. Lighthouses and church towers, the little towns of Aldeburgh and Southwold, and Orford with its castle; the square mass of the nuclear generating station at Sizewell, the House in the Clouds at Thorpeness, the radar masts at Bawdsey, the church spires of Felixstowe and Harwich, and in the far south the cliffs and the tower of the Naze. All of these could be seen clearly, and between them the alternate stretches of low cliff and shingle bank.

Views of the coast are perhaps the most extensive and interesting in such a generally low-lying area as East Anglia, and one does not need to be at sea. From the cliffs at Felixstowe, one can take in the panorama from Walton-on-the-Naze to Sizewell. From Salthouse Heath there is a superb view of the Norfolk coast extending from the hills above Sheringham in the east to the woods at Wells in the west—a prospect that can be seen gloriously reversed by looking inland from Blakeney Point.

If we look more closely, we discover, and I mean that in its old and exciting sense, a coastline that is the most interesting single feature, and certainly the most impressive and fascinating feature, of the region. This is a coast that has the supreme restfulness of sheer simplicity of line and form in the long, gently curving sweep of breakers and shingle and cliff, combined with the intense interest of swiftly changing marsh and salting and shingle bank, habitats that have fostered some of Britain's finest nature reserves. For all the apparent simplicity, there is considerable variety in the beauty of wide, tree-lined estuaries, the background of dune and heath and forest, the charm and character of little towns that have escaped the horrors of south-coast suburbaniza-tion, and that would be immediately recognized by George Crabbe, Daniel Defoe or William Cobbett.

Some horrors there are, mainly north and south of Great Yarmouth, and facing the Wash, in the shape of holiday camps and caravans. Sprawling and ugly these may be, but they are now kept in bounds, and sufficient unspoilt and splendid coastline survives in Norfolk and Suffolk for the Countryside Commission to have designated more than half of it as 'areas of outstanding natural beauty' and as 'heritage coast'. The enhanced official status should ensure a better chance of protection and survival.

Before describing the coast in more detail, it is worth remembering how it has come to be as it is. Long before the Ice Age there was no East Anglian coast; indeed there was no East Anglia. While the chalk was being laid down, the sea level rose and drowned the whole of Britain except for what are now known as the highlands of England, Wales and Scotland. Round our region's coast as it is now, we can see the chalk at Hunstanton, and in the cliffs at one or two places in north Norfolk; and we can see the shelly crags and the peat laid down in later ages. In the cliffs, especially in north Norfolk, are found the bones of the mammoths and woolly bears and other animals long extinct, that frequented Britain when it was still part of the Continental main-land. It was finally cut off when the ice melted and the sea rose, leaving East Anglia with a coastline which probably had the general shape we now know, but which has been changed greatly in detail by wind and weather and tide. Frost and wind and rain have helped the sea to eat into the soft, earthy cliffs, and the material eroded has gone to silt up river mouths and to form beaches elsewhere. The tidal currents, helped by the winds, have carried sand and shingle along the coast to form long shingle banks in front of old harbours. Inside the bars, harbours have become choked with silt and mud, and saltings have evolved into salt marshes and later into enclosed fresh marshes, helped by the hand of man. All these processes in the distant past were somewhat inter-mittent, and occasionally were reversed or slowed down by rises and falls in sea level until medieval times. Since then coastal changes have in general proceeded more steadily, apart from occasional dramatic storms and floods which in a night have upset the trends of centuries in particular localities.

Erosion of cliffs in Norfolk and Suffolk, and the build-up of shingle banks especially in north Norfolk, and the silting up of creeks, have continued year by year, and quickly enough for any of us in his own lifetime to be able to see and note considerable changes. In recent years, notably in the twentieth century, man has intervened in a much bigger way to stem or deflect the natural forces. The need to increase food production, to develop East Anglian ports and resorts, and to stop houses falling into the sea, has led to sea defence works which both in themselves and in their effects, have caused profound changes in the coastal scene. The enclosure of marshes around the Wash I have described in the chapters on the Fens, but it has happened on quite a large scale in north Norfolk and parts of east Suffolk. The effects on the cliffs and beaches are mentioned later. Port developments, especially since the Second World War, have been spectacular and fascinating in many ways, but they have been very damaging to the landscape and to wild life habitats. Defence works of ancient times have been joined and altered by the fortifications of two world wars in this century, but much of the more recent work was temporary in nature and has been removed.

A low-level, low-speed flight in a helicopter—or even a study of successive editions of one-inch Ordnance Survey maps—would give one an excellent picture of the East Anglian coast, and reveal many of the present features and the ways in which the coast has changed over the years, and how it is still changing. But by far the most rewarding way is to walk the beaches and cliffs and thus to see not only broad panoramas but to study and understand all the fascinating detail, even down to grains of sand, that make up the whole, ever-changing picture.

3

Norfolk Coast and Broadland

WOLFERTON CREEK on the east side of the Wash is a convenient dividing line between the Fens and the coast. To the south lie the vast areas of reclaimed marshes beside the mouth of the Great Ouse. To the north, between the Wash and Snettisham and Heacham Marshes, is a bank nearly six miles long, created by the southward drift of shingle. This bank has occasionally been over-topped by storms, as in January 1953, but the protection of the marshes has since been augmented by a raised bank. The shingle bank itself is scarred by long lagoons left by old gravel workings. These have become so attractive to sea birds, wildfowl and waders that the Royal Society for the Protection of Birds have created a large bird reserve at Snettisham. At both Snettisham and Heacham the austere beauty and solitude of the coast have been desecrated by long lines of caravans, chalets and huts, but it is unlikely that they will be allowed to spread further.

At its northern end the shingle bank merges into the modest beginnings of the cliffs at Hunstanton. They are the one notable natural feature, except for the extensive tidal flats, of a small, pleasant resort that has little else that is old or interesting. These cliffs, which are the end of the chalk hills that run through the Chilterns and the East Anglian Heights, are only about a mile long from end to end and hardly exceed sixty feet in height, but they are banded uniquely in layers of white chalk, red chalk and—lowest of all—rusty-brown carstone in two layers, the upper softer and paler than the lower. On the beach, near the cliffs, are great boulders of carstone and humps of blue-grey Kimmeridge Clay, named after the Dorset outcrop at the other end of the chalk web of southern England.

The foot of the cliffs is littered and obscured with large slabs of the red, white and brown rocks, sharp in outline when newly fallen, more rounded after pounding by high tides. The chalk forming the upper layer of the cliffs is stratified horizontally, but it splits vertically and the slabs that fall are angular in shape. On the ledges of the chalk, fulmars nest and may be seen effortlessly gliding parallel with the cliff-top, and wheeling sharply to land beside their mates on the nests. They carry on a quaint, guttural conversation quite different in tone from that of other sea birds. Starlings and sparrows fly in and out of holes where they also find nesting places.

Although the sea left these cliffs upstanding when its level fell centuries ago, it continues, with the help of rain, frost and wind to attack them and to erode them quite rapidly. They are seen to the best advantage on a late afternoon with the sun lighting them up, and on a day of exceptionally low tide when their full extent can be seen panoramically, and the great interest of the extensive beach is revealed. For some way out it is firm, flat and sandy, then comes a wave-rippled zone just short of the 'live' belt covered with worm-casts and inhabited by starfish, crabs and cockles, between the humps of carstone covered with seaweed and mussels. The sea bed a little farther out is the site of a submerged forest, and other marine creatures live in the peat and wood which provide evidence of times when the Wash and the North Sea were dry land joining Britain to the Continent. Today this vast intertidal area of the Wash, with its wealth of marine life, is one of the biggest and most attractive feeding grounds for thousands of waders and wildfowl, especially in winter. Having wandered out to low-water mark, one turns back to see the whole line of the colour-banded cliffs from end to end; the white chalk thickening gradually from south to north before dipping down and disappearing, the red chalk a fairly shallow layer of constant depth, and the brown carstone tapering away to the north.

Beyond Hunstanton the coast turns eastwards, and the cliffs give way to sand and salting, mud and marsh, running for nearly thirty miles of natural beauty, most of it protected and unmarred. From Holme-next-the-Sea, where the Peddar's Way reaches the coast, to Weybourne, where the cliffs rise up again, is a glorious stretch of coast and country which honesty compels me to acknowledge as superior to the less dramatic and simpler beauty of the coast of my native Suffolk. The coast road from Hunstanton to Cromer runs along the old coastline, at the foot of the hills, still the edge of terra firma, but now the traveller looks out northwards over a remote, mysterious 'no-man's land' of salt marsh and sand dune, shingle banks, winding creeks and grazing marshes, a land penetrated by tracks, some open and wind-swept, some sheltered between hedges of thorn and elder, leading to the tidal mud and sand and the grey North Sea. Here are thirty miles of paradise for the student of botany and birds and coastal evolution, and of sheer delight for the amateur of natural beauty. The National Trust and Cambridge University, and many students and graduates from elsewhere, have written treatises on the features and changes of this fascinating area, especially of Scolt Head Island and Blakeney Point which have been National Trust nature reserves since 1923 and 1912.

Near the western extremity of this earthly paradise is—or was— Thornham Island, a much smaller feature, illustrating in a nutshell the development of the north Norfolk coast. Since the beginning of this century, an island of sand and shell appeared west of the harbour channel. In 1939 it was in the shape of a crescent about half a mile long. It had achieved sufficient stability to withstand the waves and was being extended east and west by drifting beach materials. It was already colonized by typical coastal vegetation, and the sand flat sheltered by the crescent was being slowly transformed by the deposit of mud and the growth of marsh plants, particularly *salicornia*. By 1961 the crescent had been filled in by sand over the mud, and had advanced westwards to become joined to the coastal dunes. Attachment to the south was apparently prevented by a small tidal creek connected with the drainage of grazing marshes and the flash called Broad Water. There were, according to J. A. Steers writing in 1952, two similar islands east of the harbour channel, but they had been greatly damaged by erosion. Since then they, and the spit on the north side of the creek draining Titchwell Marshes, seem to have disappeared completely.

On the beach at Titchwell, visible only at times of the lowest tides, are the remains of an ancient forest, now seen in the shapes of black trunks and stools and beds and lumps of peat eroded by the sea and pocked with thousands of little, elongated bivalves. In 1949, the tide breached the sea walls and overran the grazing marsh which had been enclosed many years before. The wall was not repaired, and in the 1970s the Royal Society for the Protection of Birds took over the whole marsh as a bird reserve particularly suited to waders.

On this coast, salt and fresh marshes alternate, but the trend towards complete enclosure and the consequent creation of fresh marshes seems to have been halted by a timely recognition of the unique scientific interest, and the value to wild life, of the natural features. From the hill between Burnham Westgate and Burnham Deepdale one can see a wonderful panorama in which Brancaster Saltmarsh contrasts with Deepdale and Norton Marshes which are now enclosed by a bank and used for grazing cattle and growing corn, but which still contain winding flashes of water, once tidal creeks running into the channel separating Scolt Head Island from the mainland. The Island, one of the National Trust's most interesting nature reserves, is about three and a half miles long, with a western tip of shingle similar to that of Blakeney Point, and dunes and saltings constantly changing and developing. One goes out there from Brancaster Staithe where the warden lives in the old Dial House; but for an overall scenic view, look from the hill and see it across Brancaster Harbour and Norton Creek where dozens of white and red-sailed dinghies sail on the blue water of a brimming tide, as a cool breeze setting onshore raises a faint haze over the hot land on a summer's day. These small boats themselves, in large numbers, are signs of profound change, mostly since the second war. All the little harbours and villages have been discovered by towns-folk in search of peace and beauty and recreation, and many cottages have been lavishly restored, obviously far beyond the means of most local people. We must hope, selfishly, that the people and boats do not become too numerous, but at least the summer season is short, and with the protection of nature and of various organizations, the scenery and wild life should survive relatively unspoilt.

In the summer of 1967, the twelve miles of marsh, dune, wood and foreshore between Scolt Head Island and Blakeney were declared a National Nature Reserve, the second largest in England. All the land, as distinct from the foreshore which is owned by the Crown, belongs to the Holkham Estate of the Earl of Leicester, whose great-grand-father was 'Coke of Norfolk', the first and probably the greatest of those who made the English deserts fertile. Coke was the inspiration of several other East Anglian landowning nobility who followed many years later and worked a similar transformation in the Breckland. Here at Holkham, the northern fringe of the estate along with the coast, has kept its interest and beauty and is being protected for posterity by official designation in agreement with the worthy successor to en-lightened landowners. The history of Holkham and the Earls of Leicester is truly a remarkable one, illustrating how much we owe to the landed aristocracy for the beauty and prosperity of much of our coastline, and probably more so in East Anglia than anywhere else in Britain.

At the western extremity of the Holkham Reserve, the little River Burn flows through the meadows, past the combined wind and water mills of Burnham Overy, the windmill that the Norfolk artist Edward Seago painted as 'The Landmark', and the splendid old watermill and cottages on the main road. It flows into the head of a tidal creek and winds its way past Overy Staithe in a crooked channel fished by little terns and common terns from Scolt Head. A bank, protecting the enclosed Overy Marshes, runs along the east side of the creek out to Gun Hill where the dunes overlook the lowest reaches which are dignified by the name of Burnham Harbour. These dunes are quite high and, stretching for over four miles, protect the whole of the western half of the reserve between Burnham Harbour and Wells Harbour. Here, especially since 1850, natural processes have had considerable assistance from the Holkham Estate. A belt of Corsican pines, first planted in the 1850s, and obviously maintained ever since by further planting, and helped in more recent years by silver birch and poplar, have consolidated the dunes of Holkham Meals and helped the creation and protection of the enclosed marshes behind them where several hundred acres are now grazed and cultivated. A road, seemingly part of the overall grand pattern of the great landscaped estate, runs northwards from the gates of the Park, across the coast road, to Holkham Gap, a low point in the dunes, where people are able to park their cars and bicycles, and to walk among the pines and on to the beaches. The view through the pines, across the wide golden sands to the blue sea is superb, and is complemented by the wide panorama seen when one looks back through the trees, across the green fields to the old coastline marked by the background of low hills with the woods of Holkham Park and the little town of Wells.

As well as protecting the area for its general beauty and interest, and encouraging people to enjoy and understand it, the Nature Conservancy Council are studying the continuing changes. Some of these are a continuation of the long evolutionary history, modified by wise estate management, but the increase of visitors in recent years has brought new problems. Vehicles are prevented from penetrating into the dunes, but the concentration of many feet through the gap between the car park and the beach, and elsewhere, leads to quite serious erosion. Duck-board paths have been laid on the busiest pedestrian routes, and some small areas have been fenced in to enable a study to be made of recolonization by maritime and sand-dune vegetation. Much can be learned here that is useful both to the student and to people concerned with the management of rural areas accessible to the public.

Holkham Meals and the beaches run east as far as the coastguards' lookout and lifeboat station and the large caravan camp at the mouth of Wells Harbour. The little port is still used by ships with cargoes of several hundred tons of grain. They sail in from sea through the winding off-shore channel and then up the long straight channel under the bank on its west side. This channel marks a sharp division between different aspects of this coast. The western bank protects the end of the enclosed marshes I have already described. To the east lie natural salt marshes riddled with little creeks, stretching for seven miles along the coast to Blakeney. Opposite the lifeboat station at Wells a spit of shingle unattached to the mainland has developed with some areas of sand dunes and two little belts of pine trees. J. A. Steers refers to these as 'Wells Meals' but he cannot explain their origin. The tongue of shingle appears to be extending eastwards rather than westwards as at Blakeney Point and Scolt Head. To me this phenomenon seems comparable with the little island at Thornham, but Wells Meals, with the harbour to the west and the great expanse of saltings and lateral creeks to the east, seem very unlikely to link themselves to the mainland. It will be interesting to watch their progress.

Reclamation of the salt marshes between Wells and Blakeney has probably been prevented or delayed by the existence throughout the middle of the twentieth century of an artillery range and camp at Stiffkey. Although military activity is now much reduced, large-scale reclamation still seems unlikely because of the inclusion of Wells, Warham and Stiffkey Marshes and the very extensive foreshore in the National Nature Reserve, and the acquisition of Morston Marshes by the National Trust in the 1970s.

Blakeney Point lies at the end of the shingle ridge which runs westwards for about eight miles from Weybourne, where the cliffs of Cromer and Sheringham tail down to sea level. Behind the bank, between Weybourne and Cley, are grazing marshes and reed beds; between Cley and the Point itself are the dunes and saltings behind the long bar that shelters the channels running out from the little ports of Cley and Blakeney to the sea. It is famous mostly for its birds which attract so many ornithologists especially in spring and autumn. One must be thankful that it is not an easy place to get to, but the effort is well worth while.

On a perfect morning one late September we set off from Cley village and walked past cottages where house martins were still feeding young at the nests. Across the valley of the River Glaven, once an arm of the sea, we went with the sun at our backs, up past Blakeney Church which has a massive west tower and a tiny east tower in which a light still shines to guide mariners at night; and down the narrow winding High Street to the Quay where a brimming tide had covered half the road. The boat slid away smoothly on the first of the ebb and into the vast expanse of blue water between the shingle and the marshes. It came, after about half an hour, to the beach near the old lifeboat station which now serves in summer as the warden's house. Here the dunes form and reform, subject to wind and storm and the erosion by rabbits and people.

The half-dozen passengers made their way past the National Trust sign with its oak leaves and acorn, across the dunes. They saw, as they advanced, a small group of people behind the lifeboat station, with arms raised, peering through binoculars into a cluster of wild lupins. The new arrivals crept up and joined the group, to see netted, ringed and released, a tired little bird who could not have appreciated his importance. He was a young, red-breasted flycatcher, a bird that breeds in eastern Europe and is seen only very rarely in Britain. Some of the little crowd of people returned in the boat while there was still water enough to get back to Blakeney; some remained round the warden's house in the hope of seeing more rare migrant birds. We were the only ones to set out to walk the five miles back to Cley. It took from ten o'clock in the morning until four in the afternoon; it was rough going but it did not seem a yard too long.

At the Point and the entrance to Blakeney Harbour, the scene was superb in the brilliant sunlight. Channels and pools of sparkling water threaded through golden sand, some rippled, some smooth, some mottled with shingle. Behind the saltings and marshes stretched the wonderful backcloth of the coastal hills. The shapes and shadows changed as the sun moved round behind the little villages, each distinctive, each with its church, strung along the lower slopes just above marsh level—Salthouse, Cley, Blakeney and Morston. Away to the west, faint in a blue haze, stood the granaries and maltings of Wells, and beyond them the trees of Holkham Park and the Meals. And over and around it all were limitless light and air and sea and sky. Gulls ranged along the seaward side of the shingle ridge. Larks and linnets and other small birds flitted and sang among the low bushes on the other side between the shingle and the tidal area where *salicornia* and sea blite were spreading to trap the sand and mud deposited by the falling tides and thus to build up the salt marshes. Redshanks and other waders fed on the mud and sometimes flew over with their piping calls. During the day hundreds of lapwings flew westwards in ragged formation. At the end of four miles of shingle, dunes and saltings, the coastguard station marked the seaward end of the road that ran inland across the marshes towards the low tree-clad hill above the flint and red brick and tile and whitewash of the village of Cley; and the great white-capped windmill marked the end of our expedition.

This is a magnificent mill, maintained by the Norfolk County Council. It has a tall red brick tower and white cap and sails which shine in the sun when seen from near or far, even from Blakeney Point. The houses of Cley, of brick and pebble and pantile, are crowded on a low hump, and the lower ones look out northwards across the marsh to the North Sea. From here to Salthouse, the main road hugs closely the winding edge of the hills, and a dyke runs along the seaward side separating the road from the marsh. Much of this marshland area is now a nature reserve of the Norfolk Naturalists' Trust. The reserve is varied—marsh grazing, reed beds, shingle and lagoons— ideal for many species of breeding birds, including several rare species, and a safe resting place for the thousands that winter here or pass this way on migration in spring or autumn.

At Salthouse all the houses are on the landward side of the coast road, and the church stands high and well back from the marsh. Turning at the tiny village green by the Dun Cow, one looks up a narrow lane flanked closely by a wonderful group of barns and cottages—again of red brick, pebble and pantile—as impressive as the great stone barns and stone cottages of other counties. This local style of building runs right along the north Norfolk coast. On our journeys from the south, we first see it soon after we have crossed the upper Bure at Saxlingthorpe. The materials and styles are combined in a vernacular as strong as in the stone areas of the Cotswolds and Northamptonshire. A rich red brick for the quoins and frames and for decorative patterns, even on some barns; large rounded, grey and brown pebbles for infilling, and brightish red or shiny black pantiles on the roofs. The overall effect is very bright and fresh, even in older buildings, and in delightful contrast with the green of arable and woodland and the brilliant blue sky and white clouds. The platitudes about the Norfolk light are indeed true. It is clear and sharp. On the north coast, particularly in bright weather, the shape and form of the hills and the woods and churches and houses are emphasized as one looks into the light; and as the sun works round from left to right, the shadows too move round and show the steepness and roundness of the quite considerable hills and the dark masses of the woods and the light and shade of the churches.

From the top of the hill at Salthouse one looks back over the sea from a height of about 200 feet. On the heath are gorse, heather and sorrel, rosebay and bramble. From the plateau, where people picnic on the old wartime concrete bases, is a splendid panorama, ten miles to the west over Cley Marshes, Blakeney Point and Harbour, Stiffkey and Wells saltings to the 'stop' of Holkham Meals; six miles east to Sheringham over the dramatically hilly landscape of Weybourne, fashioned in glacial times. In contrast with this widespread scene, are the details and colours of the immediate surroundings, heather blowing brilliantly, red sorrel, purple rosebay, the bright green of mosses, the black soil and the grey sand of the tracks, and the pink grasses shimmering in the fresh wind.

From those glacial hills, intriguingly named Telegraph and Muckleburgh, there is a view over the pantiled roofs of the village to Weybourne Hope. I would rather call it Weybourne Gap because the end of the road where the longshore fishing boats are beached lies between the lower slopes of Muckleburgh Hill and the beginning of the cliffs of north Norfolk. It is from this spot that the sea has built up the shingle bank for eight miles westwards to Blakeney Point. In travelling from west to east along this fascinating coast I have gone against the natural westward movement of materials and the consequent accretion, as we have seen especially at Scolt Head and Blakeney. However, not far beyond Weybourne, the southward-setting tidal currents divide, and from Sheringham the movement is eastwards and southwards along the rest of the Norfolk and Suffolk coasts, with a general picture of erosion of the cliffs and accretion of shingle banks and bars on the lower parts.

Weybourne Hope, or Gap, is an important milestone of great interest. The cliff face is of a lightish-coloured, chalky clay containing squarish, chalky stones and scattered, huge knobbly flints. It is severely eroded by nature and by people playing, digging and geologizing, and presents a very grotesque sight from the beach. The light, chalky layer is capped by an intermittent and contorted iron pan rusty in colour and containing many stones. Sandy material and thin topsoil, growing barley nearly to the edge, complete the face of the cliff. A short climb up the slope to the east reveals, when one turns around, the long, gently curved line of the shingle disappearing into the distance, with its fringe of white foam and sea spray. The cliff top, despite, or rather because of, its poor soil and exposure to wind and salt, supports an interesting variety of plants. In parts it is carpeted with buck's horn plantain. Birdsfoot trefoil and ribwort plantain are numerous, and a colony of thrift or sea pink makes a brave show of colour on the very edge overlooking one of the great gullies left by massive landslides. Such falls must be quite frequent in these cliffs of soft, glacial sands and clays, but I have never been fortunate enough to see one. In 1972 a naturalist visiting the coast near Sheringham described how, while she was watching nesting fulmars, "a huge elbow of the cliff collapsed. First cracks appeared and trickles of sand cascaded to the beach and shortly afterwards great masses of sand and glacial clay toppled and crashed with a noise like thunder. The reverberations were followed all along the cliffs by a tremendous outburst of cackling from all the fulmars, which reacted like pheasants when alarmed by thunder or by a jet plane breaking the sound barrier."

We looked at that part of the coast in June of the same year, and descended from the beautiful, hilly, wooded country of Beacon Hill and Roman Camp, over 300 feet above sea level. West Runton, a little resort with the atmosphere of the Edwardian days of L. P. Hartley's novels, lies just inland from a 'gap'. The wind roared as through a funnel, blowing the fine, stinging sand into our faces. The cliffs, especially east of the gap, were sandy in colour, very high, almost vertical, and evidently of harder material than at Weybourne to the west or Mundesley to the east. Fulmars were nesting on ledges near the cliff tops. The upper part of the beach was fine sand, but as the tide was very low we were able to see that the lower beach was covered with huge, knobbly-shaped flints, some barnacled, some with round holes, and many of them about eighteen inches long. These are about the biggest flints one is likely to see, and here they have earned the unique distinction, in East Anglia, of the notation of 'rocks' on the Ordnance Survey map.

The high cliffs of glacial materials continue eastwards beyond Cromer, where the coastline turns away in a long curve to the south-east. The evidence of one's eyes of serious and continuing erosion is confirmed by a study of successive maps published during the past hundred years. Buildings have tumbled to the beaches; coastal roads have been severed by cliff falls and have had to be replaced by new roads farther inland. At Overstrand the so-called High Street is blocked by barriers and a section can be used only by pedestrians. Foundations and floors of buildings are—or were when we saw them in 1972—precariously embedded in the vertical sides of a 'bay' where a large section of the cliff had fallen away to the beach far below. There are—or were then—several occupied houses on the seaward side of the High Street, but their future must have been very short. Where cliff falls have left a slope for a long enough period, it has become overgrown and partly stabilized by grass and other plants, but undermining at lower levels by frost, wind and the sea leads to further falls.

On parts of the Norfolk and Suffolk coasts attempts have been made, and are still being made, by local authorities to prevent further erosion. Near Beacon Hill, Trimingham, contractors were at work at the foot of some of Norfolk's highest cliffs. They were of soft, sandy material and very liable to erosion and landslips. A line of wooden stakes with infilling of steel piles, was being constructed along the coast, a short distance from the foot of the sloping cliffs, to contain the sand falling from them and to defend their base from attack by the waves. New groynes, at right angles, were already collecting beach material and thus strengthening the defence of the cliffs. Necessary and desirable though these works may be, they will inevitably make the coast less interesting and revealing. Where cliff falls used to leave steep or vertical faces, the various strata could be clearly seen, and in parts of the coasts of Norfolk and Suffolk they contained the flint tools of early men, the fossilized shells of ancient marine deposits, the teeth and bones of long-extinct animals, and the remains of plants of prehistoric times. All that will be left if the engineers achieve their objective of stability, will be fairly uniform slopes clothed with a mixture of natural and introduced vegetation. This will be much less interesting, and change will be much slower and less dramatic, but one can understand the desire of the authorities to halt the erosion which over the centuries has taken away so many homes and other buildings and land. At Sidestrand the church was threatened in the mid-nineteenth century, and was rebuilt in 1881, about a quarter of a mile inland, beside the main road.

Beyond Mundesley, where sand martins nest in the few remaining

Orfordness, Suffolk

Cley Mill and Blakeney Church

Trimingham—the lost road

Bacton North Sea Gas Terminal and Church

Horsey Mill and Dyke

Norwich—Pull's Ferry

Wroxham Bridge and new hotel

Great Yarmouth Custom House and Commissioners' Offices

Seals on Scroby Sands off Great Yarmouth

Woodbridge Tide Mill during restoration

Lowestoft Harbour—stern trawlers

Thorpeness Mill and the House in the Clouds

Ipswich Dockside Mills

Sailing Barges on the Orwell

vertical areas of sandy cliffs, the country becomes more flat and open, and the cliffs gradually decline in height past Bacton and Happisburgh to Sea Palling and Waxham. Between Paston and Bacton lies the great complex of the North Sea Gas terminal, which has been operating for some years, following the controversy that attended its progress from the drawing-board. A fair attempt has been made to lessen its effect on the countryside by keeping the buildings low and using red bricks which seem however too bright and a near miss for the old, glowing red bricks of Norfolk. Grassy banks have been formed to hide the security fencing, and trees have been planted. But, alas, in the long, hot summer of 1970, many of the trees had died, and there seemed to be no indigenous bushes such as gorse and broom. The tall radio towers stand up starkly and the buildings are interspersed with a conglomeration of pipes. Seen closely the whole thing is startling and reminiscent of science fiction. From a distance seen through the typical coastal haze, it all appears like a mirage.

After the cliffs and lighthouse of Happisburgh, the marram hills run for several miles, from Sea Palling in the north-west, past Waxham, Horsey and Winterton, to the cliffs of Scratby in the south-east. These dunes, which act as a barrier between the North Sea and the Broads, have built up in front of the old coastline with its marshes at Horsey and its low cliffs at Winterton and Hemsby. Part of the village of Winterton stands on the edge of what were cliffs, and presents a some-what unusual picture, having a group of white-walled, thatched-roofed, circular, holiday chalets, ingeniously imitating the round form of the white, disused lighthouse. At Hemsby, two parallel lines of dunes, one on the old coastline and one on the beach, are peppered with little wooden bungalows dating from fifty or more years ago, and now linked by an untidy network of poles and overhead electricity lines over the marram, bramble and sea buckthorn.

The best of the dunes, about 260 acres, north of Winterton, is a National Nature Reserve, and is part of the 'area of outstanding natural beauty' between Waxham and Winterton. The dunes here are wide and high, and much of their area is well stabilized with marram and other grasses. There are patches of cross-leaved heather, an unusual sight in such surroundings, and in some damper areas are a few dwarf willows and birch. Water and peat accumulating in hollows have created conditions suitable for the natterjack toad, now a rare creature receiving special care and legal protection. Here too the common lizard lives and can be seen on hot sunny days. Several impressive blow-holes are left to illustrate the vulnerability of these dunes which were in fact breached by the tidal surge of 1953. One particularly low area of bare sand remains about a mile north of the coastguard station at Winterton. A bank of sand has been created across this area just behind

4

the beach and marram grass planted presumably to stabilize it and prevent another break-through of sea floods into the broads. From the higher points are views inland over what looks like continuous woodland but is in fact a panorama made up of small woods, scrub, hedgerow trees and tree-lined dykes and broads. Five windmills, formerly windpumps draining the marshes, can be seen, but in the early 1900s there must have been many more.

From the southern end of Winterton to the beginnings of Great Yarmouth, a distance of six miles, the sandy cliffs and beaches are fringed with thousands of chalets and caravans that came mostly in the first half of this century before effective controls existed. Depressing in their appearance and sheer size, these camps are a source of pleasure to countless holidaymakers, and an outstanding example of rapid manmade changes on what was until the early 1900s a bleak, windswept and largely deserted coast suffering constant attack by the sea. Change continues in that many of the caravans are being replaced by bright, little brick and glass chalets, and more of the camps are building large dance halls and swimming-pools. The villages of Hemsby, Scratby and Caister have been so swamped by all this and by many new houses and bungalows, that it is only by making a conscious effort that one notices the old cores with the parish churches, village inns and cottages with whitewashed walls and pantiled roofs. Winterton has suffered less than the others, and still has its old pattern of narrow lanes and old houses, and a fine church tower that is a landmark for miles around.

Having rather summarily dismissed the remainder of the Norfolk coast, except for Great Yarmouth which I shall describe later, I return to Horsey, where the best place to appreciate the closeness of the Broads to the coast, is the gallery at the top of Horsey Mill, a red-brick tower mill once used to help drain the marshes. Restored and maintained by the National Trust, it stands at the head of a dyke used by some of the Broadland craft from Horsey Mere and the network of Broads and rivers that lie inland. North and east one sees the sand dunes along the coast—south and west the reed beds and dykes and grazing marshes, and the open waters of the Mere.

This is a curious corner of East Anglia, and is indeed unique in Britain. Stretches of arable alternate with wide flat areas of grazing marsh and reed beds, with broads and rivers cluttered, where the roads cross them, with cafés, caravans, chalets, house-boats and yachts. But away from the roads all is quieter, and the marshes and reeds stretch away in the distance, to the line where the low hills and the trees begin again. Great banks of cloud hang over the dunes that mark the coastline, and the towers of churches and windmills stand out as splendid landmarks in a land that is nearly bare of trees except in small oases. Apart from the churches, the buildings and villages on this north-east shoulder of Norfolk are not attractive. Indeed some of the villages are pathetically mediocre, and made even more so by the rather shoddy accompaniments of the holiday traffic on the coast and the Broads. The little timber cafés and chalets and the caravans look even sadder when the summer crowds have deserted them.

The Nature Conservancy in their Report on Broadland in 1965, described it as "an extensive system of marshland, inter-connected waterways and shallow lakes or Broads lying in the valleys of the Rivers Bure, Yare and Waveney and their tributaries". From the land much of Broadland is very remote and almost inaccessible; much of it can be reached and seen only by boat. These peculiarities have helped the proliferation of wild life, but a serious threat has developed in the past fifty years from the greatly increased recreational use. It has caused a reduction of wild life in many areas and its withdrawal into more confined and protected areas; and a consequent strengthening of concern and action by conservationists. But the very fact that the Broads is an almost totally interconnected system has made it very difficult to stop or control the spread of people and boats and pollution. Because of the serious problems arising in recent years, Broadland is probably one of the most studied, documented and planned parts of Britain.

It was in 1960 that a paper published by J. M. Lambert and others, following years of physical and documentary research, established that the Broads were created by peat excavation in Saxon and Norman times. These continued for several centuries, but were flooded in the 1200s because of a slow rise in sea level relative to that of the land. In places it was possible, however, to continue excavations until much later; indeed in a few shallow workings until the mid-nineteenth century. The very extensive early workings thus became large areas of fairly shallow open water, mostly connected with the river system draining to the sea at Great Yarmouth. Since the Middle Ages, the evolution of the Broads has followed a very complex pattern affected by natural processes such as the changing sea level; and by human management, use and neglect. Those who wish to study these changes in detail can do so in other, specialized publications, and by study in the field. It will be sufficient for me to refer to general changes and trends, before describing a few typical parts of Broadland.

It seems certain that without human intervention, natural changes would have followed an inevitable succession. The very slow-moving waters of the rivers and broads would have gradually filled with detritus or silt on which growth of reed and sedge would have been followed by bushes and trees such as willow and alder. The ultimate fen carr or woodland, has come about in parts of Broadland, but in most of its area the natural succession has been slowed down, arrested or changed by man's activities, deliberate or otherwise. Where possible, he continued to dig peat for fuel and to cut reed and sedge, and alder coppice. All these had important economic uses, some of which, mainly reed and sedge for thatching, have continued on a reduced scale to the present day. Much of the old marshland was drained to create pasture and continues as such; some has recently been converted to arable, with varying degrees of success and with a continuing risk of flooding, for example in the Waveney valley near Beccles.

Dykes and staithes were created to facilitate the local transport of the reed, sedge and peat 'crops' in an area which was then and still is largely inaccessible by land. Main rivers were kept clear for commercial navigation by longer distance craft under sail until superseded by steam and later by oil. When commercial sailing craft died out before the middle of the twentieth century, the only trading craft left were comparatively large vessels plying round the coast and to and from the Continent, and the only river suitable for their use and with commercial potential, was the Yare between Great Yarmouth and Norwich. Apart from the need to keep the channel dredged to a sufficient depth, there are the effects of such traffic on the banks, on natural conditions and on other users. The greatest and most rapid influence on Broadland has been its 'discovery' in the late nineteenth century, and its subsequent use as a great holiday and recreational centre. Cruising boats were first advertised for hire in the 1880s, but the greatest growth in use has been in the past fifty years. During this time the busy season has extended at both ends until, in the late 1960s, it covered over five months of the year, and involved an estimated total of 260,000 people annually. In addition to the holidaymakers in their hired boats, chalets, caravans and hotels, there are innumerable private motor and sailing craft, and many thousands of day trippers and fishermen. To meet this demand, villages such as Wroxham have grown unnaturally full of boat-building workshops, boat-hiring premises, landing places, moorings, car parks, caravans, chalets, shops and cafés, which have caused a complete metamorphosis in little more than half a century. Much of what one sees in, for instance, Wroxham, Potter Heigham, Horning and Stalham, is far from pretty, and some of it looks positively shoddy and reminiscent of shanty towns of the mid-West. To be fair, I must admit that more recent developments have tended to be much better designed.

Between the bases and mooring places, the traffic of so many boats causes erosion and damage to river banks, undermining of trees, pollution of the water, and a general disruption for a long summer season of the natural peace and wild life. Fishermen also erode the banks, and some of them, like other users, contribute to the unsightly litter that disfigures the most heavily used localities. Eroded banks have to be piled. Plant, animal and bird life, except for the ubiquitous swans and ducks who follow the fleet, tend to be driven away from the busy places into protected and other less accessible rivers and broads. The more sensitive plants and animals, especially fish and insects, are affected by pollution including the drainage into rivers and broads of the residues of agricultural fertilizers from the arable fields on the sides of the valleys. They cause abnormal growth of algae which absorb most of the oxygen from the water, and prevent or restrict the survival of other plants and of animal life. Pollution is now much reduced by the enforcement of byelaws requiring sealed sewage systems on hired boats, and discharge from them only to proper disposal plants.

Natural consequences of unusual human activities are seen in the effects of coypu on the ecology of Broadland. During the 1930s and 1940s some of these large South American rodents escaped from nutria fur farms and spread rapidly through an area ideally suited to them. Breeding at any season, and having litters of four or five, perhaps twice a year, they increased enormously to become a serious agricultural pest. They feed on reed and sedge and on crops, particularly sugar beet, in fields adjoining the rivers and broads. Since 1960 trapping and shooting campaigns, and the occasional severe winter, have greatly reduced their numbers, but in such inaccessible areas many undoubtedly survive. By destroying reed and sedge, coypus have created some open water, but it is too shallow, and soon becomes recolonized with plant growth once the animals have been eliminated.

The centre for discussion of the Broads and their problems is Norwich, for there in particular are the headquarters of the County Council and the Regional Office of the Nature Conservancy. Apart from this, Norwich deserves a place in this chapter, for it is a port at the tidal limit of the Yare, and has a yacht station and boat-hiring yards for Broads cruisers. My brief description will be mainly of these aspects, as the best-known features, including the Cathedral and the Castle, are fully described in many other books.

From the sea and the Broads, Norwich is reached by small commercial ships and Broads cruisers sailing for nearly thirty miles up the narrow, winding Yare from Yarmouth. For all this distance there is only one bridge. the railway swing-bridge at Reedham, and road traffic can cross at only one point, by a small, rather primitive, chain ferry also at Reedham. The river flows through a flood plain that was once a wide arm of the sea; most of the marshes have been drained, but some areas remain as reedy swamps and broads.

At the approach to the city the river lies between high wooded parkland on the south and the steep hillside at Thorpe St Andrew with scattered, large houses set among the trees. An electricity generating station and gas works by the river used to receive their coal by ship; the electricity station now uses oil which arrives in small tankers, but the gas now comes by pipeline cross-country from Bacton. Small ships, up to about 600 tons and 150 feet in length, sail up the Yare into the Wensum at Trowse, and pass through the Carrow Road lifting bridge, taking in cargoes of timber and grain, and bringing out scrap metal and barley. But it does not require much exploring and research to realize that the activity of the port is not as great as it used to be. Along the river above the Carrow Road bridge, up as far as Foundry Bridge, the first fixed bridge as one travels up from seawards, are the remains of old quays and rail sidings and riverside buildings which were obviously connected with water-borne trade. Until well into the twentieth century sailing wherries, the local counterpart of the Thames sailing barge, and dumb lighters, carried cargoes up and down the Yare, and maintained a picturesque link with past days before rail and road transport became dominant. Now one wherry, the *Albion*, is preserved by a trust, and sailed for pleasure.

Just below the Carrow Road bridge are the Boom Towers, circular flint towers, one on either side of the river to control the passage of ships. They are at the south-eastern end of the two-mile wall which was built around the west side of the medieval city; the northern and eastern sides were bounded and defended by the winding River Wensum. Parts of the wall can still be traced, but cannot really be seen to the best advantage as they adjoin the line of the dual-carriageway inner ring road. As at Great Yarmouth, the town was still contained within the wall until the end of the eighteenth century.

Between Foundry Bridge, with its Victorian cast-iron parapets, and Bishopbridge, a fourteenth-century stone bridge, Broads cruisers are moored along the eastern bank in the shade of the trees of Riverside Road. On the opposite side is the ancient house and archway at Pull's Ferry where a short canal was constructed in Norman times for boats bringing stone for building the Cathedral which can be seen from here in all its glory across the green meadows. The quarter of the old city around the Cathedral is undoubtedly the most beautiful and unspoilt and it is a platitude to say it must not be missed. From the peace of the Cathedral Precincts, it is but a short walk to the busy Market Place overlooked by the Scandinavian-styled City Hall of the 1930s and flanked by the splendid church of St Peter Mancroft and the flint and stone Guildhall of the 1500s. The City Hall, from its elevated position looks across to the huge, square keep of the Norman castle, now a splendid museum where one can learn a great deal in the extremely well-designed galleries about the history, archaeology and natural history of Norwich and Norfolk. From the high mound on which the Castle stands, there is a very fine view all round of Norwich old and new, and in particular one can see how much of the medieval pattern within the walls has survived. There is, however, the regrettable intrusion, as in other cities, of huge, rectangular, office blocks of the 1950s and 1960s, which have destroyed the scale and character of parts of the city and spoiled the setting of some of the thirty pre-Reformation churches and other old buildings. Notwithstanding this, Norwich remains a city full of interest but I must leave it now to return to the Broads.

One fine day in early May 1973, I travelled, with others, in the Norwich City Football Club's luxury motor coach from Norwich to Wroxham on a mission, the nature of which I shall declare later. I noticed that many of the old, shacky wooden shops and other buildings in Wroxham had been replaced by permanent brick buildings, including a pleasant pedestrian shopping centre. The approaches were flanked by basins and boatyards, and I had the impression that the boat-building and hiring industries had grown very much since my previous visit. The boats were now larger and brighter, and aggressively modern in design, and very unlike the typical old Broads cruiser of pre-war and immediately post-war years, though a few of the old survive. We boarded a water-bus in a little backwater near Wroxham Station, and sailed under the old bridge which bore innumerable grooves and paint marks on its underside. We passed between the many boat-building and boat-hiring yards that stretch for half a mile downstream. Even so early in the season, there were many boats on the move; small day launches, water-buses, motor cruisers, and, on Wroxham Broad, a few sailing yachts. It was the first time I had noticed a distinct vernacular style of building, with timber frames and cladding, round timber supports, and reed-thatched roofs; the whole building on stilts and painted black and white, often with a boat dock below and water front and rear. Many of them were obviously built as summer-houses, but some of the more ambitious ones appeared to be permanent residences. Set back here and there in the woods, and approached by private waterways, were large, red-brick houses, some of them reed-thatched.

As we emerged from the built-up area, a change in the speed limit allowed us to accelerate from five knots to seven, between alder and willow woodland or carr where the trees stood with their roots in the water. We could see the results of, on the one hand, natural growth and succession, reeds, scrub, woodland and associated silting up, and on the other the steady process of erosion by the flow of water and its disturbance by the passing and repassing of thousands of boats. The lapping water eats away the soft earth between the trees, and then undermines the trees themselves. Lumps of clay bank collapse into the river and one by one the trees follow suit. In places, some vegetation and trees are being cleared; in others dead trees stand or lie and give the locality a depressed and derelict air, especially by the entrance to Salhouse Broad. Rubbish collects round the roots and must be even worse later in the summer.

Wroxham Broad, a fine stretch of open water backed by trees, accommodates a very large modern sailing clubhouse, dinghy park and moorings, and there is room for the larger sailing yachts to spread their wings. Salhouse Broad is smaller, but is accessible to the public from the land, and the slopes around the old oak trees are therefore badly eroded. Large areas have lost all their grass and just sandy soil remains, the erosion of feet being undoubtedly assisted by the weather. On the west bank of the river, the tree fringe is thin in parts and reveals the reeds and scrub developing behind it around Hoveton Great Broad, part of the Bure Marshes National Nature Reserve. Woodbastwick Marshes and Fen, south and east of the river, appear to be an impenetrable jungle. In an area of about 500 acres, there were, in 1845, 114 acres of open water, 345 acres of grazing and mowing marshes, reed and sedge beds and 51 acres of woodland and carr. By 1880–84 the respective figures had changed to 15, 409 and 86; in 1958 to 15, 190 and 305. Thus we see the dramatic growth of woodland and carr with the decline of the old traditional uses. These figures are illustrated in a much more vivid way by maps in the Nature Conservancy's 1965 Report.

Hoveton Little Broad is still a very pleasant wide stretch of water, overlooked by several large houses on the high ground to the north. Nearby on the riverside is an old red-brick tower mill converted tastefully to a summer house, with its own little garden and mooring. There are many more signs of affluence as one nears Horning. The north bank has many quite large chalets, with their own boats and moorings. On the other side are some rather sad-looking ancient houseboats, each with its own little private plot and landing place, reminiscent of a riparian Pitsea or Vange. Lower Street, Horning, contains a row of quite large new red-brick and roll-tiled houses, backing on to the river, each with its own boathouse or mooring place. Then follow lawns and trees and chalets, a less sophisticated version of Maidenhead, but including nevertheless an arboreal walk up to a hotel for lunch in idyllic surroundings complete with a flock of white doves.

We saw a good deal of natural bird life here in early May, but wondered if in the height of the season there would be any except ducks, swans and sparrows, and of course the white doves. Our short cruise showed us, and the government minister we had brought for just that purpose, the great conflicts and the need for a balance between conservation and exploitation. While some forms of pollution are to be controlled more effectively, there will still be pollution by noise, exhausts, rubbish, agricultural chemicals, and disturbance by the sheer numbers of people and boats, though one can hardly be surprised that they come in their thousands to such an essentially attractive area.

In the Yare valley just below Norwich there is a marked contrast between the gently undulating arable plateau and the flat flood plain about a hundred feet lower. It is quite a narrow flood plain until the river gets beyond Surlingham. The proportion generally for the whole of Broadland of 'reclaimed' marshland to unreclaimed fen is tremendous, except in one or two of the northern rivers. In other valleys such as the Waveney and the Yare, it is easy to see the value to wild life, and the great interest, of the few remaining unreclaimed areas, of which there is quite a long stretch north and east of Surlingham. Aerial photographs show it clearly, and also the various habitats within it, but they can be seen and appreciated very easily on the ground in the vicinity of Wheatfen Broad. Walking from 'dry land' towards the broad and river, one sees the successive natural stages in reverse. First is a climax oak woodland—very tall, thin oaks, with a few ash, beech, sycamore and rowan, and a great deal of natural regeneration looking hopeful for the future. Through it are several parallel, shallow drainage ditches, taking water to the river. Then one emerges into the reed marsh with scattered alder, oak and other scrub. One marsh, the Parish Marsh, had been burnt in March 1972, about two months before we walked through it, but was recovering well. We were told that there might be time for some plants to become established, though perhaps only temporarily, that had not been present in the reed beds. There is a thicker belt of scrub on the outer edge of the marshes and some open water in the centre. From a tree platform about twenty feet up, it is possible to see what areas were once open water, probably within living memory, and easy to imagine how soon, with all the flourishing vegetation in such damp conditions, the days of the remaining open water will be over.

There is quite a feeling of the jungle about it all, and it provides good homes and feeding for birds. These include heron, mallard, great crested grebe, moorhen, Canada geese, redshank, reed bunting, sedge warbler, grasshopper warbler, willow warbler and many woodland birds such as cuckoo and nightingale. The illusion of being in the jungle persists if one tramps in the swampy heat through the reed beds, with the peat squelching underfoot, to the river. Here it is a broad river with large willow trees, and used by many motor cruisers and the commercial shipping of the port of Norwich. There is some erosion of the banks, but a narrow fringe of reeds helps to protect them. At the 'inland' extremity of this fascinating nature reserve, one grass meadow east of the lane is grazed by cattle. To the west of the lane, a clear dividing line, is gently sloping arable land.

A short distance upstream, the Norfolk Naturalists' Trust have 250 acres at Surlingham Broad, making with Wheatfen Broad and its surroundings, a considerable area of protected land and water. It is liable to flooding in winter, but I doubt if it ever gets as desperately in

need of water in summer as do some of the fenland reserves of Cambridgeshire, such as Wicken Fen, which have been left at a higher level
than the surrounding drained and shrinking peatland arable.

Hickling Broad, having the largest area of open water in Broadland,
also attracts many people, but the numbers are not so great, nor the
pressures so intense, as it lies at the north-eastern extremity of the
network of waterways. The water of the Broad, and of Horsey Mere
nearby, through their proximity to the coast, is more brackish than in
most other parts. This has given them an unusual aquatic flora, a good
variety of fish, and exceptionally rich bird life. The Norfolk Naturalists' Trust owns 1200 acres of Hickling Broad and land around it, as a
nature reserve. Many students and specialists visit the reserve to study
particular subjects, but many amateurs like ourselves go for the beauty
of the place and for the delight of seeing birds and flowers and
butterflies.

The approach is by a narrow lane from the village. The last half mile
is a track between flat, wide fields and reed beds. When we went in
August 1966, only a few could visit the reserve at a time. With a
permit, we met the warden, George Bishop, since retired, at Whiteslea
Lodge, an old, white, weather-boarded, reed-thatched building
standing by the water. This used to be a marshman's cottage, and later a
shooting lodge from which the wildfowlers set out in gun punts to
slaughter winter duck by the hundred from butts set in the marshes.
The guns are gone and now the Trust welcomes those who come with
binoculars to see the wonderful variety of birds that live on or visit the
Broad and its surroundings. George Bishop, a quiet-spoken, keen-eyed
man, with white hair and a tremendous interest in his job, poled us
and his big golden Labrador, Sandy, in the canoe-shaped punt with
flared bows to part the reeds, across to the hides which lie in remote
narrow waterways away from the main channel where the holiday
yachts sail or motor through to the River Thurne and the rest of
Broadland.

We left Sandy to doze contentedly in the sun, in the bottom of the
punt, while we climbed into the first hide to look out across a small
lagoon filled with sunlight from a blue sky flecked with white clouds
chased by the cold north-west wind. But cold though it was, the light
was perfect as we watched the feeding waders and the lapwings and
coots, and the duck that flew strongly around and wheeled down on to
the water with a splash and a slide. One or two coypu, like giant rats,
crept out of the reeds and sunned themselves on the bank and splashed
about in the shallow water. While we watched the wild life on the
lagoon, the red and white and blue sails and the motor cruisers passed
to and fro behind the barrier of reeds, seemingly unaware of the birds
and the watchers so near to them. From the second hide, on letting

down the flap, we saw the flamingo that George Bishop had seen earlier in the day. Now, in brilliant sunshine, and wading in blue water, it was an amazing sight, not only for its strangeness here in Norfolk, but for its size and startling beauty. The pale pink of the neck seemed almost white in contrast with the brilliant orange, or was it salmon pink, of the wings; and the red bands round its 'knees' and 'ankles'. For a moment, as something startled the flamingo into spreading its wings of orange edged with black, I had a full view in my binoculars, but it did not take to the air, and we continued to watch it for some time. We found the other birds, ducks, waders, wagtails, moorhens, coots, pipits and a heron, less spectacular, but nevertheless fascinating at close quarters as they fed on the land, water or mud.

On leaving the hide, we found Sandy lying quietly in the sun, seemingly asleep but actually alert. We glided back across the channel, between the yachts, to Whiteslea Lodge, after circling the area we had previously seen from the elevated lookout platform. From the ground it had been possible to see only the reed beds on the far side of the narrow channel and sails passing in the distance, but from twenty feet up we could see across the expanse of the Broad, back to Hickling village, with the church and great brick tower of the windmill, now without its sails. In the distance, to the north and east, stretched the low line of the sand dunes, broken by the tower of Martham church, and the huge concrete water tower at Caister-on-Sea. Near at hand the reed beds were intersected by narrow channels of clear water, and here and there stood the stark, unconcealed 'hides' of the nature reserve. Before we left, George Bishop told us about some of the well-known people who had visited Hickling Broad, including the Duke of Edinburgh, and we saw a picture of King George VI with Aubrey Buxton the Norfolk naturalist, at a coot shoot in 1951. Shooting rights continued until 1965, and provided a useful income for the Trust, but the warden was pleased to tell us that there was now no shooting on the reserve. He also told us about one of the earliest bird photographers, a Miss Turner, who had spent many days in hides and boats, often in severe weather, photographing birds on the Broad.

In the January of 1968 the local newspaper carried photographs of George Bishop feeding the large flocks of ducks, geese and swans on the ice which prevented them from getting their natural food. This was an aspect not seen by the Broads holidaymaker, and was also in contrast with earlier years when the ice would have been broken to give access for wildfowlers. George Bishop retired soon after that winter of 1968. During the years that followed, interest in the reserve and the demand for access increased so much that facilities for visitors were developed considerably to include a three-mile water trail and additional hides. This work was done by the new warden, Lt. Col. Sankey and his staff, and won a Countryside Award in 1970, European Conservation Year. During the first three months after its opening in May 1970, well over 1000 people were taken round the water trail. Lt. Col. Sankey, alas, died in 1975, but the Trust carry on managing the reserve in the face of ever-increasing human activity, trying to interest and educate more and more people. It is in most respects a very successful venture, but since 1975 there has been an alarming decline in aquatic animal and plant life here and elsewhere in the Broads. The Trust, the Nature Conservancy Council and other bodies have initiated extensive research into the causes and possible solutions, but the situation at Hickling, with all its protection and management as a National Nature Reserve, illustrates how quickly and insidiously conditions can change in Broadland. It is, as the Nature Conservancy said in their report in 1965, a region "in which natural processes and man's activities have combined to create a unique environment. ... Much of it is ecologically unstable and the restorative processes of nature cannot keep pace with the demands on them." To regulate all the activities, some of which inevitably conflict with others, and to protect the best natural features and wild life and the local industries and agriculture, in the face of the steadily growing demands for recreation, is an almost impossible task that has kept the many interested bodies worried and busy for years. In 1978, as an alternative to a National Park, the local authorities, water and navigation authorities, set up a new Broads Authority which it is hoped will result in more effective co-ordination and control.

The Bure, the Yare and the Waveney, all winding their slow way through flood plains, once extensive arms of the sea, converge on Breydon Water, a wide estuary where the ebb tide runs straight and fast between the mud flats, feeding grounds for many wildfowl and waders especially in winter. The impressive remains of the Roman fort at Burgh Castle overlook the river and the marshes dividing Norfolk from Suffolk. Here the holiday sailor returning to Great Yarmouth leaves the Broads behind him, and comes to the ancient town which has grown over the centuries to cover four or five miles of the sand spit across the common mouth of the three rivers. Before taking his motor cruiser back to its berth at the Marina on the Bure near the Caister Road, he may, if he has the time, sail under the Haven Bridge and down to the harbour mouth and back. In this five-mile extension of his holiday he may see enough clues to ancient and modern history to persuade him to explore Great Yarmouth further before finally leaving it. This section of the river is lined with quays on either side. On the Gorleston side large quantities of timber are still imported and stored. A little further downstream, huge sea-going tugs for servicing North Sea oil rigs are moored beside enormous rectangular barges on which large, box-like, steel buildings are being constructed. Nearer the sea, the older houses of Gorleston stand among trees on higher ground overlooking the river, which takes a sharp turn to enter the sea between short, projecting piers. This is the point at which the citizens of Great Yarmouth, in the mid-sixteenth century finally succeeded in arresting the southward growth of the sand spit which for several centuries had seemed set on completely closing the harbour mouth. Even today work continues on repairing and improving the banks and piers which still suffer from the results of scouring and silting.

On the way back up-river, our sailor sees something of the industry that has spread in this century over the sandy acres of the South Denes. A huge frozen-food factory, built to take locally landed fish, now freezes mainly locally grown vegetables. The herring fishery, which was Yarmouth's main industry for centuries, came to a sudden end within ten years of the Second World War as supplies of North Sea herring virtually disappeared through over-fishing. The low buildings of the Fish Wharf, where the fish was landed from trawlers to be packed by Scottish fishergirls, still stand but like most of the buildings old and new along this reach of the river, they are occupied by firms connected with the North Sea oil industry. Having suddenly lost its thousand-year old herring fishery, Yarmouth was fortunate a few years later in becoming the main centre for the explorations and drilling for gas, and then to serve a similar role in the development of off-shore oil fields in the southern North Sea.

Between the Fish Wharf and the Town Hall, the splendid old houses of South Quay are reminders of past prosperity. Once merchants' houses they are now offices for the Customs and Excise, solicitors and shipping firms, and are fortunately well preserved. They cover a long period from the sixteenth to the nineteenth century, but their various styles harmonize and present a picture reminiscent of the North Brink at Wisbech. The Customs House of 1720, with a beautiful Georgian red-brick and stone front, and an early nineteenth-century porch, is the finest. It is now linked at the rear with a large new government office block in a very original and pleasing modern style with flint-faced walls, small, pointed windows and a slate roof with three pyramidal 'towers' like malting ventilators. On the edge of South Quay, near the Customs House and the flint and stone offices of the Port and Haven Commissioners, is an old, grey, 25-ton crane, built in 1907 by Cowan and Sheldon of Carlisle. A circle of spiked, cast-iron railings encloses it like a squire's tomb in a country churchyard. Beside it is a notice— "Dangerous Cranes at Work"! Between the crane and the road, are disused railway lines over which, until as late as 1968, freight wagons were hauled by shunting engines, with cowcatchers, preceded by a man carrying a red flag. Hall Quay, by the Town Hall, has some impressive Victorian buildings which overlook the quay where

holidaymakers embark on trips upriver to the Broads, and seaward to
the seals of Scroby Sands.

Our Broadland sailor now turns into the Bure and steps ashore at
the North Quay, a short distance from the north-west tower of the
Town Wall built in the thirteenth and fourteenth centuries to enclose
the medieval town. Although the Wall is broken by roads and buildings, enough remains for us to trace its whole length of about a mile to
a point at the far end of South Quay where a tiny plaque on the cut-off
end of the Wall records the demolition of Southgate in 1812.

Outside the Wall it is easy to trace successive waves of expansion
towards the sea and the beach, starting in the early 1800s east of the
Market Place, and continuing through the nineteenth and twentieth
centuries to give us what is now the biggest seaside resort between
Southend and Skegness. South of the Marine Parade, which is reminiscent of Blackpool in the bustle and multiplicity of its popular amuse-
ments, are reminders of earlier days. The fine, grey brick quadrangle
of St Nicholas Hospital was built as a naval hospital in 1809–11. Nelson,
who returned to Yarmouth after the Battles of the Nile and Copen-
hagen, is commemorated nearby in the Nelson Column. It was erected
on the South Denes in 1817, about twenty-five years before his
monument in Trafalgar Square, but, at Yarmouth, it is Britannia not
Nelson who stands at the top at an identical altitude above the ground.

Back within the town walls, we can still trace the main features of
the medieval pattern in the three principal north-south streets and the
Market Place. At the north-east corner stands the Church of St
Nicholas, reputed to be the largest parish church in England. First built
in the twelfth century, it became ruinous in Georgian times but was
restored in the nineteenth century, only to be burnt out in 1942 and
rebuilt in the late 1950s. The medieval tollhouse suffered similar troubles
and was again restored after the war. A few other old houses near it
remind us that until the 1940s the old town had a unique feature of
great interest in the Rows. Over 150 narrow parallel lanes, from 2 feet
6 inches to 6 feet in width, ran across the town east to west from King
Street and the Market Place to the Quays. W. G. Hoskins attributed
this remarkable pattern to a perpetuation of accesses between fishermen's plots along the river in medieval times, and a colleague of his at
Leicester University suggested that the Rows had been successively
prolonged westwards as the shore receded with a general fall in river
level in relation to the land. The pattern has virtually disappeared since
1940, through war-time damage and by post-war redevelopment to
provide better housing and roads; a process which resulted by 1966 in
the unfortunate loss of many buildings of historic interest. In that year
the Borough Council published a Town Centre Appraisal which
pessimistically concluded that most of the historic centre and most of

the few remaining historic buildings would have to be sacrificed in further redevelopment if the town was to retain and enhance its status as a sub-regional centre. Proposals in 1967 paid a little more heed to conservation and suggested retaining thirty-five Rows. By 1977 rather fewer had survived, but some can still be seen as narrow gaps between shops in King Street and the Market Place, and along the Quays. In spite of this, Great Yarmouth between the walls and the river, is still a fascinating town in its history and its visible relics.

4

Suffolk Coast and Estuaries

THE general structure of Norfolk and Suffolk, sloping gently from north-west to south-east, has given the two counties very different coastlines. They both have smooth lines because of the crumbling nature of the cliffs but the coast of Suffolk is broken every few miles between the broad waters of Breydon in the north and the Stour in the south, by wide estuaries and small streams.

Beyond the hotels and houses of Gorleston, the huge holiday camps of Hopton and Corton lie just behind the low, crumbling cliffs. Along this stretch, sea defence works are, as at Trimingham, reducing the cliffs to stable slopes covered with grass and largely devoid of interest.

At Lowestoft the sea has built up a shingle Ness, the easternmost point in Britain, projecting some way in front of the old line of the cliffs. North of the town is an area of raised beach called the Denes where the scrubby bushes attract many migrating birds on their way north and south.

The old town stands on a ridge about fifty feet above the wide beach on which were the curing houses and the net-drying grounds of the fishermen. Some relics remain in the form of dilapidated brick and pantiled buildings, and scattered posts, and the area is still reached from the High Street by about a dozen narrow alleys known as scores. These are similar to the rows of Great Yarmouth except that in Lowestoft they need long flights of steps to get up and down what were once the coastal cliffs. At the north end of the High Street stands the lighthouse on top of the cliff about a quarter of a mile back from the present coastline, which has been alternately built up and eroded. Many successive sea walls around the Ness have been pounded to rubble during the past hundred years, but a large area has been built over since the harbour was created in 1831. Houses and factories associated with the fishing industry spread over the beach in Victorian times. Many of the houses have disappeared in the twentieth century, and large factories for the processing and freezing of fish and vegetables have appeared.

The herring fishery is still here, though on a smaller scale than before the war, with modern diesel trawlers instead of the steam trawlers and the picturesque sailing drifters which survived until the inter-war years. The fishing fleet continues to use the outer part of the harbour, while inland other industries have transformed the muddy tidal creek known as Lake Lothing. There is a base, with tugs and ships, serving North Sea oil rigs, but this activity is not on as large a scale as at Great Yarmouth. On the south side, near the swing bridge, is a quay and large crane built to receive and handle heavy engineering components for Sizewell nuclear power station; the facilities remain, awaiting a decision on when the second station will be constructed. Upstream, imported timber is unloaded for a huge joinery factory. Near this are the shipyards, building small but specialized ships, such as tugs, ferries and fast naval vessels, for customers all over the world. The quays and buildings and the ships under construction are impressive features in this rather confined waterway between the two halves of the town.

South of the harbour mouth, the scene is still very much a Victorian one, with long terraces of tall, grey brick boarding-houses and hotels. The southern arm of the harbour mouth has carried, for about twenty years, a building of great interest to ornithologists. The seaward end of the South Pier Pavilion was faced with corrugated asbestos, with a narrow ledge about twenty feet up. This ledge was discovered by kittiwakes who established what was then their only nesting site between the cliffs of Yorkshire and Dorset. Since then, other small colonies have been nesting, along with fulmars, on ledges on the cliffs at Hunstanton and on the north Norfolk coast. It now seems, regrettably, that the kittiwakes will no longer be able to nest at Lowestoft; the Pavilion is to be rebuilt, and the old Royal Hotel which when empty accommodated a few nests, has already been demolished.

Pakefield, now a suburb of Lowestoft, was, until the turn of the century, a separate village with a thatched church and quaint, narrow streets of fishermen's cottages. Long before and after 1900 the village suffered serious erosion of its cliffs, and house after house tumbled to the beach, even into the 1940s. J. A. Steers, in *The Sea Coast*, records the loss of land east of the church: 1883–1905, 100 feet; 1905–1927, 270 feet; 1927–1947, 250 feet. One has to read between the lines of these cold statistics to realize what they meant to the people of Pakefield as the years went by and the sea advanced to demolish their homes. Dozens of small houses in and near Beach Street, which led down to the lifeboat house, and many others between there and the church,

5

disappeared during the first forty years of the twentieth century. In spite of all the obvious dangers, several new roads were laid out and new houses built east and south of the church in the early 1900s.

However, by about 1950, this section of the coast seemed to have become more stable. In the years that followed, a concrete wall and promenade were built as an extension of the Lowestoft promenade, along the foot of the Pakefield cliffs to a point just north of the church. The cliffs were graded to a gentle slope, presumably their 'angle of repose', and partly grassed and partly concreted. Natural forces, helped by wooden groynes, built up further protection in the form of a wide shingly beach which now extends at low water to approximately the line where the cliffs stood in 1884. It is awe-inspiring to look over this wide beach and to remember that its area was covered less than a century ago with a network of narrow streets and many houses. The landward part of the beach, slightly lower than the shingle ridges between it and the sea, is sandy and is acquiring additional stability by the growth of marram grass. Alexanders, mallow, ragwort and bind-weed in their various seasons, grow and flower on the cliffs and banks, preserving some of the old, quiet atmosphere away from the formal seaside civilization of Lowestoft. Longshore fishing boats lie on the beach, and near the church are some of the old pantiled and thatched cottages of red brick and pebble. The church stands firm and square with its thatched roof and sturdy tower. Its east end is only 50 feet from the top of the low cliff; in 1884 the distance was 700 feet! In calm weather there is a feeling of peace and security, but even as recently as 1973 steel piling was being driven in beside the wooden groynes to help in the accumulation of a protective beach. I imagine it will be a long time before the older people in Pakefield feel completely safe, for they remember what has happened in their lifetimes, and they know that, only a few miles to the south, the cliffs are still crumbling and slipping away year by year at Covehithe, Easton and Dunwich where villages, towns and harbours have long ago disappeared under the waves.

Leaving behind Pakefield, and Kessingland, a rather drab village that has also suffered a good deal from coastal erosion, I come to the 'real coast' of Suffolk, the coast I have seen and walked at all seasons and in all weathers from Arctic to sub-tropical. It is remarkably undefiled and has a wonderful variety of scene and atmosphere in the thirty-four miles from Benacre Ness to Felixstowe. This is the part of the Suffolk coast which in 1970 shared with the north Norfolk coast the double honour of designation as an area of outstanding natural beauty and recommendation by the Countryside Commission for special protection as a 'heritage coast'.

As we noticed from the Dutch ship, the Suffolk coast has alternating lengths of low cliffs and shingle banks behind which are 'broads' that get progressively silted up and choked with reeds until very little open water is left; they have, as at Covehithe and Easton, been further curtailed by the coast-line advancing inland.

I remember a visit with members of the Suffolk Naturalists' Society to Covehithe and Benacre in mid-March 1969. Although we had heard the weather forecast, we were not really prepared for the mighty and bitter blast that met us at the cliff top. It roared in straight off the sea which it had whipped into a fury of sandy, foaming waves rolling on to the beach at high speed. The air was full of spray and the beaches to north and south merged quickly into a misty haze. As we walked north along the cliff, our ears were frozen and our eyes streaming, but we soon had the first and most splendid sight of birds on this strenuous and exhilarating day. About forty geese in beautiful, fluid V-formation, flew southwards over the sea, with a strong, confident flight that appeared unshaken by the roaring gale. We could not identify them, but the spectacle in itself was enough and one we would not have seen in summer.

The wood by the broad was still fringed on the seaward side by the standing grey skeletons of oaks killed by the sea water of the floods in early 1953. The living trees farther back were still bare of leaves, and the whole scene was in utter contrast with my first memory of it on a warm, sunny April day about ten years earlier. Then, the woods and reed beds were full of the song of chaffinch and blackbird, and reed and sedge warblers. Now we saw only a few mallard floating on the broad and a heron standing on the far shore against the dark woods, silent but for the roar of wind and sea.

It is hard to understand how plants grow and survive on a coast where conditions are so hostile for so much of the year, for even in summer, cool, salty breezes and mists come in off the sea. Yet even in late winter, it was apparent that the shingle had a prolific growth of plant life, ranging from lichens to gorse, broom and hawthorn. In addition to the scattered natural growth, was an area recently planted with rows of marram grass. It was too early to see any building up and consolidation of sand around the plants whose success in stabilizing loose sand, especially on the coast, follows from its remarkable ability to form fresh shoots and roots when submerged by the rising sand. It can, provided the sand does not accumulate too rapidly over the plant, continue to grow upwards through many feet of sand.

The marram was a reminder of the rapidly changing conditions on the coasts of Norfolk and Suffolk. The banks of sand and shingle north of Benacre Broad are clearly subject to change with every gale and storm and high tide. Wind and wave move the sand and shingle, and wash up great lumps of dark, woody peat from the North Sea bed.

These are made up of vegetable matter, part-way to the coal stage, and contain many twigs and small branches. One can also find remains of insects, for example the wing cases of beetles. Lumps of amber, a fossilized resin, sometimes with insects embalmed in them, are also found in these masses of peat. They evidently come from the Dogger Bank where once lay the delta of the Rhine with silty lands covered with vegetation.

At Benacre, as at Covehithe, Easton and Minsmere, the little river has become barred from the sea by a shingle bank built up by sea drift; and a lagoon or broad has formed behind the bank. In time broads like these become silted up and reed beds encroach on the open water. South of Minsmere in particular the silting has led ultimately to grazing meadows.

Going south from Covehithe, we were reminded of the erosion by the sea of this coast over the centuries, with the disappearance of villages, churches and houses, and even towns such as Dunwich; a strange combination of direct destruction and of the choking of rivers and ports by the accumulation of silt and sand and shingle. The rate of erosion on parts of the Suffolk coast has slowed down very much since 1940, but as we saw very clearly on this March day in 1969 and again in 1975, the cliffs are still crumbling rapidly. Gales, sea spray, rain, frost all eat away the soft earthy and sandy cliffs. Cultivation to within a yard of the edge must increase the seepage of rain through the cliff face and hasten the process of disintegration. It is hard, incidentally, to believe that any worth-while crop can be grown on the light sandy soil at the cliff edge, or that fertilizer will stay in the land long enough to increase a yield already limited by biting winds and salt spray.

Farther south, at Covehithe Broad and Easton Broad, we saw more effects of human activity. On the beach were several dead gulls, guillemots and razorbills, and a diver, victims of oil on the sea. Some were only slightly oiled, but others were completely covered in vile, black slime. They had been blown ashore by the easterly gale and left stranded by the receding tide. Here and there were congealed lumps of the black oil that had killed them. The beaches were littered as never before with driftwood which has its uses, and with ugly and useless litter that will not rot away. Coloured plastic cups, bottles and containers, glass bottles and electric light bulbs, were scattered widely, and as much as a hundred yards inland by the onshore gale. Much of this rubbish must be thrown overboard from ships, and creates awful conditions for those who visit our coast in summer.

Above Easton Broad, many old trees had died and were standing in the dead bracken, through which bluebells were pushing in the hope of flowering before being swamped by the new fronds of bracken in the summer. One or two dead trees had fallen to the beach and lay like grotesque, grey skeletons. South of the broad the cliffs show bands of shelly crag, sand, bluish grey clay and rusty, soft sandstone, and contain many fossilized shells. Here too the weather and the farmer are still working on the cliffs, and as they crumble, sand and shells trickle down, and huge lumps of the greasy, blue clay fall on to the exposed layer of sandstone. As at Pakefield, it is fascinating to compare the Ordnance Survey maps from 1885 to 1971 for the coastline at Easton Bavents. Losses were 200 feet from 1885 to 1903, 180 feet from 1903 to 1927, 330 feet from 1927 to 1971; a total of 710 feet. This was about the same as at Pakefield until the 1950s, but at Easton and Covehithe the erosion continued after 1950 and is still going on in the late 1970s. Some authorities claim that Easton Ness was once the easternmost point of Suffolk, and thus of Britain, but the present position of the cliff line is two miles west of Lowestoft, and there is no Ness at Easton.

The gale was still keeping the small birds out of sight, except for the occasional brave skylark, soaring and singing over the fields. A pair of swans, a red-breasted merganser and several mallard were enjoying the comparative calm of the broad behind a low shingle bank. They had apparently discovered, as we did later, that the fury of the gale seemed to spend itself on striking the cliffs and beaches, and a hundred yards inland conditions were relatively peaceful. Southwards, the little town of Southwold became more prominent on its low hill, surrounded by the sea and marshes. It has more than once become an island in times of flood. The white lighthouse and the great flint tower of the church stood up boldly above the houses. Another man-made change was seen in the marshy area between Reydon and Southwold. This had been drained by dredging out the waterway of Buss Creek and creating grazing meadows in place of marsh and mud. Until a few years ago there were lagoons and patches of shingle where terns nested and waders fed; here we had seen our first spotted redshank. Today we saw only starlings and lapwings.

We turned inland and followed the route of the Southwold light railway, which closed in 1929 after fifty years, across the common to the bridge over the River Blyth. Then the path curved away from the railway, through the gorse on Walberswick Common, towards the tall church tower, reminiscent of Covehithe in its size and ruined nave. Walberswick lies on a ridge that must in the Middle Ages have been a promontory between two sizeable arms of the sea, now the Blyth to the north and Westwood Marshes on the south. They carried many ships and barges until the rivers and harbours became silted up and Dunwich disappeared into the sea. Now they are some of the most attractive areas in the country for birds and other wild life, and there-fore for naturalists. From the coast to the head of the Blyth estuary, and southwards, lies a fascinating area of reed and marsh, heath and pines

and tidal mud flats, all covered since 1972 by a National Nature Reserve
agreement between the landowner and the Nature Conservancy. At
Blythburgh bridge, a sluice has been proposed to prevent tidal flooding
of the meadows upstream. It will be interesting to see what ecological
changes result, apart from the inevitable reseeding of some old rough
grazing meadows and the conversion of others to arable, and the
consequent changes in the valley landscape. Without the sluice, the
influence of salt water goes some way inland; bladderwrack grows on
posts at the river's edge, and small crabs are left stranded at low tide.
The meadows near the bridge are no doubt poor grazing, but they
attract shelduck and redshank, and the reeds along the brackish ditches
offer nesting sites for reed and sedge warblers.

Walberswick has kept much of its old and picturesque appearance,
but behind its façades great changes have taken place with the lavish
restoration of old cottages and houses owned by weekenders and retired
people from London. The riverside is an intriguing, untidy, old-
fashioned mixture of sand and shacks and boats, and the ramp survives
from which the old car ferry used to drag itself to and fro on chains
across the river to Southwold. The view of that beautiful little town is
unfortunately marred from Walberswick by the caravan camp on the
other side of the river. From the green where our walk ended, we could
hear the roar of the gale and of the waves on the shingle beaches,
reminding us how the lives of the local people in past centuries have
been ruled by the elements and how their environment and their
fortunes have been changed by the wind and the sea. The view to the
south from the shore is over a wide, slow arc of sandy beach to
Dunwich where the earthy cliffs rise below the woods, only to fall
again to sea level behind the Minsmere beaches. Beyond, massive but
somehow insubstantial at seven miles' range, is the square block of the
Sizewell nuclear power station. In spite of this modern feature, the
overall scene is one of peace and simple beauty, though the building of
a second, much larger power station will greatly increase the effect on
the landscape.

From the old coastguard cottages on the Dunwich cliffs, one looks
out over the reed beds and flashes of Minsmere. On a June day with a
strong wind from the south-west and small white clouds scudding
across a blue sky, there is a fairly rough grey sea, with white breakers
along the curving shoreline, but no sea spray hanging over the beach to
obscure the visibility. All is clear and bright and seems to become even
more so as the day wears on. In this sort of landscape, perhaps as much
as in any other, the colours change greatly with the season. In midsummer, the reeds are predominantly green, with a few faint streaks of
old, dry reed among the new. The heather is still dark brown and the
corn green in the fields rising above the reed beds. On Westleton Heath,

not far away, the pale, dead grass runs like broad streams between the dark heather. There are scattered elder, hawthorn and gorse bushes, with a background of woods with greens of various shades and forms; and the wind sounds like the sea as it blows through the heather and the thorn. On a bright winter's day, the sea is a sheet of dazzling silver, and the reed beds straw-coloured, relieved with gleams of open water. In the marshes of the middle distance were, until a few years ago, the grey silhouettes of two wind-pumps and two old pumping windmills. The dark, almost black pine forest contrasts with the dull purple of the new shoots in the birch scrub. The slopes are golden and brown with dead bracken and dry heather, but the gorse is green and flowering in golden profusion. The 'inlet' below the tail of Dunwich cliffs is fascinating at any time, with its sea of reeds and shoreline of alder and birch scrub, and a few skeleton trees evidently killed by salt water.

How unpredictable and unseasonable conditions can be on this coast! The shore and the broads at Covehithe and Benacre can be lashed by the fury of a gale in summer, and they can be idyllic on a still, sunny winter day. Peaceful conditions are experienced more often just away from the coast, on the estuaries where the boisterous effects of wind and tide give way to the normally quiet ebb and flow between the wide banks, as on the Butley River. In a flat calm, a few days after a southerly gale, it is seen from the low hill at Boyton as a winding silver stream, with the shingle bar of Orfordness and the open sea beyond. The air is crystal clear and the Orfordness lighthouse and the Shipwash lightship are easily seen against a shallow border of sky under a canopy of dark, indigo cloud. On the eastern horizon huge masses of sunlit cumulus appear to be sailing on the sea. The river, on the early ebb, glides seaward from the west like oily ink, from the Sudbourne woods, blue in the distance. While the light lasts there are the sharp contrasts of colour in the golden stubble, the green pastures with sheep and cattle, and the red Suffolk brick and pantile of the cottages and farms. The tide soon leaves a narrow belt of mud, occupied quickly by a string of gulls, redshank, dunlin, ringed plover and a few oyster-catchers. A curlew calls as it flies over, but a heron flaps silently by; rooks congregate in the top of a dead tree. In the pale blue water of the dykes are white swans with their grey cygnets, and a few black moorhens. Duck, put up by occasional distant shots, fly high and strong against the luminous sky. Down river, a man in a dinghy puts off from his yacht at anchor in the calm, silent water. Beyond, lies the eternal sea, and as the river and the daylight ebb slowly eastwards, the lights flash brightly from the tower of Orfordness and the lantern of the Shipwash.

A footpath from Chillesford skirts round Decoy Wood and across open country sloping down to the reed beds and marshes by the upper reaches of the Butley River. The path curves along the side of the low hill, overlooking the creek and the mill and the dark, distant forests. In warm spring sunshine, the nutty scent of gorse and the heat reflected from the wiry turf make this feel like the land of the lotus-eaters. A turn suddenly reveals the reddish-orange cliff-face of a small pit cut into the hillside, with layers of shells laid in the red crag and sand. The sand between the shelly bands is riddled with hundreds of holes made by nesting sand martins. The birds come and go swiftly and constantly, chattering quietly as they fly, their shadows passing and repassing over the sunlit face of the pit. Here and there a rabbit sits basking in the sunny entrance to a larger hole, evidently reached from ground level somewhere above the pit. Redshank circle over the marsh, piping insistently in protest at human disturbance.

The head of the Butley estuary is silted up and covered with reedbeds which are cut in rotation year by year. The bundles lie on the west bank near Butley Mills and are used for thatching, and occasionally for reed fences. In contrast, the River Ore between Slaughden Quay at Alde-burgh and its mouth at Shingle Street, is broad and deep and flows fast between the river walls, with only a narrow belt of mud at low water. With the consolidation and maintenance of the walls since 1953, it seems there can be little further change, except south of Butley River. Here, outside the river wall that encloses the grazing marshes, are saltings in an advanced stage of evolution, with a mixture of low shingle ridges and tidal mud and runnels. When I walked over this area in 1972, it was extensively colonized with sea purslane and grass had taken over the drier parts. These saltings are covered only by very high tides, but they are cut by several narrow runnels where the sea purslane thrives especially on the muddy banks. As it grows, it traps the silt and the runnels gradually fill up and disappear.

The shingle ridges here and at Shingle Street farther south were apparently created by the sea bringing material southwards along the coast before the Ness grew to its present length. Orfordness itself is one of the most spectacular natural phenomena on the coast of Britain, surpassing in length and in interest the better known Chesil Bank in Dorset. The River Alde, winding its lovely way from Snape Bridge between low wooded slopes on the north and marshes and cornfields on the south, once reached the sea at Aldeburgh. But, upon reaching a point only fifty yards from the sea, it is deflected southwards for eleven miles by a long shingle bank that was built up by the sea over the centuries. J. A. Steers, who made an intensive study of Orfordness, considers, although he admits that the old maps and evidence are inaccurate and unreliable, that the southern tip reached a point—Stoneyditch—opposite Orford in the Middle Ages, and remained roughly in that position for many years. Once the spit grew southwards, the fortunes of the port declined as the harbour entrance grew more distant and more difficult.

In 1952, shortly before the great sea floods of early 1953, Professor Steers posed the question—"what would happen if the sea broke through?" the narrow neck of shingle at Slaughden. He thought it very unlikely to happen, and, that if it did, the sea would be likely to replenish the shingle before the river could make full use of the gap. This is what actually happened on the night of 31st January–1st February 1953, and in the period that followed, but surprisingly Steers did not refer to the Slaughden gap in the "Appendix on The Storm of 1953 and its Aftermath" which he added in 1960 to the third edition of his book.

Significant physiographical changes are now confined mainly to the southern end of the spit and to Orford Haven and Shingle Street, but its past development can best be understood by a study of aerial photographs which reveal clearly the pattern of ridges from end to end, except where parts were used for wartime bombing practice, and later for defence research and radar establishments. From the beginning of the twentieth century, Orfordness has attracted the attention of governments looking for remote and inaccessible places on the east coast for defence works. The latest threat, as yet unresolved but strongly opposed, is the possibility of a nuclear power station that would be developed in stages over a long period to become the biggest in Britain. In the meantime, the botanists and ornithologists study Orfordness while they may, and the Nature Conservancy Council seeks to extend its National Nature Reserve over the area where the Central Electricity Generating Board are doing their feasibility study. Farther north, on the Lantern Marshes site of the short-lived radar station, the British Broadcasting Corporation have established a transmitting station for overseas broadcasts.

The Butley River joins the main river, the Ore, opposite the tail of Havergate Island where the avocets nest. There is also a colony of black-headed gulls whose noisy cries carry across the water. But one can appreciate just what a remarkable sanctuary this is only by getting a permit and spending a day on the island with the warden. Reg Partridge, until his death in 1974, used to wait at Orford Quay for the day's visitors. His son has taken over as warden and, with comparable skill and knowledge, steers the little motor launch quietly down-river, keeping as far as possible out of any waves raised by a fast-flowing ebb against a strong south-west wind. On the left the lighthouse and the ugly concrete 'grandstands' of Orfordness give way to the narrowing shingle bank; on the right low hills form the western horizon. A narrow belt of mud begins to appear along the shore of the island, and a whimbrel wheels overhead and lands on the Ness. A sandwich tern ranges to and fro over the river, head turning from side to side, and dives for fish with an impressive splash.

As we come ashore, voluntary wardens help us from the boat. We walk up the beach past a delightful weathercock in the shape of an avocet and chicks, and a post showing the level of the 1953 floods which covered the whole island. The sea walls enclose large areas of rough grass and muddy lagoons where the levels of the water, except in times of rare disaster, are controlled to give the right conditions at the right time for the island's seasonal bird populations. As on the Butley River, we are distracted from the birds by the delightful scenery, much of it seen before but from different angles. It is reminiscent of the Norfolk coast seen from Blakeney Point, but on a smaller and more subtle scale. There are dark woods, pale golden corn and stubble, brown plough and green pastures, and mellow red farms and barns.

The distant town of Orford is embowered in trees. Between the tall keep of the Norman castle and the church tower are the old red and grey roofs and walls of the houses. The river is quieter as we return upstream, the town comes nearer, and in the brilliant afternoon sun, it is seen in its full beauty with the broad river as foreground. From here the peace and beauty are virtually unmarred and we can feel ourselves back in the times before the motor vehicle, for old houses conceal from the river the solid mass of cars in the Market Place, on the Quay and behind it, and the late summer bank-holiday crowds driving round looking for somewhere to stop their hot metal boxes. Any return from the sea gives this contrast, and the regrettable return from romance to reality, but here the shock is greater than returning to a large port where one expects to find the bustle of people and cars and trains and cranes.

It is impossible to write about the coast without straying to the heaths and the woods, and, of course, much of the coast is approached through them.

On a fine late April day, Staverton picnic place, between the road and the old oak woodland, is filled with warmth and light in which bird song brings the feel not of spring, but of early summer. In the old oaks, birch and beech we look at first in vain for the chiffchaffs and willow warblers whose songs delight our ears. The willow warbler's clear, sweet, descending trills make one feel summer is near. A tree creeper flies with nesting materials to a hole behind the loose bark, only six feet from the ground. A pair of great spotted woodpeckers flies over, and early swallows and redstarts are seen. It is interesting to compare this area with Thetford Forest and what is left of the Breckland. There is a subtle, indefinable difference, due perhaps to slight differences in soils, contours and patterns of planting and cultivation;

but probably due mostly to the nearness to the sea of the forests east of Woodbridge.

There are relics of past splendours between Chillesford and Sudbourne. The road is lined with rhododendrons, and fine specimen trees stand in the old park in startling contrast with the dark though beautiful uniformity of the utilitarian forests of the 1920s and 1930s. Iken Heath is no longer a true heath, though small clumps of Scots pine stand in the vast stony fields. There is a view of the Alde estuary, a beautiful expanse of blue water. Iken church stands on its little wooded promontory overlooking the river, and on the far side the heaths and woods stretch away towards Aldeburgh. Faintly in the background are the two lines of tall, grey pylons marching away to the west from Sizewell.

Then you pass the long, curving front of Snape Maltings, with their brick walls and wooden steps and sack hoists, and the arch and the clock, and the Virginian creeper beautifying it all. There is the old inn, the Plough and Sail, whose silhouette sign reminds you of the days when plough and sail were indeed closely connected in places such as this. If you want to get to the coast, you must resist the temptation to explore the Maltings and to see the famous concert hall, which was opened in 1967 to provide a home for the Aldeburgh Festival events that had outgrown the capacity of the local halls and churches. It is described in a later chapter.

By the Maltings, at the limit of navigation, the road until 1960 passed over a little hump-backed bridge, picturesque in warm, red brick, especially when seen from the river. Built in 1802, it eventually became an obstruction and a danger to modern traffic, and like the bridge over the Blyth Navigation at Blyford, it was cleared away and replaced by a flat, wide modern bridge, over which you can drive without realizing it is a bridge, and without even seeing the river unless you are on a bus. At the top of the hill, on the common opposite the church, is a bus shelter built with bricks from the old bridge, and with a top shaped like it.

The common, like many other Suffolk heaths and commons in the twentieth century, has been cleared of gorse and heather, and ploughed and cultivated. It survived as heathland until the 1960s, but other similar areas between Snape and Aldeburgh were not cleared until the mid-1970s. These landscape changes were taking place in post-war years, while Aldeburgh, formerly the preserve of fishermen and wildfowlers, and discerning outsiders, was becoming increasingly famous as the home of the festival started by Benjamin Britten and his friends in 1948.

The town today shows many signs of the fame and prosperity brought to it by the festival directly and indirectly. It has a bright, well-kept and busy look about it, but fortunately both the sea front and the centre of the town still have much of their Victorian and Edwardian atmosphere. The pattern of the lower, older, part is long, straight and narrow, parallel with the coast, with little streets and alleys connecting the High Street with the beach. On the beach itself, below the hill on which stands the parish church, is the sixteenth-century Moot Hall. This small, but impressive, timber-framed building, with red-brick infilling, was once presumably in the market place in the centre of the old town. The destruction of medieval Aldeburgh by the sea must have been as dramatic, on a smaller scale, as that of the much larger port and town of Dunwich, but by comparison little seems to have been recorded about this phase of Aldeburgh's history.

South of the Moot Hall most of the houses and hotels have their backs to the sea, or crouch behind high walls. The lifeboat is launched from the beach, and a quaint little nineteenth-century tower houses a coastguard station. Beyond the town the beach merges into the narrow shingle bar which is the north end of Orfordness. Since the sea broke through in 1953, a concrete sea wall has been constructed on the seaward side of the narrowest section, where it is now a mere 40 feet between the face of the wall and highest tide levels in the river at the back of the bank. The wall runs as far as the Martello tower which in recent years has been restored and converted into holiday flats, another enterprise by the Landmark Trust who specialize in rescuing unusual historic buildings. This tower is, I believe, unique in having the ground plan shape of a four-leafed clover instead of a circle. It stands in a circular walled pit, now cut on the seaward side by the new concrete sea wall. The single small door, reached from landward by a wooden footbridge, has slits for drawbridge chains, and a small window on either side. There are very small windows on each of the bulging 'wings'. The tower is of yellow and brownish bricks, with stone frames for the door and window openings, and stands on a raked plinth of granite blocks. It seems to have been remarkably well restored and is a splendid feature in a very open setting.

To the south one looks along the shingle bank to Orfordness light-house and the radio masts on the marshes. Inland of the river, and behind the reclaimed marshes, farms and woods stand on the higher ground. Northwards, between the marshes and the sea, the little town has spread over the low hill near the church, while in the foreground many yachts are moored on the river at Slaughden near the modern buildings and dinghy park of the yacht club. This particular scene has changed considerably since the 1940s when it still had what I can only describe as the natural, untidy charm and interest of tidal waters used mainly by local fishermen and wildfowlers.

At that time, with the tarred wooden huts, and old fishing boats, by the marshes and the mud, it was probably little changed in appearance since George Crabbe, Aldeburgh's native poet, wrote such grimly, realistic descriptions of the town and its people whom he described as "a wild amphibious race"! He is still quoted in nearly every book on the Suffolk coast, and the story of *Peter Grimes* was taken by Benjamin Britten from *The Borough*, a long poem written in 1810.

North of the Moot Hall an open road runs between the marsh and the shingle to Thorpeness, a seaside village that was planned and built mainly between 1910 and 1930. In the early days of the village's development, the 60-acre Meare was dug out from the marshes that receive the waters of the Hundred River—another small Suffolk river barred from the sea by a shingle bank. The picturesque houses, country club and other buildings, including tall water towers disguised as fairy-tale houses, stand on a maze of little roads, many of them still unmade shingle tracks. A fine white post mill, moved in 1923 from the neighbouring village of Aldringham, to pump water up to the tank over the House in the Clouds, was restored in the late 1970s for use as an information centre for this part of the heritage coast.

There is an exhilarating walk from Thorpeness northwards along the beach to Sizewell and Minsmere, but the road turns inland through heath and woods to Leiston. This is a curious little town, the centre of which has been dominated for over a century by the high brick walls of Garrett's engineering works. The works moved to a new site near the station a few years ago, but the future of the old site is still uncertain. Ideas, good in theory, have been advanced for a new town centre, with shops, offices, houses and community buildings, on this large block of land, but government policy for areas near nuclear power stations would not allow the town to grow more than a little. Even without the power station, it seems unlikely that there would be much natural growth in such a small country town that has no special attractions.

Turning off the main road beyond Leiston, we pass along narrow, winding lanes to Eastbridge with its little inn, the Eel's Foot, which like the inn at Snape is reminiscent of earlier activities in an area where many people were indeed amphibious. The lane emerges from between low banks and hedges to a glorious panorama to east and west. The sun and the massive black and white cumulus clouds, showing the threat of a storm, hang over the marshes and the gleam of the New Cut and other dykes and waterways. A vast reed bed stretches away to the foot of the dark, primitive woodland and heath on the slopes above. A marsh harrier circles slowly over the reeds, harried itself by lapwings and scolded by blackbirds and ducks. An early ring ousel rests on a field by the road, and a snipe flies round and round, with a regular side-slipping dive that makes the characteristic drumming noise.

A walk along the willow-lined road, through the woods and up to the Walks, reveals many birds of marsh, woodland, heath and water. From the open hillside is a view across the marshes to the sea, over reed beds and meres, trees, gorse, bramble and woodland, indeed the whole wonderful range of habitats that have made Minsmere one of the most famous bird reserves in the world. Remembering some rather odd questions by otherwise intelligent people, perhaps I may be forgiven for mentioning that the birds here all come and go of their own free will, on migration or for the breeding season, or as summer or winter visitors. The large number of species is due to the wide variety of terrain and water and mud, much of it natural, though the reserve has been made more attractive to a wider range of birds by the deliberate adaptation of natural features. New lagoons have been formed for wildfowl in winter and waders in summer, with seasonal control of water levels. Shingle islets have been created to encourage the nesting of terns. But the beauty and glory of Minsmere is that the birds are free, and one never knows from day to day what new species will turn up or move on.

After such a walk on a spring day, we turned back to Eastbridge. A snipe had settled on a tall electricity pole and sat there for over half an hour, silent but for an occasional cry. The sun was getting lower and the lurid orange sky held the threat of a storm in the heavy black clouds. Moving on to Westleton Heath, now protected as one of the few remaining wild heathland areas of East Anglia, we saw many small birds gathering to roost in the bushes as the light faded. At Dunwich were the sheer simplicity and perfection and peace of the curving beach sweeping away to north and south, and the low, even waves breaking softly from a calm sea. Spray masked the beach under the crumbling cliffs towards Minsmere. The other way the curve was backed by the marshes and woods and the tall church tower of Walberswick. Farther north, we could just still see the church tower of Southwold and the white lighthouse from which the light was already flashing red in the coastal sector.

Then back once more to Eastbridge just to sit and look and listen as the last of the light faded and the stars began to appear. The snipe, now unseen, was again on the wing and drumming overhead with an eerie, elusive sound like an angry bee. There came the cautious squawk of a disturbed moorhen, the alarm notes of a late blackbird, the quiet chuckle of a pair of duck just visible flying low over the road, the piping call of a redshank, mysterious rustlings in the reeds, and the distant bark of a dog. Then lastly, soft slow footsteps approaching and passing—a lover and his lass under the stars.

There is a frightening contrast between the seemingly unchanging peace and beauty of much of the Suffolk coast, and the sinister changes and developments, past, present and future, in the name of defence. We have seen the Roman fort at Burgh Castle and the Norman castle at Orford. From Aldeburgh southwards along the shores of Suffolk and Essex stand the stout, round Martello towers, part of our defences against the possibility of invasion by Napoleon. In gaps between the towers we have seen the tall pylons and wide screens at Bawdsey Manor where radar was developed during the Second World War; and on the marshes between Aldeburgh and Orford the vast defensive radar system completed in 1971 and dismantled in 1973. Orfordness itself still has the crude concrete remains of a weapons research establishment.

From these awful illustrations of man's effect on the coastal landscape, I resume my account of the estuaries, knowing that I ought to refrain from describing each and every one, but they are so beautiful and so varied and show such fascinating evidence of changes, that perhaps I will be forgiven for doing so.

The estuary of the Deben takes a winding course between low hills, pine woods and marshes, to its narrow and vigorous exit to the sea. At its mouth the shingle banks change with every tide and storm, and sailing dinghies and yachts approach and leave with caution. It is not many decades since sailing barges frequented the river, using the various farm quays, some of which can still be found on the map and on the ground, and the quay at Woodbridge near the head of the estuary. This small town, worthy of exploration for its antiquity and beauty, is famous for the proximity of two unique features, one on either side of the river. On the town quay stands a tide mill, on a site first mentioned in 1170. The present building dates from the eighteenth century, and worked by water power until the main wheel shaft broke in 1957. It is the last remaining complete tide mill in the whole North Sea area and has, fortunately, been restored in the 1970s by a trust, financed by private and public funds. The full story of the mill and details of its restoration can be read in a booklet published by the trust, but I must mention the transformation during the first two years. The roof was retiled, the whole timber frame stabilized and renovated, and the fifty-year-old corrugated iron cladding replaced by white weather-boarding. The mill stands in such a commanding position that everyone, public and artists alike, tended to overlook the ugliness of the corrugated iron, until 1973 when the full beauty of the building reappeared. The machinery is being restored, but normal working is unlikely to be resumed as the mill pool is now a yacht harbour. However, the future of the mill as a splendid historic feature of the estuary and townscape is assured, and the public will be able to use the building for various community purposes.

On the east side of the estuary, up on the hillside, less than a mile from the tide mill, is the site of the Sutton Hoo ship-burial. This was discovered, in a group of barrows, in the summer just before the outbreak of the Second World War, which undoubtedly eclipsed what was even then proclaimed by experts as likely to prove "the most significant, as it is certainly the most splendid, archaeological discovery ever made in the British Isles". The discovery, and what was unearthed, have been fully documented since, and make fascinating reading, while the Sutton Hoo treasures on display at the British Museum make a visit worthwhile without any other justification.

These two sites at the head of the Deben estuary widen our view of history in the area, and illustrate the length of man's settlement here and his influences on the landscape.

Returning to more recent times and to the changing moods and conditions of the Suffolk coast, I recall two remarkable extremes. On a Saturday afternoon in July 1961, it was 92°F on the Air Ministry roof in London. Thirty miles away, in our little town garden in Chelmsford, it was probably even hotter. The next morning, to get some relief from the heat, we rose before the birds and reached Pin Mill before the peace of Sunday had been disturbed by the arrival of newspapers and milk. Our fellow men still lay abed, but turtle doves, finches, swifts, swallows and skylarks were sharing with us the delights of a perfect summer morning.

On the estuary the small boats rode smoothly on the ebb-tide running away into a blue haze which thinly veiled the wooded slopes. We walked in the cool shade of old oaks at the edge of the saltings, and saw many of the birds of woodland, field, marsh, river and sea. Willow warblers, whitethroats, wrens, long-tailed tits, blue tits and great tits, dunnocks and tree sparrows, flitted about among the lower branches and in the undergrowth; rooks, jackdaws, magpies, starlings, thrushes and blackbirds, seemed to prefer the upper branches. Out in the open, families of greenfinches and goldfinches were busy in the bushes and thistles; a couple of dozen peewits, including a number of young, sat on a bare field. All except the silent peewits sang their praise of the beautiful morn. Linnets in small groups fed among the sea lavender near the landward edge of the saltings. Beyond, on the broadening expanse of tidal mud, half-a-dozen curlew and as many redshank were feeding and occasionally flying and uttering their thrilling calls. Nearby the black-headed gulls, noisy as usual, sounded in marked contrast to the quiet gabble of the shelduck whose young were still quite small but mobile both on mud and in water. A line of seven swans flew low over the river, heading seawards, but too far away for us to hear the beat of their wings. A nuthatch moved silently and nimbly up and down the trunk and under the branches of an old dying oak.

As we walked back through the trees, the power of the sun increased and promised yet another blazing day. The birds were a little quieter, except at the water's edge where the gulls and duck were still active.

A few yachts' crews were now awake and preparing to slip away down-river; the towering sails of a barge were set to catch the first of the breeze ruffling the water.

On our journey home we noticed that the greater heat inland seemed to have quietened the birds once more, but by eleven o'clock we were meeting the population of the city streaming towards the coast in cars and coaches to meet the midday sun.

A year and a half later, in January 1963, we had recently moved to Suffolk, and were in the middle of one of the longest and severest winters ever known to most of us. Sunday 13th followed the coldest of many cold nights, with the temperature down to about 0°F, 92 degrees lower than on that summer afternoon in 1961.

This Arctic morning was overcast and visibility none too good. Snow still lay deep in the gardens and on the fields from the New Year blizzards. As we drove along by the Orwell estuary, we saw, fleetingly, hundreds of waders on the mud, and ducks and coots on the river. A couple of hooded crows foraged on the foreshore, where the receding tide had left stranded ice floes. The walk along the shore and under the trees of Freston and Woolverstone Parks in the depth of the severest winter for about a century, gave us an insight into the conditions wild creatures have to endure. As far as Woolverstone Hall the tide-line was thick with dunlin, knot and redshank, with a few curlew and a solitary grey plover. The variety of duck on the river was much wider than usual, and included a single eider being harried by a greater black-backed gull. Cormorants decorated the navigation and mooring buoys, indeed one at Butterman's Bay had a line of four. In the woods and undergrowth were all the woodland and field birds that one ever saw, including our first bramblings seen at very close range and as tame as chaffinches. Among the ice where the stream entered the tidal river at Pin Mill were about seventy-five swans huddled closely together in the forlorn hope of getting food from the few people who were stirring abroad.

The severe frost continued day after day, until the morning of Saturday 26th, when there was a quick thaw, that was, however, to be halted by renewed snow and frost a few days later.

The upper reaches of the Deben estuary were frozen over, a happening almost as rare as on the Thames at London Bridge. At Woodbridge the whole river as far as the eye could see was covered with rough ice, just beginning to break up with the thaw, and the first of the ebb taking the support from under it, but there was no clear water except in the pond above the Tide Mill, and in small patches where the floes had been broken up between the boats in the yacht basin. The ice was about a foot thick. It was not clear and smooth like fresh water ice, but white and granular, becoming mushy and wet in the hollows due to the thaw. The sun came out during the afternoon, and on a larger, smoother area a little downstream, children walked and slid and cycled! Around the basin, the boat-yards and the Mill, the tide had been over the bank, but had now fallen about a foot. Finches and pipits, sparrows and starlings were feeding around the Mill and many went scavenging on the ice. A cock chaffinch lay stiff and dead on an ice floe by the Mill. About fifty swans, including a number of young, fed noisily on grain that had been scattered on the ice for them. Occasionally one or two would fly down from another flock a quarter of a mile away, and land sliding and scrambling to a standstill. A little removed from the swans, but much tamer than usual, were a hundred shelduck, a couple of dozen pintail duck, fifty coot, and small numbers of other duck. Occasionally some of the duck flew overhead, and the shelduck and pintail were especially beautiful in the afternoon sunlight. Near the far shore were several waders, including a pair of curlew. Altogether it was a remarkable spectacle, to be seen perhaps only once in a lifetime.

Although the severe frosts continued into March, the head of the Orwell was not frozen solid like the Deben at Woodbridge. The Orwell has a deep channel used throughout the year by many large and small ships carrying cargoes to and from Ipswich.

The best approach to this town, one of the oldest and most interesting in Britain, is from the sea, up the long, winding estuary between the beautiful woods and parkland, in which consultants in the 1960s envisaged skyscraper flats overlooking the Orwell from the north. These featured as part of a suggested 'linear town' between Ipswich and Felixstowe, one of several alternative ways of accommodating 70,000 people from London. Another firm of consultants engaged later, appeared more sensitive to the beauty of the estuary and the better features of the town, but even they suggested low-density 'executive-type' housing on the slopes of Freston and Wherstead overlooking the upper reaches from the west side. This part of the planned expansion was successfully opposed, and the banks on either side are now part of the designated area of outstanding natural beauty covering the Suffolk coast, heaths and estuaries. There was considerable relief in 1969 when the government decided not to authorize a London overspill scheme but some damage had already been done in the town centre by the premature building and extension of shops and offices, many of which remain vacant in 1978.

While the parkland and hillsides of the upper estuary now seem safe from house building, it seems certain that a large, high-level bridge will be built as part of the Ipswich Southern Bypass. Controversy has continued for several years on whether there should be a bridge or a tunnel. Cost will, I think, rule out a tunnel, and the bridge is likely to be a long, flat, rather graceless structure like the M2 bridge over the

Medway. However, it may well be less conspicuous than a suspension bridge with very high towers, and it is to be hoped that the crossing will be close to the southern edge of the town rather than a mile downstream at Freston Hill. The east end of the bridge, and the new road will, if constructed on the 'inner line', cut across Gainsborough Lane. The views of the estuary from the vicinity of this narrow country lane are popularly supposed to have inspired some of Gainsborough's landscapes while he lived in Ipswich in the 1750s, but this is not easy to prove, as he was less consistent than Constable in naming the scenes he painted.

Since 1900, the upper estuary has been much narrowed by the reclamation of land for industry, and for tidal quays to accommodate ships too large to enter the enclosed dock. One sails up-river between the tall pylons that carry power lines from the Cliff Quay Generating Station which uses about 500,000 tons of sea-borne coal each year. It is a large, post-war, brick building with three tall chimneys that have come to be accepted as impressive landmarks. This is as far as industry has extended downstream, and from the bend at Ostrich Creek, the sailor gets a vista northwards, past the cranes, ships and factories of Cliff Quay on the starboard side, to the entrance lock of the Wet Dock, and to the town on its slopes beyond.

The east side of the river here was known as Hog Highland, where, until the early 1920s rough grassy hills sloped down to a sandy beach frequented by local people and their children. Cliff Quay was started in 1923, and progressively extended to nearly a mile in length, and is now backed by factories, timber yards and oil storage tanks. Opposite, a new West Quay, for handling container traffic, has been constructed since 1970, and further constricts the width of this reach.

We now come to the heart of the port, which originally consisted of the quays along the outer, northern side of the river just below Stoke Bridge and immediately adjoining the old centre of the town. A look around the Dock and New Cut today, and a study of old pictures from 1870 to 1920, make one realize the great changes that have taken place. The building of the Wet Dock in 1841 by cutting off an L-shaped portion of the river at the head of the estuary, stimulated building activity on the quays, of large brick maltings and flour mills, and the works of Ransomes, Sims and Jefferies, all of whom relied on sea transport for the import of raw materials and the export of finished products—and of the gas works. All these had large, impressive, and in some cases handsome, buildings of red brick, some with white brick ornamentation and black engineering brick plinths, and a new Custom House was completed in 1844. The scale of these Victorian additions and replacements was larger than that of previous buildings, but the closely built-up character of what had been the outer bend of the river was maintained. Stoke tide mill which stood at the head of the estuary and beside the first bridge, was extended then superseded by much larger buildings of mill-like style. They in turn survived until the 1970s; their disappearance has left a characterless blank in the views up and down the river.

The flour mills and maltings of the 1800s were extended piecemeal up to the 1960s. Until the 1920s the additions were mainly picturesque brick gables and pinnacled towers, clad in grey corrugated iron, and extensions over the quayside to facilitate direct unloading of grain into the buildings from the holds of ships. In the late 1920s and early 1930s very tall, plain, reinforced concrete silos were added, and soon became familiar features of the dockside scene, but post-war additions have been more assertive and the tallest is a most unfortunate close neighbour of the Victorian Custom House, now the offices of the Ipswich Port Authority. It seems regrettable, incidentally, that the Authority controlling such a prosperous and growing port has allowed its own distinguished offices to become so shabby. A very impressive range of maltings on the far side of the New Cut was damaged by fire a few years ago, and is becoming increasingly derelict, pleasing no-one except the black redstarts who nest there in small numbers as they did on bombed sites in London.

Ransomes, Sims and Jefferies have migrated from the dock to new buildings outside the town and their old quayside factory has given way to an open area for storing goods, especially vehicles and trailers, in transit. No longer can we see pig iron from north-east England being unloaded from ships and going into the works where through open doors was the exciting, fiery spectacle of molten metal being transformed into ploughshares and other farm implements. Even the gas works, which received large supplies of coal by sea and exported coke, have gone, and 1977 saw the end of the fifty-year-old gasholder, the first of a number of 150-foot giants built in various parts of England. So landmarks come and go, and the character of the port changes.

The natural general shabbiness and busyness of the 1920s has given way to a more worrying decay of the older buildings that still stand between and behind the new ones of steel and concrete, and I fear further deterioration may not be arrested in time to save what is left of the visible reminders of centuries of the port's history.

There is still much exciting and interesting activity, particularly under Paul's and Cranfields, where, in a narrow space used by road and rail, chutes and tubes drop into lorries and tankers the flour and animal foods which are the end products of the grain, beans and other materials that have been sucked out of the holds of ships lying at the quayside.

In Fore Street there remain a few splendid old houses, formerly belonging to merchants with their quayside space at the rear. Old pictures show small sailing ships, such as collier brigs, lying at the quays, and even well into the 1900s, the Wet Dock was full of large full-rigged, ocean-going sailing ships and the local Thames sailing barges.

The medieval town was enclosed by ramparts on the curved alignment of the Anglo-Saxon ditch round the north and east; the west side was protected by marshy ground between the tidal Orwell and the River Gipping, the course of which was diverted before 1674 along the south-western edge of the town. The first half mile is still there as a reed-fringed canal beside Alderman Road Recreation Ground. The canal was cut short in the mid 1850s at Handford Mill, and the section that had acted as a head of water for Stoke Mill was culverted, and the marshy ground built over during the years that followed. More or less on the line of the vanished river, there now stands a great wall of modern office blocks. Their massive, monolithic forms contrast unfavourably with the rugged, irregular mass of the dockside buildings, and spoil the view across the town from the station. Between them and the present river is a low-lying area that still floods occasionally if a very high tide prevents the discharge of storm water from the town's drains. Flood protection works in the 1970s, consisting of new weirs, channel deepening and concrete river walls and steel piling, have considerably reduced the risks, and have incidentally substituted a rather hard, formal look for the old muddy, crumbling banks and wooden quays I knew in the 1920s as I wandered along the river and dockside absorbing the atmosphere that was to remain with me always.

I have written of Ipswich mainly as an historic port, but I cannot leave it, particularly as it is so little known by outsiders, without remarking that any visitor, or indeed inhabitant, will find much to interest him in the dozen medieval churches, old houses and beautiful parks. The Ancient House is the most elaborate pargetted house in Britain, while much can be learned of local history in the museum and art gallery of Christchurch Mansion, a handsome, red-brick Elizabethan house in a well-wooded park just outside the line of the old ramparts.

The Stour is the broadest, and yet, for most of its length, the quietest of the Suffolk estuaries. Like the Orwell it has seen great changes at its extremities, mostly during the past hundred years. Until the early years of the twentieth century, the water meadows of Flatford merged into the saltings at the head of the estuary, and Constable's view of Dedham Vale looking east to the broad, gleaming waters of Mistley, was as yet unmarred by the plastics factory beside the railway. It would be hard to find a worse example of utterly insensitive and outrageous development, and it has grown piecemeal into the great mass of buildings, chimneys and pipework and rubbish that now divides Dedham Vale from the beautiful tidal waters. Manningtree and

Mistley, two charming places that hug the Essex shore, owe their existence to the river, and have old quays and massive maltings, probably sharing with Snape the honour of the largest and finest group in East Anglia. Beneath them, in the channel which here runs close to the foot of the hill, was one of Britain's largest herds of swans, now somewhat less in numbers because of declining activity, and therefore less food, at the maltings. The channel, now little used except by small boat sailors, takes a winding course between square miles of tidal mud beloved of waders and wildfowl. This estuary is of such importance as a feeding, wintering and roosting place for many thousands of birds, that it has been declared a 'site of special scientific interest', and is likely to be managed by the Nature Conservancy Council as a national nature reserve. Their interest was stimulated by the proposal, now dropped, to create a vast new airport on Foulness and the Maplin Sands in south Essex, which would have displaced many thousands of sea birds and waders from their old haunts and feeding grounds.

Arable fields and a few parks and woods cover the rising land behind the Suffolk and Essex shores, where, because of their inaccessibility by water, there are no riverside settlements, and the landscape is mostly unspoilt. On the Suffolk side, at Holbrook, in a splendid position overlooking the broad river, stands the Royal Hospital School, built in the 1930s to house the school formerly run by the Admiralty at Greenwich. It is, as Nikolaus Pevsner says, "neither imaginative nor inventive, but it is in its scale and formality certainly impressive", with the tall stone bell-tower acting as a landmark for many miles around and dominating the long, low range of buildings of red brick dressed with stone.

At Shotley, the naval training establishment, H.M.S. *Ganges*, does not get a mention by Pevsner, consisting as it does of a miscellany of rather indifferent twentieth-century buildings; the only impressive features are the water tower and the great white mast with its yardarms and top button. The training establishment, standing on a high promontory between the Orwell and Stour estuaries, was originally based on the old wooden man-of-war that was moored off Shotley from 1899 until the 1920s. After several years of doubt and speculation, H.M.S. *Ganges* closed in 1976, and discussions go on about the future of its buildings, playing fields, houses and civilian employees; another example of dramatic change connected with defence. From Shotley one looks across to the quays and cranes and ships of Felixstowe and Harwich and Parkeston, all of which have suffered or enjoyed great 'sea changes' and fluctuations of fortune. The point dividing the Orwell from the Stour is perhaps the best from which to study these changes, and enjoy the beauty and interest of the landscape and seascape. One of the best occasions is that of the Pin Mill Sailing Barge Match, usually in mid-August. The huge red ochre sails move down the Orwell against a background of dark woods and hedges and pale, golden cornfields. With a southerly wind they come down the reach, a long leg and a short, spaced out regularly soon after the start. Past Shotley Point they are able to bear away to the south-east, past the cranes and tanks of Felixstowe Dock. Watching the great, solid, yet graceful and fascinating silhouettes, I remember the 1920s and 1930s when every tide carried a fleet of sailing barges up or down the Orwell to or from Ipswich. The last fully-rigged barge in trade gave up as late as 1971, and the barges that take part now in the annual races on the Thames, Blackwater and Orwell are privately owned and most of them have been converted for use as yachts. But they have kept their sturdy hulls and long spars, and their magnificent and unique sail plan and rigging. In the 1960s when the races got into their swing again, many barges carried new white sails which, after a year or two became a dirty grey, and looked much less beautiful than the traditional colour which is their hallmark. By 1971 most of them again had red ochre sails which, with the black hulls, names picked out in gold and the coloured transoms, make up a remarkably beautiful boat, bearing in mind the bluff bows, hard chines and straight sides. All in all, the sailing barge is a remarkable blend of power, grace and efficiency.

Having sailed round an offshore buoy, the barges come back into Harwich Harbour through scenes very different from the pastoral banks of the estuaries. On the one side are the great container cranes, warehouses, flour mills, tanks and ships at Felixstowe; on the other the wharves and cranes, and the church and town hall of Harwich. In the channel is a great variety of moving craft, private and commercial. Sailing between the barges, on her way from Bremerhaven, is the German passenger ship, *Prinz Hamlet*, a large white vessel with buff funnel. Like an oversized millionaire's yacht, she pursues her zigzag course in from the sea, and rounds swiftly to dock at the new Navy Yard Wharf at Harwich. The barges continue up the Stour, past the muddy bay of Bath Side which has been considered in recent years as a possible site for a large power station or for a long quay linking Harwich and Parkeston. They pass Dutch and British ships at Parkeston Quay and sail away into the quieter waters beyond. One by one their hulls are eclipsed by Erwarton Ness, but the sails are still proudly visible as they round the mark buoy and turn eastwards to sail again through the busy waters of the harbour. With the great barges and dozens of yachts, the motor launches and pilot boats, and the various ships at anchor or moorings, it is a fascinating scene, contrasting very strongly with the simple beauty and loneliness of much of the East Anglian coast. The passengers boarding the ship for the afternoon voyage to the Hook of Holland are fortunate to be sailing on a day when there is the wonderful spectacle of the great red-sailed barges at their best in a fresh southerly wind under a stormy sky.

In the long history of the harbour there have been many impressive scenes, other than barge matches, but for excitement and intense activity, the evening of 11th July 1977 probably surpassed them all. Thousands of people stood in a cold north-east wind on the shores at Harwich and Landguard Point waiting for the departure of the Royal Yacht *Britannia*, carrying the Queen and the Duke of Edinburgh who had spent a hot sunny day in Norwich and Ipswich as part of their Silver Jubilee tour of Britain. The yacht lay alongside the quay at Felixstowe, dwarfed by a huge Townsend Thorensen passenger ship, and guarded by the naval frigate F101. Other North Sea ships and ferries seemed to have delayed or advanced their arrivals and departures so as to see the *Britannia*. The harbour on the Felixstowe side was crowded with hundreds of small sailing and motor boats, twisting and turning to hold places if they could from which they would be able to see the Royal Yacht and her royal passengers depart. Four sailing barges with all sails set cruised majestically up and down in the lee of Land-guard Point, and a large hot air balloon drifted low across the harbour to disappear westwards into the darkening sky. At about 9 o'clock, the Royal Yacht *Britannia* edged slowly away from the quay, turned towards the sea escorted by the frigate and by many small yachts, and was finally lost to view as she sailed into the dusk on her way to the Humber.

Apart from the changes from century to century and year to year, estuaries such as these change from hour to hour. After a day of wind and great activity, high water and sunset can bring flat calm. On such an evening at Shotley, the freighters and yachts, lightships and dredgers, lie silently at rest. A white ketch motors smoothly up the Orwell. The passenger ship *Winston Churchill* glides quietly downstream in the dusk, to turn at the bell buoy southwards to the open sea. A few gulls drift on the water, and half a dozen dunlin circle low and land at the water's edge just as the tide begins to leave the mud. Beyond the head of the estuary, the sun sinks behind low, grey clouds and the distance is shrouded in haze. The lights on the quays and on the ships grow brighter against the darkening sky, until one can see little else but the lights and their reflections in the calm water of the broad river.

From the deck of our Dutch ship, the southern limit of the panorama was the Naze at Walton; not strictly a part of East Anglia, but to me it seems to belong to it. The low promontory slopes down to the north, turning its back on Essex and the Thames, and looks towards the Suffolk coast.

Like the rest of the East Anglian coast, the mood of the Naze changes with the seasons, from day to day and from hour to hour. Often it is cold, windswept and inhospitable, except to the many migrating birds which use it as a resting place on their flights north or south. In summer it can seem very different. As one comes through the town, the streets may be packed with holidaymakers driven off the wide, sandy beaches by a keen north-east wind and a high tide. The wind drives the waves on to the shore in a foaming, sandy procession, and with a steady roar audible from a distance; the sun is bright, but the distant air is hazy. The broad acres of green turf slope down from the Naze Tower to the tail of the cliffs and give way to shingle and saltings. The soft red crag cliffs have crumbled here and there into landslips, overgrown with bramble and thistle, and inhabited by goldfinches, sand martins and rabbits. The gulls and waders call on the mud-flats as the tide recedes from the winding creeks and the saltings.

Faintly seen across the broad bay are the white hotels of Dovercourt, the grey lighthouses and church spire of Harwich. The sun shines on the white superstructure of a big tanker at the Felixstowe jetty, and on a passenger ship heading away to the north-east for Denmark. Felixstowe itself is just discernible. Around the dock are the huge old R.A.F. seaplane hangars and the new cranes, and the great silver propane gas tank. Farther on are the spire of St John's Church and the mass of woodlands at Bawdsey Manor overlooking the mouth of the Deben. Suddenly a host of tiny white sails appears in a mass off Dovercourt, presently dispersing as the race proceeds. Here, more than anywhere else on the East Anglian coast, one sees in striking contrast the natural features and peacefulness close to but not yet overwhelmed by the activities of a thriving and rapidly growing group of ports. The naturalist and the ship watcher can both enjoy their pursuits. The Naze is safe from development, being protected by the local authorities and by the Essex Naturalists' Trust. Going back from the saltings up to the tower, one sees, against the declining sun, the tall masts of hidden yachts in their calm anchorage in the Backwaters, and, beyond them, a familiar country sight in the 1960s and 1970s, distant clouds of dark stubble smoke rising into the summer sky.

Soon, we hope, the naturalist and the ship watcher will be able to enjoy the wonders of another promontory, Landguard Point, which is visible from the Naze. It is at first glimpse a barren shingle spit, built up by the southward drift, protecting Harwich Harbour from the worst of the sea and wind. It has long been defaced by old gun emplacements and other defence works, and more recently by the digging, importing and processing of shingle. For a century it was a prohibited place, occupied first by the Army, then by the Royal Air Force, and again by the Army. For the interested serviceman and for the privileged few, it has been and still is a wonderful place from which to watch the ships approaching and leaving the harbour. Landguard tapers to a very sharp point, with a deep channel close in to the beach on the harbour side. The passenger ships, tankers and container ships pass by day and night, but alas we no longer see more than an occasional sailing barge beating in or out.

The Point itself has much to fascinate the amateur and professional naturalist. In spring each year, the little terns and ringed plovers return to lay their 'invisible' eggs on the upper beach. The parent birds, if disturbed, fly round calling wildly, trying to drive the intruder away from the nest or to distract his attention. The ringed plover can be seen running along the ground performing remarkable antics, dragging its wing and twisting and turning in such an odd manner that one really does forget to look for the nest and young. On the shingle, seemingly without moisture except for sea spray, mist, and deep seepage of sea water, grows a striking variety of coastal plants, some of them rare. The more spectacular are easily recognized, sea holly, yellow horned poppy, sea cabbage and spur valerian, but there is a host of tiny plants carpeting the dry shingle and sand, of species many of which only the experts can identify. This a splendid place for the botanist, and much of its interest must be due to the exclusion of the general public for so long. The birds and plants have been in greater danger since the land was sold by the Ministry of Defence and became more accessible. The nests of little terns and ringed plovers are particularly vulnerable to wandering, unwitting feet on the beaches, and the plants on the shingle are liable to extinction by people and cars. Local naturalists are hoping that the most interesting part can be safeguarded by management as a nature reserve with controlled public access.

Here is an epitome of the whole of the region's coast and its changing features. At Landguard we see the development of a shingle spit and its colonization by plants and birds, and the history of its use for defence from the time of the first fort in the sixteenth century. The fort was rebuilt and extended in later centuries, culminating in the vast, grim buildings with their high walls and deep, dry moats, prison-like barracks and cavernous magazines and gun emplacements. The future of the fort, an important historical monument, is still uncertain though many possibilities have been considered. A little to the north are the giant hangars built over half a century ago for the Royal Air Force seaplane station, and now used as warehouses for Felixstowe Dock. The fort stands derelict, but virtually indestructible, overlooking the harbour which, since the Second World War, has seen the spectacular growth of the three 'Haven Ports', and a tremendous increase in small boat sailing.

Across the harbour lies Harwich where the Victorian atmosphere lingers in the neighbourhood of the old pier whose importance was superseded first, at the end of the 1800s, by the creation of Parkeston

Quay a mile up-river, and then overshadowed by new quays and cranes on the other side in the 1960s. Farther over, the mud flats and marshes and saltings of the Walton Backwaters, and the craggy, crumbling cliffs of the Naze, all remain quietly subject to the changes wrought by natural forces that have worked continually on our East Anglian coast since its first emergence from the post-glacial seas.

5

East Anglian Heights

THE chalk lies under the whole of East Anglia but, apart from a few remote outcrops near Ipswich and an area of north-west Norfolk, it shows itself mainly in a belt stretching from Royston eastwards and north-eastwards to Newmarket and Bury St Edmunds.

My acquaintance with those low, rolling chalk hills began in 1930, when, for a brief year, the first away from my beloved Suffolk, I lived by the Cam a few miles south of Cambridge. From the footbridge of the little railway station at Whittlesford, it was possible to see the low hills to the south-east, on the borders of Cambridgeshire and Essex. I was fascinated by them and their mystery, and having even then a geographical turn of mind, I knew they were the East Anglian Heights.

We acquired bicycles and got to know the hills more intimately. Following the Cam valley up through Great and Little Chesterford, between the hills, which actually necessitated two short tunnels on the railway near Audley End, then, leaving the valley and climbing over a spur past the wooded park, we would race down into Saffron Walden, a delightful old market town with a magnificent church and picturesque streets. It was, and still is, a gem, and although in Essex, it seemed then and still seems now, to turn to Cambridge and to belong to East Anglia rather than to London. Sometimes we would go eastwards to Pampisford, and up the valley of the River Bourne, to Linton, an attractive old village lying below an impressive rise of 200 feet known as Rivey Hill from which there was a wide panorama of cornfields and woods. Westwards from home, the main road ran through open country past Duxford Airfield and approached the hills at Royston. Just beyond the town, the chalk hills loomed over the road, and gave a tremendous view northwards over the thousands of flat acres stretching beyond Cambridge towards the Wash. Royston was in fact in Hertfordshire, but lying on the north-facing slope it seemed even more than Saffron Walden to turn its back on the Home Counties and to belong to East Anglia.

Northwards from Whittlesford lay Cambridge, and thence we went occasionally by train. The Gog Magog Hills were on the right, a spur of the main hills, thrusting out towards the city beyond which lay the flat, unexplored mystery of the Fens. This is not the place to describe the unique splendours of Cambridge, which interested me even at the age of nine, and which fascinated me more deeply on later visits. But the city is the focal point of these hills and of the lower land between, and from the hills one can see the distant towers and spires, no less exquisite and evocative than those of Oxford. I will return briefly to this theme later.

All too soon, in 1931, we moved again, south into Essex, and for several years I travelled daily to school by train over the watershed between the valleys of the Stort and the Cam, but I did not realize the significance of this until I came to write about it forty years later. On my journeys to and from school, I seesawed over the hump which divided London from East Anglia. The River Stort flowed south to join the Lea which in turn flowed into London and the Thames. The life of Harlow, then only a large village though the inhabitants insisted on calling it a town, and of Bishop's Stortford the nearest market town, lay under the influence of London, and thence the office workers and the city magnates travelled daily, or 'commuted' as we would now say. Going to school at Newport, the first village over the hump, I travelled easily against the tide and penetrated each day during term from London-bound Essex just into the chalk hills of East Anglia, the presence of the chalk being clearly evident from the large pit in the hill-side not far from Newport Station. The school faced across the valley of the Cam to the wooded slopes of Shortgrove Park, especially glorious in autumn. The other way, to the north-west, were bare, rolling downs, low but wide and open. I learned that these hills, over which I struggled so wearily and reluctantly on mid-winter cross-country runs, extended a very long way to the south-west and were part of the great web of chalk radiating from Salisbury Plain over southern England; and that the other way, through the borders of Essex, Suffolk and Cambridgeshire, they dipped under the Breckland, rose again as the 'downs' of north-west Norfolk, and finished with a dramatic flourish in the bizarre red, white and brown cliffs of Hunstanton. For a ten-mile radius south-east of Hunstanton is an arc, crossing the line of Peddar's Way, of rolling country with huge, open fields and long, straight, hedged roads, and the feel of chalk country

about it. It is nearly all arable now, but at Ringstead Downs, the
Norfolk Naturalists' Trust have preserved twenty-five acres of chalk
grassland on the side of a little valley. Here and there in other parts of
this corner of Norfolk are small pits which show how close the chalk
is to the surface.

My early impressions of the East Anglian Heights were vivid and
lasting and were confirmed when I returned after a long absence. It is
still a different and more delectable world in the Cam valley than by
the Stort. Heading north from London there comes a point, just beyond
Elsenham on the railway, or beyond Ugley on the road, where you
realize that you have left the London clay behind. You are suddenly in
the chalk, and the land tilts gently away from London; the very air
seems different. Road and rail come together about a mile short of
Newport, in sight of the large white pit, and continue through the
delightful old village and past the school. They go on along the valley,
past the great beeches and chestnuts and the beautiful stone mansion of
Audley End, and through the Chesterfords where the hills on either
side are quite impressive.

Just north of Great Chesterford, the traveller by road could easily be
diverted from his intention of going to Cambridge, by continuing on
the line of the Icknield Way which crosses the valley at Ickleton and
heads away towards Newmarket. For a brief period, from 1848 to
1851, the traveller by train could, if he chose, have followed a similar
course by changing at Great Chesterford on to the branch line via
Pampisford to Six Mile Bottom and thus to Newmarket. That line,
intended as a shorter route from London to Norwich, has left its mark
on the countryside almost as impressively as any of the Roman roads,
pre-Roman tracks, and the linear earthworks of other ages, that run
with it and across it. Succeeding editions of the Ordnance Survey maps
tell the story of how the banks and cuttings have become overgrown
with trees, and how the sections of line at ground level have been
ploughed over and cultivated with land on either side. These ground
level sections have disappeared from the map, but can still be clearly
seen on aerial photographs and even on the ground are seasonally
revealed by a band of poorer corn or sugar beet across the field. This
line must surely have been one of the shortest-lived of all railways, for
a mere five years contained its whole life from the formation of the
company to the running of the last train, but it has left fascinating
traces that seem likely to last as long as the relics of the work of the
Romans and others that make this part of the chalk hills of such
absorbing interest to students of history and landscape. The trees along
the banks and cuttings form an admirable complement to the belt of
beech along the Roman road and to the thick woods of neighbouring
eighteenth-century parkland. The line is punctuated by the little brick

cottages that were built to house the level-crossing keepers. The remaining traces of this old railway, closed over 120 years ago, make an impressive archaeological monument by any standards and one must hope that they will be respected and protected as such. The site of the junction with the main line at Great Chesterford is affected by the new motorway from London where it crosses the valley to run into the line of the Icknield Way at Stump Cross. If and when the A11 is 'improved' beyond that point, the line of the old railway and of the Icknield Way should be left untouched if possible.

These chalk hills were once forested, but because of their generally lighter soil covering, not as thickly as the boulder clay to the south, while to the north were the swamps of what later became known as the Fens. The belt of chalk, all the way from Salisbury Plain and on through the sandy soils of the Breckland, became a corridor of movement on the north-east to south-west axis, and the scene of transverse defence works to control the movement. As populations grew, and the woods were cleared, the Breck was cultivated in a desultory fashion limited by its barrenness and the innumerable rabbits. The chalk was more suited to sheep and much of the south of Cambridgeshire carried sheep up to 1800 on an unbroken tract of chalk grassland untouched by the plough. Now we can only try to imagine what it looked like by observing the land covered by the young, green corn in the spring.

The area was transformed into arable in a short period of fifty years with what must have been dramatic effects on the flora and fauna. Natural wild life of almost every kind retreated to what are still its main habitats. As the Cambridgeshire and Isle of Ely County Council commented in their 1965 report on nature reserves, "we must be grateful to the Romans and men of the Dark Ages who left their roads and embankments which, besides being fine archaeological monuments, should also be regarded as important biological monuments, preserving all that is left of chalk grassland communities in our part of East Anglia". Thus the Devil's Ditch, running from the edge of the Fens at the village of Reach, well into the chalk hills at Wood Ditton, and the Fleam Dyke and the Roman road, Via Devana, give miles in length, but only a few yards in width, of rich chalk flora, and are refuges for birds and animals in country that, apart from a few areas of parkland, is wide, open, intensively cultivated arable. Perhaps we should add our thanks to the builders of the Chesterford to Newmarket railway which must surely be after 120 years a valuable retreat for wild life as well as a fine archaeological relic.

The main crop in this belt of low, rolling hills is corn, and we get the annual sequence of colour and activity, and apparent lack of activity, usual in corn-growing country. There are short spells when the fields are busy with the noise of tractors or combine harvesters, but for much of the year there is little sound but the song of the lark and the yellow-hammer and the sigh of the wind trailing over the long, rounded acres. At all seasons it is a beautiful countryside, more subtle than the Cotswolds or the South Downs, but equally impressive in its way as the others with their much greater height.

One late summer we returned from the Cotswolds, travelling through the East Anglian Heights from Royston to Saffron Walden. The harvest was farther advanced here than in Gloucestershire. Many fields had already been ploughed again and the chalk showed through the thin topsoil. Between Royston and Barley and Chishill was an area of country as wide and rolling and hilly as much of the central Cotswolds around Turksdean and Notgrove. There is a series of view-points on this journey that compel one to stop. From Whiteley Hill, just out of Royston, one looks south and south-east over the borders of Hertfordshire and Essex, where an 'environmental disaster' was threatened in the late 1960s and early 1970s. Nuthampstead was on the short list for the third London airport. What a disaster indeed this would have been! It beggars description and hardly bears thinking about, but more than thought came to the rescue successfully. The threats of noise, concrete, motorways, new towns and all that goes with a vast modern airport, were, after due consideration of the alternatives, redirected to Foulness and the Maplin Sands in the opposite corner of Essex; but the development has not yet been started there and the future remains uncertain.

From just north of Barley, one looks back towards Royston, and northwards over the lowlands of Cambridgeshire to the white plume of the cement works and the great white cliffs of the chalk pit at Barrington in the more lowly chalk ridge west of Cambridge. East-wards lie the hills around Great Chishill and the old, white post mill, with the church just beyond on higher ground. We cross the highest land hereabouts—about 480 feet above sea level—in the area where the three counties meet, Hertfordshire, Essex and Cambridgeshire. The landscape in all its beauty is shared between them and shows again the impossibility of keeping rigidly to county boundaries in a survey of the East Anglian region. From just east of Great Chishill one looks away down the gentle valley, with its interlocking spurs, to where it joins the valley of the Cam at Audley End; a distance of six miles, all golden stubble and brown plough, dark trees and hedges, with peewits flying over and calling plaintively; a superb view having much in common, even in scale, with parts of the Cotswolds.

Within the hills the villages are few in number, but instead of being widely scattered, as in the Breckland, they tend to be in groups, and there are few isolated houses to mar the rest of the wide, rolling acres. Great Chishill, Heydon, Chrishall and Elmdon lie in such a group, and

Cambridge—King's College Chapel

Bury St Edmunds—Crown Street

M11 at Coploe Hill, Ickleton

Saffron Walden Corn Exchange

Newport School

Beeches at Wandlebury, Cambridge

Letheringham Church and Abbey Farm

Easton Farm Park—the new dairy

Suffolk Punch and Red Polls at Benacre

Cottages at Lavenham

Flatford Mill and Willy Lott's Cottage

Wood Walton Fen—Great Raveley Drain

one wonders why they came into being on the highest part of these dry chalk hills. However, a tiny stream rises near each of them and there must have been springs of water at these points, and an area of richer soil. Elmdon and Heydon are delightful villages embowered in trees which give shelter and make more dramatic the splendid views from the fringes, especially to the north. From Heydon one again looks out over the green slopes and levels to the city of Cambridge twelve miles away, but one sees also two very prominent and comparatively recent man-made features in the otherwise rural scene. At Barrington are the chalk pit and the cement works which we have seen from elsewhere. Beyond them are the eight huge, white, circular dishes of the Radio Astronomy Observatory, spaced evenly along five kilometres of the old railway between Lord's Bridge and Trumpington.

At Heydon, on the steeper slopes, are traces of ancient cultivation in the form of strip lynchets. Here too, running north-west as straight as a die down the hillside, is an overgrown, chalky lane on the route of Heydon (or Brand) Ditch, one of the old transverse defence works that cross these hills at intervals for about twenty miles. Even more impressive are the strip lynchets at Coploe Hill, a spur just above Ickleton. They form a series of slopes and banks along the contours, parallel with the ridgeway road. The banks are steep and are lined with tree hedges of white may, which, perhaps unexpectedly, are so common in Cambridgeshire not only in the chalk hills but also on the fringes of the Fens around Cottenham and Haddenham. Indeed, in 1972, I had the general impression, which may well have been true, that the hedges were more noticeable up here on the chalk than some years ago. It is by no means a bare landscape and still has quite a lot of hedgerow trees and the straight belts of trees that shelter the farms and granges.

In this smoothly rolling country, now virtually all arable, there are some signs of what lies underneath. In winter the chalky stones and flints can be seen, and the soil of some fields is so thin that their complexions are white by comparison with the brown of those fortunate enough to have a deeper and richer topsoil. More revealing still, and more accessible than the great commercial pits, is the little, abandoned roadside chalk pit. Its vertical, white cliff-face and overgrown floor are rewarding to both the geologist and the naturalist. One such pit at Strethall has an arc of sheer chalk beneath very thin topsoil. In the chalk is a horizontal line of flat, black flints about an inch thick, merging at one end of the pit to huge, knobbly flints. They are as usual covered with a hard white layer of chalk, and are black and smooth when cracked open. This is one of the hardest and most durable of materials, used by men in ancient times to fashion tools and weapons of amazing sharpness, and in later years continuing to the present day, either whole or faced, in walls and buildings. The knobbly flints and

7

other large stones are used extensively through the chalk hills of East
Anglia and in north-west Norfolk, in walls and barns and houses, while
the faced flints, black, hard and shiny even after centuries, set in intricate
patterns between bands and quoins of building stone or brick, adorn
many splendid churches, and some of the more elegant houses of the
region. The chalk itself in which the flints are found is not usually hard
enough for use as a building material, but some hard chalk known as
'clunch' is found here and there and used in barns and houses and in
some of the more modest churches in the Breckland and north-west
Norfolk. On the floor of the pit at Strethall, earth had been spread in
rough ridges, probably to discourage access by vehicles. Here in June
were many flowering plants—scarlet pimpernel, crosswort, mayweed,
forget-me-not, white campion, with thistles and knapweed to follow.
Some of these are common elsewhere, but some, including the greater
knapweed, are plants of the chalk country.

The high, open, stony land around Strethall and Littlebury, west of
the Cam valley, has for many years been the breeding ground of the
stone curlew, a bird that became quite rare in its main haunt, the
Breckland, with the planting of the forests and the 'reclamation' of
waste land for arable and pasture. Here on the East Anglian Heights,
the more intensive cultivation of the arable land, and the virtual
disappearance of fallow fields, seemed likely to deter the stone curlews,
but they appear to have adapted themselves to nesting in the young
growing corn where indeed they are better protected from predators
than on bare, stony fields. Contrary to the forecasts and fears of the
experts, this shy and rather specialized bird has adjusted its habits to
changed conditions both here on the chalk downs and in the Breckland
where it is now nesting in forest rides, young plantations and arable
fields, albeit in small numbers everywhere; it is still one of the rarest of
British breeding birds.

From Strethall there is a great view along the little valley beside the
strip lynchets of Coploe Hill, and on down the Cam. In clear weather,
with the help of binoculars, one can see several well-known Cambridge
landmarks about twelve miles away; King's College Chapel, white
stone with pinnacles at either end; the great spire of the Roman
Catholic Church; and the massive tower of St John's College Chapel.
In the summer of 1972 we noticed a new landmark, unidentified until
later in the day. It appeared to be a very tall and bulky brown tower,
and not a thing of beauty, rising above a spur of the Gogs. In the middle
distance were wooded hillsides on the far side of the Cam. It is very
noticeable that for its whole length from Newport to Cambridge, the
east side is much more wooded and varied than the west.

In June most of the countryside was green, with corn and some
sugar beet, and an occasional fallow field. Here and there were flocks

of folded sheep; before 1800 it would have been nearly all sheep pasture. Open narrow roads run between the fields and everywhere the skylarks sing over them. From Fox Hill, between Stapleford and Wandlebury, is another, closer view of the city and its towers and spires, but this panorama is now marred hideously by the great slab block, broadside on, and the new landmark we saw earlier, the huge, twin-linked chimneys of the new Addenbrooke's Hospital on the southern edge of Cambridge. These buildings seem to me to be monstrous and completely out of character and proportion with this delicate, open landscape and with the scale and beauty of the churches and colleges beyond. The Cambridge Preservation Society rightly advertise their success in the 1950s in preventing the spread of Cambridge towards the Gogs, but the new hospital has a disastrous effect on the Green Belt that was officially established around the city in the years that followed.

In spite of this preposterous sight, it is impossible not to be lured away from the lovely chalk hills into the busyness and beauty of the city. Recent visits have confirmed the fascination of early acquaintance. Much is the same, much is changed or changing. The railway station, that uniquely long, one-sided wonder of my childhood, with eight lines radiating to as many counties, is much as it was, though several of the lines are closed, and no longer we see both L.M.S.R. and L.N.E.R. trains at the one station. Now they are all British Rail diesels, not much different from those of the rest of Britain. The station is as far from the city centre as ever, but no longer can we go by tram, with the exciting possibility of the wheels falling off, an adventure cheerfully suffered by the returning undergraduate, Ricky Elliot, in *The Longest Journey* which E. M. Forster published in 1907. But on the way we can still see the landmarks that Elliot saw—the 'florid bulk' of the Catholic Church, the 'Venetian Palace' of Addenbrooke's Hospital (the old one!), and the 'Roman Temple' of the Fitzwilliam Museum.

My own memories of 1930 include the punts and skiffs on the river running along the Backs, and the hordes of young men wearing flowing black gowns and mortar boards; and multitudes of decrepit, basketed, old bicycles, mostly female, either leaning in tangled masses against railings, or being seized indiscriminately and ridden erratically through the streets by those same young men. The streets are busier now and noisier, but the quiet, narrow lanes are still cluttered with old bikes and frequented by undergraduates less formally dressed, but similar in many ways to their predecessors. Most impressive of all is the eternal beauty of the old Colleges and the Backs. Inevitably one compares Cambridge with Oxford. Such comparisons are almost bound to be subjective, but I will try to be otherwise. Cambridge has neither the skyline nor the setting of Oxford. There are fewer dramatic panoramas, from the closely neighbouring hills, of dreaming towers and spires, but I think that Cambridge is just as rich in its architectural glories. Oxford has the High and Radcliffe Camera and Tom Quad, but Cambridge has King's and Trinity and the incomparable Backs. And has Oxford really anything to surpass King's Parade with the superb trio of King's College Chapel, the Old University Library and the Senate House? The beauty of this trio is enhanced by a great horse chestnut which is as fine as, and more impressively placed than the Oxford sycamore in the High, described by Thomas Sharp in *Oxford Replanned* as "one of the most important trees in the world; without it this scene would greatly suffer". While the Oxford sycamore bulges proudly over the pavement from a narrow gap between All Souls and Queen's, the Cambridge chestnut stands fully revealed on the lawn in the angle between three of the finest buildings in the city.

Cambridge is very rich in trees, especially along Trumpington Road and the Backs, and has an unusual feature in Brooklands Avenue which is lined by alternating fastigiate (Dawyck) beech and fastigiate horn-beam. For those especially interested, the Botanic Gardens contain many other interesting and unusual trees.

The city is rich in fine buildings, old and new, which make an absorbing study in themselves. Like Oxford, Cambridge has a long tradition of fine architecture and of adding new to old rather than clearing and starting again. Being a university town it has always had for its size a high proportion of new buildings in each century. A university has special needs of large, growing establishments, and their intellectual basis stimulates a keen interest in their architecture. Over the centuries the growth and the additions have mostly been absorbed happily in the timeless setting of trees, grass and water. There have been exceptions in Victorian times and in the 1930s, and in more recent years. Hawksmoor and Barry added to Wren are not as startling as Powell and Moya and Basil Spence added to Georgian, Gothic and Victorian. Some of the new buildings are very good, such as the award-winning Cripps Buildings at St John's, but others are harder for the layman to accept. What is he to make, for example, of Churchill College? To me it seems strong, determined, even ruthless in character, like the great man himself, but no doubt destined to mellow with the years and with the growth of its surrounding trees; but I am thankful that Churchill does not stand cheek by jowl with King's and Clare!

Any city, and especially an historic university city, has a strong influence on the country around it. Cambridge has a ring of dormitory villages, many of them revived and restored by the city and university workers and London commuters who prefer to live in the country. Without them, the decay of the villages would have continued with the decline in the number of farm workers, now very low in number in a predominantly corn-growing area. Cambridge has had another interesting influence on the countryside. The presence of the university, with its very strong scientific aspects, has led to the creation of many research establishments in country mansions thus preserving in some cases the historic houses and in most the beauty of their wooded parkland.

The visitor to the city, enchanted though he may be with all its beauty and wonders, needs after a time to escape from a surfeit of richness and bustle, to the restfulness of the villages and the country. The nearest and most delightful oasis is Wandlebury up on the Gog Magog Hills only two miles from the edge of the city. Here is an epitome of the history and natural features of the chalk hills of East Anglia. Sheltered from the busy main road by a thick belt of trees, lies an Iron Age hill fort, circular in shape, about a thousand feet in diameter, its banks and ditches largely overgrown with splendid beech and other trees. In and around the fort is now beautiful parkland acquired by the Cambridge Preservation Society in 1954 for the benefit of the public.

On our first visit, in high summer, we walked up through the wooded glades, past the pond and the Muscovy ducks with large families of tiny yellow and brown ducklings. Birds sang joyfully and spotted flycatchers darted and weaved from their perching places. Overlooking the clearing in the centre of the wooded circle are the stables with their clock tower and cupola and cottages. These mellow brick buildings date from the eighteenth century and stood beside a mansion of the same age on a site now marked by a raised lawn with a sundial pillar in the middle. Here then are impressive relics, as elsewhere in the East Anglian Heights, of human occupation and use in widely separated centuries. The eighteenth-century building and the tree planting in and around the circular fort introduced a measure of formality, but time has mellowed it all and there is to me no feeling of incongruity.

At first we were quite alone, but presently the stillness and peace were broken, but not rudely, by the arrival of about fifty small children with two or three teachers. They came quietly and slowly through the wooded glade, but they erupted visibly and audibly as they emerged on to the sunlit lawn. As though released from darkness, they scattered excitedly, running and leaping like lambs, and falling and rolling on the grass. Wandlebury is used by schools and others for the study of natural history, and a nature trail follows the outer bank of the fort. It starts from the stables and cuts across the lawn to a door in the high, polygonal wall enclosing what was the garden of the mansion within the fort. Inside the wall is a great variety of trees, some native, others foreign, but outside the wall most of them, planted in the eighteenth century, and the shrubs and flowers and grasses, are characteristic of the chalk country. They and the many woodland birds are described in the guide to the nature trail.

Just beyond Wandlebury, and running away south-east towards Haverhill, is the Roman road, Via Devana. On the opposite side of Cambridge, from there to Huntingdon, it has for centuries been the route of a busy main road, but here it is a green lane with white may tree hedges, and is rich with chalk grassland flora which largely disappeared from this countryside on its conversion from sheep walks to arable.

The chalk hills continue in a broad arc from Linton and Bartlow, past Newmarket, eastwards to Bury St Edmunds, and merge along their northern edge into the Breckland where the chalk lies under stony soil. Bartlow, like other places in this area, has an interesting mixture of ancient and modern archaeological relics. The railway is now disused but the station is occupied as a private house named 'Booking Hall', and the cuttings and bridges remain. The banks are covered with trees and bushes and are rich in wild flowers and no doubt in animal life. From the station a narrow path leads through thick woodland to the Bartlow Hills, four very steep-sided grassy mounds about forty feet high. These are Romano-British burial mounds or barrows, very much overgrown when I saw them, but the top of at least one could be reached to gain a fine view over the village and across the rolling hills above Linton.

North-eastwards, towards Newmarket, runs the Icknield Way, now the A11, crossed at right-angles by the succession of Roman road, earthworks, roads, tracks and tree belts, that give this part of the country such a distinctive pattern. These features cover many centuries up to recent times, but the most impressive is the Devil's Ditch, which runs for seven miles, almost dead straight, from 350 feet above sea level at Wood Ditton up in the chalk hills, to about 50 feet in the centre of the village of Reach on the edge of the Fens. Like the other parallel earthworks that cross the Icknield Way, it is thought to date from late Roman or early Saxon times, and like the others, to have been built for defence by hindering and controlling movement along the south-west to north-east axis. The 30–40 foot bank is flanked by steep dykes, that on the south-west side being the deeper. These dykes are now usually dry, but were probably made more effective in the distant past by the presence of water in parts. The Devil's Ditch is a fascinating walk in its own right, by the woods of Stetchworth, then above the cornfields, the golf course and the race course of Newmarket, where unfortunately it has been breached by a bypass of motorway proportions, and finally through lower, more open country, into the narrow village green of Reach; but its great interest lies in its history and its botanical richness. Even more than the Roman roads and other linear earthworks, this one seems to have become the home of many plants now rare not only in arable East Anglia but in the whole of Britain. The most remarkable is probably the pasque flower, *Anemone pulsatilla*, but there are many others of considerable beauty and rarity. Birds and insects are numerous, too, and the Devil's Ditch has been studied intensively by amateur and professional naturalists.

From parts of the Ditch, or rather from the top of its bank, and from many points on the chalk hills above Newmarket, one can see on clear days the great tower and lantern and the long mass of Ely Cathedral at least a dozen miles away on its low island in the middle of the Fens. At one such viewpoint near Stetchworth, a local farmer stopped and talked to us about the countryside which he obviously loved, and about the Devil's Ditch, and a new linear feature then forecast in 1967. This was to be a huge water main to take surplus water from the Fens, southwards over the chalk hills into the headwaters of the River Stour, to augment the water supply for Essex. There was to be a concrete tunnel 100 inches in diameter—"I could drive my car through it!" he told us—from Feltwell on the new cut-off channel that runs along the eastern fringe of the Fens. This tunnel, he went on, and we verified the facts later, would run underground to a pumping station at Kennet east of Newmarket. From Kennet a 72-inch pipe would take the water through the hills to the upper Stour at Great Bradley. Lower down the river, at Wixoe, there would be a pumping station to control the flow and to divert some of the water across country in other large pipes to the upper reaches of the Rivers Pant and Chelmer.

Within five years the farmer's prophecies, based of course on reliable reports, had mostly come true. The 12½-mile tunnel had been constructed, lying between 90 and 270 feet below the ground, to Kennet, then 9 miles of the 72-inch pipe to the Stour. A large, modern pumping station and control centre had been built at Wixoe, with the connecting link to the River Pant. From points many miles lower down these rivers, the water is pumped through older mains to the large reservoirs at Abberton and Hanningfield in Essex. All this is an interesting though mostly invisible feature of the East Anglian Heights, except for the pumping stations. The one at Wixoe, opened by the Queen in 1971, is a long, low, flat-roofed building of dark brick with light concrete cappings, and is of a pleasing but unassertive modern character. The fences are wooden post and rail, and the grounds are grassed among the trees old and new. On the grass, between the building and the main road, stands one of the concrete sections of the 100-inch tunnel.

From Newmarket, on to Bury St Edmunds, the chalk hills, pleasantly rolling, and ornamented with tree belts and woods, continue on either side of the road and railway. The belts are often of beech, and in places such as Hawsons Hills at Gazeley, the countryside is remarkably like the

Chilterns with beech woods on either side of grassy 'bottoms'. Many of the cottages and roadside walls are of flint set in red and white brick, both in the country and in the town of Bury. Around the town the chalk is very near the surface, and I can remember in the 1920s the chalky dust of the rough track that went from near the railway station westwards to an open area called 'the Klondyke'. In 1972, more dramatic evidence of the chalk appeared with the start of work on the Bury bypass road. A large white scar quickly appeared along the east side of the Lark valley, prominently visible from the Shire Hall and the Southgate Street neighbourhood. The raw white banks have since been graded and grassed, and trees planted to soften the effect of the new road but it remains visible, and sometimes audible, from parts of the old, monastic heart of the town.

The gridiron pattern of Bury St Edmunds originated in the eleventh and twelfth centuries, and was orientated deliberately on the great Abbey Church, the remains of which can be seen in the Abbey Gardens. The layout of the old streets survives miraculously and almost completely within the large area inside the sites of the five main 'gates', and together with the remarkable state of preservation of so many houses, churches and other buildings, make the town a constant source of wonder and admiration. Through the centuries, new buildings have kept to the old, close building lines along the medieval streets, and encroachments on to the original Market Place, by houses and shops and by the Robert Adam Town Hall of the eighteenth century and the Corn Exchange of the nineteenth, have only emphasized the essentially ancient and intimate character of the town. More open and spectacular in its size and with its large, grey brick Georgian houses, is the Angel Hill which runs round two sides of the Abbey precinct. The large houses and the Angel Hotel stand on the higher side looking over to the Abbey Gate and walls on the west side of the precinct and to the old, timber-framed houses which back on to the north side of the walls. The whole of the town within the gates can be appreciated to the full only by spending a lot of time walking around its streets, and finishing in the peace and beauty of the two splendid churches which still stand within the old limits of the Abbey, and in the old churchyard and the Abbey Gardens by the little river.

It is a strange and interesting fact that Bury St Edmunds has never advanced across the River Lark, except for the line of very old houses in Eastgate Street, beyond the site of the gate, and the twentieth-century sugar factory and other industry on either side of the railway. The medieval centre at the gates of the riverside Abbey has remained as the 'town centre' through the centuries, and all the growth has been to the north, west and south. At last a 'break-through' to the east has started in spite of great opposition from those who are jealous of the unique character of the town, from the centre of which, throughout its long history, it has been possible to look across the pleasant valley of the little river to green slopes and open country. An official pronouncement was elicited that the new buildings would be kept back from the visible slopes, but considerable apprehension persists that this will not be effective. Whether seen or not from the old town, the large housing area at Moreton Hall, between the Thurston and Ipswich roads, will be an isolated community and will not appear as a natural extension to the town. The Abbey Gardens and the Lark Valley, from Eastgate Street to Southgate Bridge, will become an urban park between the town and the bypass, instead of continuing as a delightful rural setting and limit to the medieval heart. The town, with its church towers and spires, now presents a fascinating panorama from the neighbouring low hills, but I fear that much of its close communion with the countryside will be lost if it grows as planned from 25,000 to 40,000 and especially as it grows east of the valley.

Fond though I am of Bury, thoughts of the East Anglian Heights draw me back again and again to Cambridge and the Cam. I used to travel down the Cam from the south, but now that I live in Suffolk again, I usually approach Cambridge from the east. There is no longer the thrill of passing over the hump from the London Basin, but the journey still has its share of interest and delights and reveals something of the chalk hills on the way. From Bury westwards the road undulates through the low, rolling hills but since 1975 it has been much flattened and widened with the construction of a new dual carriageway. The deep valley at Barrow Bottom has been filled with surplus soil from the roadworks and its appearance changed for the worse. At Newmarket, strings of racehorses wind through the beech groves overlooking the grassy 'heath' between the two main roads which, together with the town, are now much more peaceful since the bypass road opened. From here, too, can be seen the distant tower and roofs of Ely Cathedral. The chalk is still very much in evidence west of Newmarket where the old main road runs beside the racecourse and crosses the Devil's Ditch. When the beech shelter belts are left behind, the road runs through open country, lower but rolling still in chalky fashion. To the north are endless, misty views over the Fens, to the south the East Anglian Heights with the outlying spur of the Gogs pointing to Cambridge. The way into the city from the east is through depressingly dreary suburbs, but the traveller is always rewarded when he reaches the centre. For me opportunities for prolonged visits are still rare, but I always marvel at the unexpected and vivid impressions one can get even on a fleeting visit with pleasurable moments stolen from a day of duty.

On one such day in February, a few years ago, after a morning appointment, time was too precious to waste lunching. I walked through the busy, noisy streets and the quiet lanes, still cluttered with decrepit old bikes. After a misty morning it was still very cold in the shade, but warm in the now brilliant winter sunshine. From Trinity Bridge was a superb view downstream of the dazzling white Gothic front of St John's College. The grass was as green as in late spring, the river almost a Mediterranean blue, the long willow shoots a reddish-brown, and brightest of all the hundreds of golden crocuses seemingly alight in the sun. Blue and white crocuses and yellow aconites lined the path leading towards the revelation of Clare and King's, standing together so splendidly in spite of their different styles, and also gleaming white on this clear, bright day. From King's Bridge I heard the sharp noise of the stone-masons' saws as they worked below the walls of Clare. Mothers with babies in prams sat basking in the sun in the sheltered corners. By the time my afternoon lecture was over, the sun had disappeared and the stone of King's and Clare was no longer shining, but was quietly and softly grey. All the colour had gone from the day and the air was again chill and damp. I was caught up in the five o'clock tide of traffic and drove at walking pace along Brooklands Avenue in the stream of homeward-bound civil servants. Past the chaos of building work on the site of the new hospital, I soon came to the edge of the sprawling suburbs and in the dusk saw the low hills ahead. In that light, and in that subtle countryside, they seemed strangely impressive. Past Wandlebury, 200 feet up on the side of those hills I used to see from the train, the evening traffic streamed and flashed by from the twinkling constellation of Cambridge. Away to the south-west, beyond the Granta valley, were smaller, sparkling clusters of lights in a landscape that seemed so open and simple with few hedges and trees except for the dark woods of Wandlebury and the belts of trees planted for shelter or growing naturally along the Roman road and the old railway.

The lights of the villages will soon be accompanied by a veritable Halley's Comet of lights rushing along the hillsides above Newport, Wendens Ambo and Littlebury, and crossing the valley at Great Chesterford. This will be a six-lane motorway known by the rather sinister designation of M11. Of all the changes coming to this part of East Anglia, the M11 will, I think, be the most sudden, dramatic and serious, both in its effect on the landscape and in bringing Cambridge and its countryside nearer to London. Though it will be a two-way road, I think of it as thrusting and roaring northwards from London, through south-west Essex, and then, more brutally than the railway or the old main road, surging and scouring its way, from 150 to 300 feet wide, over the watershed at Elsenham, down the valley of the infant Cam, under the old A11 at Quendon, and from there cutting across the hills all the way to Great Chesterford. With the engineer's method of 'balancing cut and fill'—and let me admit that any other way might lead to even worse results—it will cut long scars through the spurs and raise weals across the tributary valleys. At Great Chesterford the motorway will swing across the Cam and the railway, obliterating part of the site of the junction with the old Newmarket line, and ending at Stump Cross where the A11 turns on to the route of the Icknield Way. The present roundabout, already large, and hideous with giant lamp-posts, will be made even larger. No longer will one be able to pause at dusk to remember quietly the people of the years before the Romans, and the Romans themselves, and the early nineteenth-century railway engineers, all of whom did so much to shape this countryside and who left impressive marks upon it, now mellowed by time and nature.

The scale and beauty of the hills above Littlebury are already marred by the huge pylons carrying their 400,000 volt cables. They are being joined and closely followed by the motorway, and the song of the lark and the sound of the wind will be eclipsed by the roar of heavy traffic. At Wendens Ambo an embankment and bridge will skirt the village, and the new road will pass close to a site that was occupied from the Iron Age to Roman times; in the early 1970s an extensive pattern of trenches and foundations were unearthed and remained open to view for some time. Here and all along the route, the archaeologists, co-ordinated by the curator of Saffron Walden Museum, excavated and explored and recorded before the land disappeared under the new road.

Much of the area I have described in this chapter is dramatically affected, and the full scale of the changes can now be seen. Debouching from a cutting in the hills above Great Chesterford Station, the M11 swings across the valley, blocking the view up and down the river which now flows through a long, tubular culvert about twenty feet in diameter lined with corrugated metal sheets. From this point, the extension towards the Cambridge Western Bypass veers away to the north-west, cutting through the northern shoulder of Coploe Hill, to pass west of Ickleton, the village where the wandering tracks of the Icknield Way converged on a ford across the Cam. Near Duxford, a cutting in the northern edge of the hills takes the new road down to the level of the old airfield and across its eastern end. Like other disused defence establishments, Duxford Airfield's future has been debated for years and is not yet fully settled. However it is used and enjoyed by many people who fly light aircraft and gliders, and by others who come to watch them and to see the Imperial War Museum's collection of old aircraft, recently crowned by the acquisition of the prototype of the Concorde supersonic airliner.

Will the M11 and its western extension be a disaster or a blessing?

Like all motorways it will undoubtedly be both. It will spoil much of the countryside, but it may become yet another linear retreat for the flora and fauna of this open, arable landscape. If, however, the government keep to their declared policy, admittedly a proper one, of 'landscape restoration' rather than 'road beautification' on motorways, there is likely to be only sparse tree planting and thus only limited attraction for wild life along the M11 across the chalk downs. On the other hand, the opening of the motorway should greatly improve conditions in the villages and in the city of Cambridge that have suffered so long the ever-increasing noise and vibration of larger and larger lorries and more and more cars. Could a better route have been devised? To have put it farther away from the valley would have carried the damaging effects into the very heart of the high, quiet hills. The line proposed in 1964 was much closer to the old road and railway; it would have brought the noise and movement and the great scar closer to the villages and would have spoiled much of the valley and the beautiful setting of Audley End.

A return visit to Newport confirmed my impressions of what the effects will be. The village with its long street of charming old houses of many centuries looked little different from when I first saw it over forty years ago. The school still stood back from the road, behind the front lawn flanked by trees. Inevitable growth since the Second World War had, alas, put a large assembly hall on the lawn, partly hiding the attractive front which was designed in 1878 by Eden Nesfield and added to in similar style in 1928 and 1936. Other buildings had appeared north of the lane on the playing fields which themselves had been extended and had a much more open look than in the 1930s. Across the valley, the beautiful woods of Shortgrove survived in all their glory, but the village was cursed with the constant roar of much heavier traffic. It was waiting impatiently, and perhaps over-optimistically, for a return to the relative peace of pre-war years. During the last winter before the line was pegged out and the earth-movers were expected, I went round the time-honoured cross-country route, walking not running, up and down the stony tracks and across the sticky, chalky clay of the fields, littered with small, bluish flints. The banks of the sunken lane running down towards Wendens Ambo revealed the chalk, with large flints embedded in it, only about a foot below the surface. The scenery and the solitude were impressive, and the silence was broken only by the gentle rain and the calls of lapwing and lark. I found it hard to believe that within a few years the weary runners would have to pass under a motorway at two points. They would never be far from the roar of traffic, and would no longer be able to hear their own thumping hearts and heavy breathing!

A few miles away, the town of Saffron Walden had kept the beauty and charm of its streets and of its setting hard against the Audley End Park. There had been changes, but most of the old buildings and the splendid church were well preserved, and most of the new buildings of fairly good design. The Market Place, fortunate in lying clear of the main traffic routes, was still the centre of activity though its functions may have changed somewhat. On one corner stands the early Victorian Corn Exchange whose recent history reflects such changes in the past century. It was built in 1847–8, in "a tasteless and jolly Italianate style" (Pevsner), with a pair of large stone columns on either side of the entrance and an elaborate cupola and clock tower above. Like so many corn exchanges it outlived its original purpose, and the Borough Council wanted to demolish it and redevelop the site, presumably with new shops and offices. Consent for demolition was refused in 1972 by the County Council, to whom the Borough Council promptly offered the building as a gift. It was then beautifully restored and converted to use as a public library, winning, incidentally, an award for the way in which the conversion catered for access and use by the disabled. (Twenty-five miles away in Sudbury, West Suffolk County Council carried out an equally impressive conversion, earning an architectural award, of the Corn Exchange of similar age in the Market Place.)

What of Whittlesford, where I first came to know the East Anglian Heights? Here, perhaps, more has changed than at Newport. In May of 1972, we stopped in the village street to look for the little school where I spent just a year from 1930 to 1931. It was still there, discreetly hidden behind old cottages. Children were playing in front of the red and white brick building, typical of late Victorian times, and it seemed to have altered very little. The headmistress saw us, and on learning my interest, took us through the school, now crammed with one hundred and fifty children, three times as many as there were only ten years before. The opportunity to see it still in use, with its original doors and windows and cast iron stoves, was a stroke of good fortune, for the school was to close at the end of the summer term, and move into a new building near the mill.

Down at the railway station, a mile away, there had been changes too. The station itself was much the same, but our old house, itself the original station building close by the permanent way, had gone. Cars no longer bounced over the level crossing, which was now closed, and bypassed by a new road and bridge on the London side of the station. The footbridge still stood, but the view from it was obscured by a plantation of poplars along the stream. There was a general feeling of everything being a bit more hemmed in. In fact, all up the Cam valley the trees and woods and belts have mostly remained and flourished these forty years. The landscape has thus lost a little of its austere delicacy, but it is still very delightful with a peculiar quality, and for me it has lost none of its evocative powers, both in itself and as a reminder of my early acquaintance with it. From here the roads still lead up into the little valleys and across open country into those delectable hills.

6

Farming Country

OVER the chalk hills, a main road runs past the Abingtons and Linton, and climbs to 361 feet above sea level just beyond Horseheath, before descending gently through Haverhill and joining the upper Stour valley near the Wixoe pumping station. We are now in the boulder-clay country, a broad arc of good, mainly heavy, agricultural land that stretches from the centre of Essex through 'High Suffolk' and mid-Norfolk. It is some of the best arable land in Britain for wheat and barley, and for sugar beet and other root crops, but by its very nature and what has been done to it in the evolution of large-scale, intensive farming, it is in general the least attractive part of East Anglia. It has neither the broad, rolling, airy beauty of the chalk downs, nor the sheer, flat infinity of the Fens.

At the lower end of the Stour valley, just before the river broadens out suddenly into the great estuary, we find Constable Country, where John was born and where he painted so many of the pictures that have surely given most of us our romantic ideas of what East Anglia is like. Many of the best known pictures show the country as a 'workplace', well understood by a miller's son who also appreciated, and was able to convey in his paintings, the beauty of the rural scenes where the work of farming and milling was carried on. In *The Cornfield*, sheep are being driven by a boy and a dog, down an elm-lined lane, presumably to the grazing meadows we can see by the river beyond the field of ripe corn. By the gate lies the plough, waiting until after the imminent harvest. A donkey and foal stand near the little, dammed stream, from which the boy is slaking his thirst; dark, heavy clouds give the feeling that it is a hot, rather oppressive day.

The picture now known as *Flatford Mill* would hardly need

describing if we used its original title, *Scene on a Navigable River*. With a hayfield on the right, and the mill and lock in the background, a couple of barges are being disconnected from the towing horse before being poled under the bridge, which is just out of the picture on our left. The barges are on their way up the Stour which had been made navigable in the late eighteenth century as far as Sudbury. Constable's father used to send flour, produced at the mills at Flatford and Dedham, in barges down to the estuary at Mistley where it would be loaded into his own ship and sailed round to London. *Boat Building* shows a wooden barge being constructed in a small 'dry dock' cut off from the river by a movable wooden dam, between the bridge and the millstream at Flatford. These pictures and many others, include the river and the watermills which were the most important features in those days, but on either side we see the water meadows, and on the rising ground beyond are the golden cornfields. Some less well known pictures show ploughing and windmills, and one very fine panorama looking across the valley from high ground near Old Hall, East Bergholt to Dedham and Langham, includes two men (accompanied by a dog) engaged in the mundane but necessary task of loading a cart with manure from a large heap that occupies much of the foreground. This last picture belongs now to the Museum of Fine Arts, Boston, U.S.A., but we were fortunate to be able to see it in the great bicentenary exhibition in 1976 at the Tate Gallery in London. The other three pictures are still in England: *The Cornfield* and *Flatford Mill* in the National Gallery, *Boat Building* in the Victoria and Albert Museum.

Fortunately these two London galleries, and the Tate, have between them a very substantial collection of Constable's paintings, water-colours and drawings. Many of them are of scenes in Essex and Suffolk, particularly along the Stour valley, and help us to appreciate the changes that have taken place during the last 200 years. The bicentenary exhibition inspired a number of new books on Constable, including several which returned to the old theme of finding the location of the scenes he painted, and describing them as they are now. Changes in Constable Country, or Dedham Vale as it is more commonly known today, have not been as drastic as in much of rural England, but I will return to that theme after looking at the more typical parts of the farming country covered by this chapter.

Until the beginning of the twentieth century the pattern and appearance of the boulder-clay lands were largely derived from medieval times, with the network of narrow, hedged lanes and roads winding between a complex pattern of small fields bounded by hedges. Most of the power to work the land was provided by the muscles of men and horses, with the help of fairly simple farm machinery, and the farmhouses and barns were still built of traditional materials, harmonizing, perhaps untidily in places, but nevertheless harmonizing, with the rural scene. The country was still occupied mainly by people who worked on the land, but many villages were already losing people to the growing towns. Roads were dusty, motor vehicles still rare and a cause of wonder and alarm when seen. Steam traction engines were playing an important part in ploughing and threshing, but they had, though no one realized it at the time, only a brief role to play before new and more complete mechanization arrived in the form of the motor tractor. Most parishes still had their working windmills and watermills, and their blacksmiths' forges. Rural life was, to a great extent, still self-contained except for the centuries-old dependence on the market town. We can learn first-hand from countrymen still living what life was like in the East Anglian countryside before the First World War, and we can read vivid, and in some ways amusing, accounts by gifted sons of the soil. Spike Mays' book *Reuben's Corner*, about Ashdon in the north-west corner of Essex, could hardly be bettered for a re-creation in spirit and in detail of the joys and hardships of country life and the earthy characters of the time. Things have changed so much that it is hard to believe it has all happened in our own country and in living memory

While agriculture since 1914, has been the victim of fluctuating fortune caused by national and international events and economics, the trend in East Anglia has been strongly towards increased efficiency and productivity. In particular, two world wars have necessitated desperate measures to grow more food at home to compensate for restricted imports. The population of Britain has increased enormously, and greater general prosperity in the long term has added to the demand. The growth of towns and manufacturing and service industries has taken large areas of land and has attracted farm workers away from the land to better paid jobs. To sum up, the farmers of East Anglia, with fewer men to work for them, have been expected to grow more food on less land. I suppose the rapid and continuing reduction in the agricultural labour force was the biggest spur to increased mechanization which in turn led to the need to adapt the layout of farms to use by machines and methods which functioned best and most economically on a large scale. This was recognized by the government who grant-aided the removal of hedges to create bigger fields, the clearance of woodland and conversion to arable, and the reclamation of marginal land—marsh, heath, salting and fen—to arable and grazing. At the same time, artificial fertilizers and pesticides were developed to increase productivity and to minimize the many pests and diseases that food crops attract. Both for cultivation and for the application of fertilizers, sprays and powders, the large field was easier and quicker to work with tractors and large machines. The removal of hedges and hedgerow trees and the disappearance of many ditches obviated a great deal of the unproductive work of hedging, ditching and lopping, and helped to compensate for the loss of men to the towns.

All this seems almost too well known and obvious to state yet again, but East Anglia is the most important arable region in Britain, and has therefore experienced these changes in a much greater degree than other regions. What happened to Suffolk during the twenty years immediately following the Second World War is illustrated by unusually dramatic statistics which are similar to those for the rest of East Anglia. From 1945 to 1966, the acreage of farmland in Suffolk increased (mainly by the clearance of woodland and reclamation of marginal land) from 705,699 to 731,307, and the total number of full-time and part-time regular workers dropped from 20,114 to 13,359, which meant a rise in the twenty years from 35 to 54 acres per man. The percentage of arable, always high in relation to grassland, increased from 80% in 1945 to 86% in 1966 of the total farmed, and from 566,537 to 630,780 acres. Since 1966, the number of farmworkers has continued to fall, but the clearance of woodland and ploughing of marginal land has proceeded much more slowly, particularly since reclamation grants were discontinued in 1972.

It is hardly surprising that these statistical changes were accompanied by profound social and physical changes in our countryside, or that the wholesale removal of hedges and woodland brought a tremendous amount of criticism by the general public and by naturalists and conservationists. In the late 1950s and early 1960s much of the criticism, while understandable, was subjective and ill-informed, but there was real cause for concern as so much arable country in eastern England came to resemble the prairies of the American Mid-West. In one extreme example, a farm at Stradishall in south-west Suffolk, formerly divided into 40 fields, was converted, by the removal of all interior hedges and the piping and filling of all ditches, into one vast field of over 600 acres! Many critics were suggesting in those years that farmers were acting against their own interests by such drastic action and that serious thought should be given to a return to more traditional ways of farming. There was a good deal of acrimonious correspondence in the press. At least one farmer with extreme views achieved headlines and a picture in *The Times*, and was seen on the television screen defending the lengths to which he had gone in removing virtually all the trees and hedges from a very large farm in East Suffolk.

While all this was going on, a few level-headed people involved in agriculture and conservation saw that there was an urgent need to get the two 'sides' talking to each other "on a much broader front and in more sympathetic terms", it being clear that there was a great deal of mutual ignorance and lack of understanding. The initiative was taken by the Royal Society for the Protection of Birds when, in early 1967, their Reserves Manager, David Lea, talked to Derek Barber, a Bedfordshire officer of the Ministry of Agriculture's Advisory Service. Later that year, a small group was formed of representatives of the R.S.P.B., Nature Conservancy, Ministry of Agriculture, and a farmer who was also an ornithologist. The group soon realized that not only was there a general need for more knowledge and better communication, but that improvements could result only if conservationists were able to make specific suggestions, consistent with the practice and economics of efficient farming. Eric Carter, of the Ministry of Agriculture in the county of Lindsey, had the idea, which resulted in the 'Silsoe Exercise' of 1969. It was to find a block of fairly typical land which had not been subjected to extreme farming practices, and to arrange for farmers and conservationists to state in detail how they would manage it, and then to discuss the practical possibilities of compromise.

The weekend conference in July 1969 at the National College of Agricultural Engineering at Silsoe in Bedfordshire is so well documented that I will merely say here that, after introductory talks on the general problems, the delegates split up into 'syndicates', four with the objectives of effective farming, and two concerned with nature conservation. Each syndicate produced its own detailed and costed plan for a farm of 400 acres at Tring, including various degrees of hedge and ditch removal, from one extreme to the other, and providing for various mixtures of arable and stock farming. There seems little doubt that the Silsoe conference did a great deal to increase respect and understanding, and it inspired many similar exercises, with practical results likely to enhance the rural scene, in many parts of England. Many of these exercises were assisted by the Farming and Wildlife Advisory Group based at the R.S.P.B. headquarters at Sandy Lodge in Bedfordshire; and the Ministry of Agriculture started nature conservation courses for their own staff.

Suffolk was fortunate that the Ministry's Advisory Officer for the county had been a member of the group formed in 1967, and leader of one of the farming syndicates at Silsoe. He was John Trist, an extremely knowledgeable naturalist, who had spent over twenty years as a professional agricultural adviser. In the last few years of his working life he wrote the Suffolk volume of the County Agricultural Surveys, published in 1971 by the Royal Agricultural Society of England. Concurrently, and after his retirement, he played a great part in the establishment and management of the nature reserves of the Suffolk Trust for Nature Conservation. In late 1972 he became chairman of a committee set up to study 700 acres at Letheringham in East Suffolk. Their report was published by the Farming and Wildlife Advisory Group in the spring of 1974 and a field day was held on 21st May.

It was a dull, cool afternoon when about 150 farmers, foresters, naturalists and local authority planning staff, and others, assembled in the square between the Victorian buildings of Model Farm, Easton. We heard short introductory talks, over a very efficient amplifier based in a Land Rover, by John Trist and by representatives of the Ministry of Agriculture, the Forestry Commission and the County Council; and by Mr William Kerr, the senior partner in the farming enterprise, and his sons. They spoke of the aspects they were personally involved in, including Mr James Kerr's new venture, the Farm Park which had been first opened at Model Farm a few weeks earlier.

Eight or nine tractors, each with a very long trailer, were lined up round the square to take the visitors on a tour of the farm and to see the features described in the report. We sat on bales of straw and were driven along the lanes and across the fields in a long, snaking convoy that only needed pikes, muskets or rifles to make us look like a band of mercenaries setting out to pillage and loot the countryside. The military feel of things was increased by the evidence of good planning and organization, especially in the way in which the convoy manoeuvred swiftly into positions around the Land Rover at each of the stopping places where we had a short talk by an appropriate expert. We started along a lane between open arable fields and then crossed a bridge over the little River Deben where even the 1954 Ordnance Survey Map showed a ford and footbridge. The river with its willows and water meadows still looked like a part of the old Suffolk landscape, but poplars and bat willows had been planted in recent years as a quick crop. As in many other parts of East Anglia they are much better than no trees, but they do show up as a strange new feature especially in spring when the new leaves are orange in colour. The little road parallel with the river ran along the edge of the flood plain and marked the boundary between the green lushness and trees of the valley bottom and the wide open cultivated slopes now terribly dry and dusty after an exceptionally dry winter and spring. A vast area west of this road had lost all the hedges which formerly divided it into small fields averaging about thirteen acres, and various crops were now grown on blocks of land undivided by hedges or ditches. The published Study covered 700 acres of a total farming enterprise of 1400 acres, and in that half, since the 1950s, 5 miles of ditches, 4 miles of hedges and 75 acres of woodland, had been removed. Where there had been 109 fields, of which sixty-nine were under 5 acres and only five over 20 acres, there were now only forty-nine, with ten main arable fields including one of 189 acres. The total number of enclosures, before and after, tends to be misleading, as quite a lot were, and still are, plots containing farm buildings, cottages, cattle yards and paddocks, but the overall change from small to large fields is very striking, particularly if one looks at old and new maps of the farm. The Kerrs said that fewer hedges might have been removed fifteen years previously if modern hedge-cutting machinery had then been available. From the higher ground where we paused to survey the landscape, we looked back over the valley with its trees and green meadows backed by rising ground with scattered trees and small woods, giving an overall impression of a very attractive, well-wooded countryside. Even the arable areas of the farm itself did not offend the eye as they do in some districts, as a few hedges and small woodlands remained, and the terrain was gently rolling and intersected by small valleys.

A pair of mallard rose and flew from the little pond near Cutters Grove, and drew our attention to the value to wild life of even a small pond with trees and bushes round it. The small pieces of woodland left on this farm are just large enough to shelter many birds, small animals and insects, and to enhance the rural scene, but by trying to imagine how it would look without them we realized how vital it was to keep what was left. During the past twenty years Old Park Wood had been reduced from 65 acres to 3 acres, Smilley Wood from 25 to 2, and Cutters Grove from 12 to 10. There had been small gains in the form of willows and poplars planted along the riverside meadows on areas large enough to be shown on the 1969 edition of the Ordnance Survey one-inch map.

From Cutters Grove we went westwards across the fields, past a bean crop alongside which a dozen hives had been placed for the flowering season, to Hoo Green. This is an ancient settlement where much of the old pattern of hedges and small fields, and the green itself, can be seen in spite of the presence of several modern hedges. With or without knowledge of the historical and topographical evolution of Hoo Green, we could all see and feel very clearly the tremendous contrasts with the vast fields and the wide landscape we had just traversed. Eastwards we re-entered more open country with wide views across the Deben valley towards Easton Park, the former home of the Duke of Hamilton whose huge Suffolk estate, until its sale in lots in 1919, included the Letheringham farms. The line of oaks along the road, although impressive and welcome, looked rather isolated and forlorn without hedges and with shorn road verges. Close by Letheringham Church, on rising ground above the Deben, stood the main group of farm buildings of traditional red brick and pantile, but in a fascinating setting including banks and old brick walls that indicated clearly a very long history and ecclesiastical associations. We were considering the landscape and its changes rather than history, and noted the utterly satisfying picture these buildings made especially from across the tiny valley on its west side. From within the group of buildings where we stopped to see a demonstration by Harry Searle,

District Officer of the Forestry Commission, of how (but as he readily admitted, not when!) to plant a tree, the presence of a large asbestos-roofed building was regrettable. In spite of its well-weathered roof, it still looked crudely utilitarian and out of keeping, but we could understand that many old buildings, some listed as being of architectural or historic interest, may be of little practical use in modern arable farming, and are very expensive to maintain.

After the tour, there was a discussion in the lecture room at the Model Farm, where an exhibition showed, by photographs and maps, how the landscape had changed. Apart from a few plaintive cries from naturalists—"where have all the butterflies gone?"—most of the discussion showed a good understanding of the practicalities and economics of modern farming. There was much sympathy for the problems and aims of the conservationists, and a general feeling that there had been too much destruction in the last twenty years and that it was time to call a halt. There were sincere expressions of intent to 'do something about it', and a declaration was made by the chairman that the Letheringham Report would be followed by practical action and further study.

Within a few miles of Letheringham are four farms on parts of which old patterns and old methods survive.

At Otley, Monewden and Cransford, there are several small pastures that have probably never been ploughed, and have certainly not been subjected to modern farming methods, fertilizers or herbicides. They are cut for hay in July and some of the meadows are grazed by cattle. Having been managed in this way for so long, they have, in contrast with 'improved' pastures, a rich variety of grasses, and many wild flowers including some that are comparatively rare. There are many meadow saffron or *Colchicum autumnale* (not the saffron crocus, *Colchicum sativus*, or the autumn crocus, *Colchicum nudiflorus*), blooming in September; and fritillaries, orchids and adder's tongue, and many more species to delight the botanist. These particular meadows on the four farms are managed by the farmers in accordance with agreements with the Suffolk Trust for Nature Conservation. They are not open to the public, except on occasional 'open days' arranged by the Trust. We step back into the past when we walk in from the road by the seventeenth-century farmhouse on its moated site, to the little, secluded fields surrounded by thick hedges. At the back of the farm, chickens roam freely around the old wooden coops under the huge elms, now alas, diseased and dying like so many trees and hedges in this part of Suffolk, and indeed throughout East Anglia and the rest of southern England.

Not far away, on the disused airfield at Debach, other chickens numbering many thousands, do not enjoy such old-fashioned freedom, as they are housed in huge buildings on the old runways. All around is an open, flat landscape, typical of much of the present-day country from Ipswich to the Norfolk border and beyond. On a rambling tour through the boulder clay country, we can get a vivid impression of what has been done by modern farming methods followed by Dutch elm disease. I do not want to suggest that it is all one vast prairie, for there are still many isolated areas of various sizes, with roadside and field hedges, village greens and ponds, and here and there some old woodlands that have survived for a thousand years or more. But these oases are relatively small, and serve to emphasize the extent of the new agricultural landscapes.

For miles on either side of the Roman road between Ipswich and Norwich, the lanes wind their way through a wide, windswept plateau, broken by only a few shallow valleys. It is a bleak, wet and sticky prospect in winter, with occasional, isolated oaks and elms, dead or in poor condition, standing on bare roadside banks. Here and there, as at Cay Hill near Mendlesham Green, are short lengths of road still bordered by natural-looking, untidy, mixed hedges, thick enough even in winter to hide the deep ditches and the bare fields beyond. Before the removal of so many hedges, we would not have had a view across the fields to the tall church tower of Mendlesham, an attractive village with many old timber-framed houses in its close-knit centre which gives it almost the look and feel of a small town.

At Cotton, a fine old thatched and pink-washed farmhouse stands opposite the church in its neglected churchyard. It is a beautiful, light, airy church, with wooden box pews, some with doors. Although it seems to be in a good state of preservation, the stone pillars of the nave lean several degrees outwards from the floor upwards. The countryside round here has many farmhouses of the sixteenth and seventeenth centuries and earlier, standing on moated sites, surrounded by elm, oak, ash and sycamore, which shelter also old weather-boarded or brick and tiled barns. At one moated farm, not far from Cotton, the beauty and interest of the garden are enhanced by many wild flowers, such as primroses, cowslips, violets, dusky cranesbill and Himalayan balsam.

Returning to the main road at Little Stonham, we can see evidence of historical and recent changes. The Magpie Inn has what is now a rare feature, a sign mounted on a wooden frame spanning the road. The legs on either side were cut a few years ago and the sign temporarily removed to allow the passage on a lorry of a tiny, square, thatched cottage, the Mustard Pot. This had been removed to allow road widening near Mendlesham, a few miles to the north, and was re-erected as a fishermen's shelter beside the River Gipping at Bosmere Mill, Needham Market. North of the Magpie where the low bank, or *agger*, of the Roman road can just be seen on the east side, the hedges have disappeared and a few new roadside trees have been planted. The openness gives us a good view of a fine group of old farm buildings with red pantiles well weathered with yellow lichen; the perfection of this group, next to the beautiful farmhouse, has been a little marred by a recent asbestos building. From here, and indeed from much of mid-Suffolk in clear weather, we can see the 1000-foot mast at the Independent Television Authority transmitting station. This is on a disused airfield on which there are large warehouses and a heavy-lorry depot. At Eye Airfield, a little farther north, are several factories, and a large gas compressor station, with barbed wire fences, pipework and floodlights, which will be seen as a grotesque addition to the scene for some years until the new trees round it have grown large enough to soften the effects.

A mile and a half away from the main road, the little town of Eye keeps its quiet charm in narrow, winding streets, the pattern of which was set by the outer bailey of the Norman castle at the east end of the oval. The overgrown mound, behind houses, is overlooked by the magnificent church tower, wonderfully patterned in white stone and black flint flushwork, which Pevsner describes as one of the wonders of Suffolk. At the western end of the oval we can see the pattern of the original market place, laid out like the rest of the town, in a few years after 1066, but since built over with houses, shops and the rather fanciful Victorian Town Hall which Pevsner dismissed (I think unfairly) as 'horrible'. As its name implies, Eye was built on an island surrounded by the little River Dove and a tributary, and by wet peaty ground known as the Town Moor.

East and south-east of the town, the open landscape stretches for miles over an area where I think we see the worst effects of the clearance of hedges, trees and woodland. All through the parishes of Kenton, Monk Soham, Bedfield, Tannington, Ashfield and Worlingworth, and northwards, the land is mostly flat. This fact, and the scarcity of trees, expose unpleasantly other features of modern farming. Huge new buildings, mostly of asbestos and concrete, serve as mushroom 'factories', or house pigs, chickens and turkeys in tens of thousands. We no longer see, except in a few rare and secret places, the mushrooms in the meadows or the chickens in the farmyards, and we see fewer cattle and sheep as arable becomes almost universal in this area. The present character of most of the land in these six parishes is such that the County Council, in conjunction with the Countryside Commission, has chosen them for a major grant-aided scheme to plant trees and improve the landscape following its early grant-aided clearance! But even as late as 1977, bulldozers were filling ditches and preparing a large area near Fressingfield for a major field drainage scheme, transforming the gentle slopes into one huge featureless field.

Farther east, as we approach the A12 beyond which are the lighter soils of the Sandlings, the countryside is more diverse with many woods west of Saxmundham, and several parks around Yoxford. At Heveningham the Hall stands in a huge park where a distinguished modern landscape architect, Sylvia Crowe, has been engaged to rehabilitate the gaps and damage which time and some neglect have wrought on Capability Brown's setting of the splendid Georgian mansion. Turning again towards the Norfolk border we come to the land of the Saints of Ilketshall and South Elmham, a group of villages mostly west of Stone Street, the Roman road from Halesworth to Bungay. Their historical features and significance are described in detail by Norman Scarfe in *The Suffolk Landscape*, but for my purpose it will suffice if I draw attention to the flat, open arable landscape having subtle differences which make it look less devastated and more interesting than the six parishes mentioned earlier. Houses and farms, many of them on moated sites, are widely scattered, there are no compact villages, and the little churches stand in comparative isolation. There are huge village greens and commons, with many ponds, on land which is some of the heaviest and most difficult to drain. It is a strange area seemingly cut off from the rest of the county, and nowhere is it easier to lose one's bearings, particularly with the added confusion caused by so many similar names; there are eight South Elmhams and four Ilketshalls, and some of each now consist merely of a church and one or two farmhouses.

If we turn west up the Waveney valley we welcome the beauty of the river with its water meadows, willows and alders as a relief from the boulder clay farmlands on the higher ground, but we return to the bleak, open country north of Scole on the Norwich road, particularly between Dickleburgh and Long Stratton. The pattern, or lack of pattern, continues for some distance west of Norwich, though it is broken somewhat by the wooded slopes and parkland of the Wensum valley. There is a great difference beyond Fakenham, where we soon come to the verge of the East Anglian Heights, and a rolling, chalk-based landscape that continues westwards to Hunstanton. It is still arable country, with large fields; indeed the fields here were never small and most of the roadside hedges remain, separated from the long, straight roads by wide verges. The hedges are probably at their very best at the end of June, with the lush green growth of thorn and the reddish tinges of maple so thickly leaved that they seem impenetrable. The hawthorn berries, growing and turning brown, give a bronze sheen, but the real glory of the hedges at this season is in the masses of white elder bloom—what a time the birds and the wine-makers must have later—and the delicate and ubiquitous wild rose with here and there the brighter pink of the downy rose on its green, thorny stems.

The wide verges are rich with the brightest and largest of our roadside flowers. When we travelled through the two counties in midsummer, the roadside flowers in Norfolk seemed much finer and more numerous than in Suffolk where the drought of 1974 had been much more prolonged. The corn and the beet in the fields seemed much stronger and greener. Most colourful and plentiful among the Norfolk flowers were the purple mallow, three feet and more in height, and the scarlet poppy. The thistles were not yet in full flower, but had already reached a great height. White campion was widespread. Umbellifers of various kinds, some white, some yellow, some pink, some green, were everywhere, with the greatest but the most sinister, the giant hemlock, reaching up to eight feet. In north Norfolk we found a yellow star thistle, and most spectacular of all a glorious stand of viper's bugloss among wild mignonette about four feet high on a heap of sand and earth just inside the gate of a sand pit near Glandford. An interesting fact of which we were reminded frequently was the very great variation in the size of the same plant species in different places and conditions. They grew at their biggest at the back of roadside verges, and at their lowest and smallest on the cliffs and shingle of the coast. The variation was in some cases so considerable that it was hard to believe we were looking at the same species.

On our journey back to Suffolk, we noticed a marked contrast between the country north and south of the River Yare. To the south, through the rest of Norfolk and into mid-Suffolk, the hedges were scarcer and thinner, and the verges much poorer in wild flowers; indeed many appeared to have nothing but umbellifers and grasses, except for occasional patches of poppies, mallows, corn marigolds and thistles on recently disturbed areas. New farm buildings were mostly of crude materials and there were more intensive pig and poultry units. Even the older farm buildings were of poorer quality as we moved away from the sources of materials that gave rise to the fine brick, pebble and pantile barns of north-west Norfolk.

The boundary between Norfolk and Suffolk is marked for most of its length by the Little Ouse which runs west into the Fens to join the Great Ouse on its way to the Wash, and the Waveney which runs east to Breydon Water and the North Sea. These two rivers rise within twenty feet of each other, as springs on either side of the road just north of Redgrave, and run first through areas of peat fen of unique interest in their setting in the arable belt. Just east of the road the infant Waveney is bordered by over 300 acres of Redgrave and Lopham Fens, the first and probably still the most interesting of the Suffolk Trust's nature reserves. In the early nineteenth century, following parliamentary enclosure of other land, these fens were awarded to the poor of the parishes, who took reed and sedge for thatching and for animal bedding, and cut and dried peat for fuel. These activities, which ceased about forty years ago, created conditions suitable for many different plants and insects, some of them rare, and a large variety of animals and birds. The reserve has the distinction of spiders not known elsewhere, including a species added by Dr Eric Duffey to the British list in 1956. It is the large raft spider, Britain's largest, and is found in vegetation around water-filled peat diggings. The flowers include various orchids, and the insectivorous butterwort and sundew, and on small, raised, sandy areas we find cross-leaved heath and cotton grass. Birds, especially warblers, are very numerous, and huge numbers of toads are present in the breeding season. At all times of the year, there is much to interest the naturalist, but conditions reminiscent of tropical swamps can be almost unbearable in extreme heat, as visitors found on an open day in the summer of 1976 when the temperature was over 90°F.

Between Redgrave and Ixworth there is considerable evidence of the loss of hedges and trees, and we sometimes see what was once an extremely rare sight in East Anglia, a view of clear arable land rising to a skyline bare of any features whatever; in fact hardly a view at all in spite of its extent. A great deal of sugar beet is grown in mid-Suffolk, and much of it is taken to the factory at Bury St Edmunds where the great concrete silos and clouds of steam can be seen from miles around. Close to the sugar factory is a huge, post-war, concrete block of maltings, superseding the picturesque old, red-brick, cowled buildings near the railway station. These factories are symbolic of rural changes, and remind us of the extent and importance of industries associated with East Anglian farming. The Bury sugar factory, and others in East Anglia, were built in the 1920s, and helped to sustain local agriculture during a period of severe depression; the crop continues to be a very important item in the pattern of farming activities in the area covered by this chapter. Less well known is the fact that there was an abortive and short-lived attempt to introduce sugar beet as early as 1868 when a refiner of imported sugar erected a small factory at Lavenham for extracting beet juice for further processing at his London factory.

Other agricultural industries, particularly those producing farm machinery, fertilizers and chemicals, have flourished in East Anglia, developing from small local businesses into firms known throughout the world. Ransomes, Sims and Jefferies Ltd, had its origins in a small foundry for the production of ploughshares, set up by Robert Ransome in Ipswich in 1789; and grew into internationally famous manufacturers of agricultural machinery, taking in their stride the construction of battery-operated lorries in the early 1900s and Ipswich Corporation trolley buses in the 1920s and 1930s. Fisons Ltd, the enormous firm whose name is now synonymous with fertilizers and farm chemicals, started in a small way in Ipswich in 1847, manufacturing a phosphate fertilizer. Three similar businesses were amalgamated in 1929 as Fison, Packard and Prentice Ltd, who developed the site of an old paper mill by the Gipping at Bramford, and built a large fertilizer factory at Cliff Quay, Ipswich. Description of these industries is really outside the scope of a book on landscape, but I must mention briefly Garrett's of Leiston and Burrell's of Thetford, who manufactured so many of the splendid steam engines that impressed the eye and ear for nearly a century in the fields and farmyards; some of these magnificent machines can still be seen in action at steam rallies and in fairs, and rural life museums.

Even more significant in the rural scene has been the disappearance of nearly all the windmills of which only a handful have been preserved, and only one or two, notably Bryant's Mill at Pakenham near Bury, still grind corn. In the same village is a watermill with its machinery intact, and there are hopes that it may be restored to working order. The majority of our watermills have gone, but some have been converted into very beautiful houses in idyllic settings. The work these mills once did now takes place on a much larger scale to feed the greatly increased population, in huge concrete dockside mills at Ipswich and other ports.

We can still learn something and see some of the relics of old farming methods by visiting the Museum of East Anglian Rural Life at Stowmarket, in the heart of the boulder clay country. It is in the wooded grounds of Abbot's Hall, a fine, early eighteenth-century brick house only a few yards from the centre of the town. A huge timber-framed barn contains old farm carts and implements, and other buildings have a fascinating collection including equipment from dairies and stables. A small smithy from Grundisburgh has been re-erected here, and is used for demonstrating the skills of the blacksmith. Under long-term plans it is hoped to rescue other typical rural buildings from dereliction or demolition, and to create a collection representative of the landscapes and activities of the counties of the region. Of special interest are Alton watermill and mill house rescued from the site of a large new reservoir south of Ipswich. Land adjoining the museum is cropped and grazed, and the museum itself cultivates a small area using horses and old, simple implements.

Continuing our tour through the boulder clay farming country, we can now have a brief look at a few of the surviving woodland areas in south-west Suffolk. By comparison with Norfolk, the county has lost much more woodland to arable in the past century, and has undoubtedly lost as great a proportion of its hedges; a study in Norfolk established that about half that county's hedges were removed between 1946 and 1970. The part of Suffolk south and west of a line from Ipswich to Stanton, near Ixworth, has still far more woods, large and small, than the central plateau to the north-east, but some of those which have survived have done so only after long drawn-out battles against proposals for clear felling and conversion to arable. The hands of local authorities imposing tree-preservation orders, and of government departments arbitrating on resultant appeals, have been greatly strengthened by detailed scientific and historical studies and reports by local and regional experts, notably Oliver Rackham of Cambridge University. He found that a group of woods at Barking, near Needham Market, threatened with clearance in the early 1970s, figured in a survey of the Bishop of Ely's estates in 1251. The history and the interesting flora and fauna that had developed, added considerable weight to the more obvious case for preserving the woodlands as splendid features in a valley landscape.

The case of Felsham Hall Wood and Monks Park Wood, Bradfield, was more complex and difficult, covering the whole range of history, uses and interest from earliest times to the present. It is thought that these woods originated as part of the forest which spread over the country from about 8000 B.C. when the climate was improving after the Ice Age. Like the Barking Woods, their existence in the thirteenth century is confirmed by their inclusion in ecclesiastical records; they belonged to the Abbey of St Edmundsbury. From at least that time, these woods, like others, played an important part in rural life and economy by providing timber for building, wood for fuel, and the products of coppicing for making fences, hurdles and handles for rakes and other implements. The campaign to save most of this block of woodland, the largest surviving on the boulder clay in Suffolk, culminated in the late 1960s in the purchase of 125 acres by the Society for the Promotion of Nature Reserves and a management agreement with the owners of a further 30 acres. Coppicing continues, and a small local firm still produces fencing materials and implement handles. Management in this way enables the survival of a great variety of flowering plants, and birds and insects are also numerous. Historical features include fish ponds and boundary banks and ditches. Altogether these woods are of tremendous interest, and their beauty is a source of great pleasure to specialist and amateur alike.

From Bradfield to the upper Stour where this chapter began, it is well worth the trouble of finding one's way through the hilliest and least known part of Suffolk. There is a choice of routes, but one must make a point of finding Hartest in its steep-sided little valley, and with its cottages bordering the central green; and Hawkedon, a smaller, more remote village where the fifteenth-century Hall faces the church across a more open and less well-kept green.

Stoke-by-Clare, hidden from the River Stour by the trees of the Priory, is at the west end of a string of villages famed far beyond the bounds of Suffolk, for the beauty of their streets, old buildings, and in several, for their splendid churches. Stoke itself has been transformed in very recent years by the removal of the railway line and the hump-backed road bridge which had been unfortunate barriers cutting the village green in two for over a century. The closure and removal of the railway here, and in many parts of East Anglia, was the end of a means of transport that served the farming community in many ways until motor transport took over. At Clare the station buildings are preserved as part of a small country park which includes the remains of the castle. Clare, Cavendish, Long Melford and Lavenham are too well known to need description here, but in the context of farming country it is of interest to note the evidence, in the shape of fine houses and churches, of sixteenth-century prosperity based on the woollen industry, and the fact that these gems of old England are now sur-rounded by the windy acres of modern arable farming. The exception is Long Melford which, with its beautiful village green, bordered on the west by fine old houses, by the brick wall, towers and park of Melford Hall on the east, and by the wooded grounds of Kentwell Hall on the north, still has a beautiful setting.

Most of the disused railway track from Lavenham through Long Melford, serves as a very pleasant public walk finishing at its south end in the water meadows between the old market town of Sudbury and the hills on the Essex side of the river. Here was the head of the navi-gation, of which evidence can be found in the width of the river, and the existence of basins, wharves and warehouses, and a long narrow channel that served the brickworks and chalk quarry near Ballingdon Grove. In that channel, several sunken barges, similar to the one in Constable's *Boat Building*, have been found, and one is being restored by the River Stour Trust, an active voluntary society with the objectives of safeguarding and promoting the recreational use of the river. In the centre of the town, at the top of the Market Hill, below the tower of St Peter's Church, stands a statue of Thomas Gainsborough, who was born in what is now Gainsborough House in Gainsborough Street. The house, now preserved by a trust, is used as a gallery for art exhibi-tions. In 1977, the year after Constable's bicentenary, the 250th anniversary of Gainsborough's birth was commemorated in an exhibition here which showed some of his local landscapes. They included a fine picture, painted in 1748, but not previously seen by the public, of Hadleigh Church in its beautiful setting, little changed over 200 years later, with timber-framed houses to the east and the splendid Deanery Tower, a brick gatehouse of 1495, opposite the west end.

About half-way between Gainsborough's statue and his house, the Corn Exchange, like the one at Saffron Walden, was in a fairly advanced state of decay until it was rescued by the County Council who restored its monumental Victorian façade and cleverly converted its interior into a most attractive public library.

From Sudbury southwards to Marks Tey, the branch line survives precariously, heavily subsidized from year to year. The growth of trees and bushes on its banks compensate a little for the loss of trees in the flood plain. Many of the old, grotesque but familiar pollarded willows that used to line and mark out from afar the meandering course of the river have gone, and most of those that remain have rotted and split apart or fallen. 'Improvements' to the river, to reduce the risk of flooding and to facilitate the flow of the additional water piped from the Fens into the upper Stour, have taken the form of widening, deepening and straightening the channel. Trees have been cut down, and the old, rough, naturally eroded banks have been replaced by gentle grass slopes, with low flood banks set about twenty feet back. These works, from Cornard down past Henny, have made a considerable difference to the landscape, and the new graded banks, bare of trees and bushes, are of no interest to the kingfisher and the water vole and other animals and birds. The beauty of the valley has been affected also by the death of many elms and the removal of hedges from the roadsides and fields along the steeply rising ground on either side. Here and there we are getting used to the small plantations of the quick-growing *Robusta* poplar which are quite conspicuous when the spring sunshine shows up their young, orange-brown foliage.

In spite of these changes, the section of the valley from Sudbury down to Nayland, remains sufficiently attractive for consideration as an extension of the designated Area of Outstanding Natural Beauty covering what is now popularly regarded as Dedham Vale from Nayland to Brantham. The open, boulder-clay country lies mostly beyond the skyline on the Suffolk and Essex sides, and the Vale itself is quite well wooded and remarkably unspoilt, but its vulnerability is illustrated by the existence on the hillsides of two or three large, ugly and prominent asbestos farm buildings which seem to have slipped through the net of the voluntary consultation system set up by the County Councils in agreement with the Country Landowners' Association and the National Farmers' Union. But all in all it is still a very beautiful valley, which, together with the valleys of its little tributaries the Box and the Brett, I think well deserves to be an official AONB, even though some critics, perhaps more impressed with the large-scale splendour of the Cotswolds or the Mendips, have suggested it would never have been designated but for its association with John Constable. To counter that argument, I suggest that our greatest landscape artist recognized that the valley was exceptionally beautiful, and the authorities of the twentieth century have acknowledged that it retains sufficient of its beauty and character, albeit changed in many details, to warrant special protection.

From Nayland to Brantham, where the churches contain altar paintings of Christ by Constable, we are constantly reminded of the scenes and landmarks in his pictures. To describe those scenes as they are today would take too long and might be too far removed from the theme of farming country, but farming interests are involved in the Anglian Water Authority's proposals for 'improving' the river between Stratford St Mary and Flatford. Straightening, deepening and widening are suggested to reduce the risk of flooding and thus to enable the farmland to be used for a much greater proportion of the year. Conservationists fear that the works would have similar regrettable effects to those already seen at Henny, and that the probable conversion of water meadows to arable would completely change the character of the heart of Constable Country. This is indeed the *Dedham Vale* of his famous picture (now in the National Gallery of Scotland) of the valley looking from Gun Hill, Langham, over Stratford Bridge, to Dedham church and village in the middle distance and to the open water of the Stour estuary. It is difficult to get this view now because of the growth of trees on Gun Hill, but it is still largely unspoilt in spite of the dual carriageway bypass at Stratford and the distant chimney of the plastics factory at the head of the estuary.

Dedham Mill is still used by corn merchants but has been so enlarged by brick and concrete additions that any remaining fragments of the little mill seen in Constable's pictures are completely dwarfed and hidden. From his familiar viewpoint, huge willows now mask the mill and the tower of the church.

Flatford Mill is reached from East Bergholt where the church and the detached bell-cage are of special interest, by a lane which, alas, is no longer what Norman Scarfe in 1960 described as an 'arboreal tunnel'. The last, two-way, sunken section leading down to the river has degenerated in recent years into a grossly overused road with badly eroded banks topped with tall, dead elms and ugly stumps. It is hoped that the local authorities, in conjunction with the landowners including the National Trust, will be able to effect some improvement by transferring the car park from the bottom to the top of the lane, and by clearing the dead elms and planting new trees. The scene in the late 1970s is one that would have saddened John Constable, but I think he would still find much here to please him.

The mill is in the hands of the National Trust. It is not open to the public, but let to the Field Studies Council. This, the first of their centres for a wide variety of environmental studies, was established in 1946 with help from the Carnegie United Kingdom Trustees. The weekly courses concentrate mainly on natural history, local history and landscape, including landscape painting in Constable Country, and much of the work is truly study 'in the field'. What a wonderful atmosphere and setting the students have in which to work. The main building of the mill has on the ground floor the refectory, a delightful room with white walls, and a white ceiling between the heavy, dark beams that support what was the 'stone floor' above. Large, round-headed, small-paned windows light the splendid modern refectory tables and benches made of solid oak by the craftsmen of the Papworth Everard Settlement, west of Cambridge, who have done similar work for King's College. The windows look across the placid pool of *The Hay Wain* to Willy Lott's Cottage, but the best, almost uncanny, view of the cottage is obtained by looking out from the hall of the mill through the top half of the stable-type door. The cottage, now looking rather whiter and smarter, is used as sleeping accommodation for students. Others are accommodated on the upper floor of the mill. Working facilities include the library, known as the Carnegie Room, laboratories, a studio and a dark room.

The mill, built in the 1730s, on the site of earlier mills going back to Domesday, lost its machinery soon after 1900, but it has kept its atmosphere, and still has the sack hoist projecting over the lane, and the roar of the water going over the sluice at the rear, to remind us of its original function. The warden of the field-study centre since 1949, Mr F. J. Bingley, lives in the Manor House just across the lane. It is a fine, timber-framed house, with exposed beams, dating from the sixteenth century or possibly earlier.

About two hundred yards upstream, from the other bank of the river, we are standing at the point from which Constable painted *Flatford Mill*, but now the view of the mill is completely obscured, even in winter, by trees on the edge of the towpath and on the mill island. The little dock seen in *Boat Building* is still there, and, nearer to the mill, the lock has been restored to working order by the River Stour Trust. It was officially re-opened on 29th March 1975 by Lord Greenwood (the Minister who had signed the order declaring Dedham Vale as an Area of Outstanding Natural Beauty) who came up river in a launch from Brantham to cut the tape in a snowstorm.

I return now to Easton and Letheringham which I first visited in 1974 when the report of the Farming and Wildlife Advisory Group had just been published. Easton Farm Park had been opened during the previous month, and has continued to attract large numbers of people, including many school parties, to see common farm animals, rare breeds of cattle, sheep and pigs, the magnificent Suffolk Punches, old farm machinery and waggons. This is all based on the buildings of red brick, pantiles and black boarding, erected by the Duke of Hamilton in about 1870 as a model dairy farm, close to the charming village

9

where the estate cottages and the inn have similar motifs in their barge
boards and pointed window heads. The fancy barge boards and pointed
finials on the gables have been repeated in the huge timber-framed and
timber-clad dairy opened in 1976. The dairy herd of over 100 Friesians
belongs to the neighbouring farms run by the father and brother of
Mr James Kerr, director of the Farm Park, and the new dairy has an
elevated viewing gallery and catwalk from which visitors can see the
cows brought in and milked, and the equipment for disposal of manure
and for winter feeding. The size of this new building, admirably
designed to harmonize with the nineteenth-century farm, is in complete
contrast with the Victorian dairy, a small octagonal brick building with
stained glass windows incorporating the duke's family crest, and
beautifully patterned tiled walls. In the centre of the tiled floor is a
small fountain, and round the sides are butter churns and other equipment that was used by the dairymaids. Demonstrations during the
summer months include a threshing machine driven by a Ransome's
steam engine of 1896. The Park's existence is due to James Kerr's
long-standing passion for old farm machinery, but has developed into
a major attraction with a much wider range of interests. He is proud of
the fact that in 1975 Easton Farm Park won first prize in the private
sector in the Conservation Award Scheme for Recreation and Leisure
in the Countryside run jointly by the Royal Institution of Chartered
Surveyors and *The Times*; second and third prizes were taken by the
Duke of Wellington at Stratfield Saye and Lord Montagu at Beaulieu,
both in Hampshire.

If the Farm Park becomes a little crowded, it is pleasant to take the
nature trail across the water meadows to the River Deben, and to sit in
the shade of the alders and willows. From a seat on the bank you can
see through the poplar plantation on the other side to the low, bare
slopes of the arable farmland of Letheringham, where we come down
to earth to finish this chapter on farming country. In 1978, Mr John
Kerr told me most of the proposals made in 1974 had been implemented, but unfortunately the new roadside trees had not survived the
exceptionally hot dry summers of the following two years. However
improvements had resulted from letting those hedges grow again
which had been shaved to ground level but not grubbed out, and by
managing the mechanical trimming of hedges so that new trees were
allowed to grow in them. The small areas of woodland had been kept,
with some selective felling and coppicing within them. The bat willow
and poplar plantations were being progressively felled and replanted as
the trees matured. Pines and hardwoods had been planted in an old,
shallow pit, to create a small wooded area. Plans were being laid to
plant new trees around farmhouses and buildings where people on the
spot could look after them until they were well established. All these

measures will improve the landscape and increase the variety of wildlife without adversely affecting the efficiency of a large, modern farm, and confirm Mr Kerr's opinion that farmers are much more interested in and knowledgeable about conservation than they were before the Silsoe Exercise of 1969. This attitude is reflected in official publications by the National Farmers' Union, the Country Landowners' Association, the Ministry of Agriculture and the Nature Conservancy Council. We must not, however, expect to see a return to the small fields and large woodlands depicted in the survey in 1761 of Abbey Farm, Letheringham, for William Siree by Thomas Warren of Bury St Edmunds, but it is quite startling to recall that the pattern on the beautiful coloured map which Mr Kerr showed me survived almost intact for nearly two more centuries.

7

Fenland Horizons

THE farming country of my previous chapter is the main arable core of East Anglia. It contains much typical lowland farming landscape, and apart from the beauty and and individuality of many of its villages and small towns, its history of agricultural innovation and progress, and the predominance of barley and sugar beet, it has little to distinguish it from the Home Counties and parts of the Midlands. To the west of the broad belt of High Suffolk and mid-Norfork, are the East Anglian Heights, now almost entirely arable country, and the Breckland where many acres have been reclaimed for agriculture between the huge pine plantations. Beyond those two distinctive parts of the region is the largest area of top quality agricultural land in Britain—the Fens.

I have chosen to write of them separately from the other farming country partly because they are physically separate from it, but also because they have a character, history and problems so different from the rest of East Anglia. There is far more to the Fens than sugar beet, celery and strawberries!

The main part is about forty miles from Cambridge northwards to the Wash and about forty miles from Peterborough south-east to Mildenhall, but a wide tongue goes on northwards for a further forty miles to Lincoln, and a broad belt of similar country curves across south Lincolnshire past Boston and Skegness and up the coast as far as Cleethorpes. However I must omit the Lincolnshire fens, except for Sutton Bridge and the mouth of the Nene which serves the inland port of Wisbech in Cambridgeshire. For my western boundary of the Fens, and indeed of East Anglia, I am using the long straight track of the main railway line to the north between Huntingdon and Peterborough.

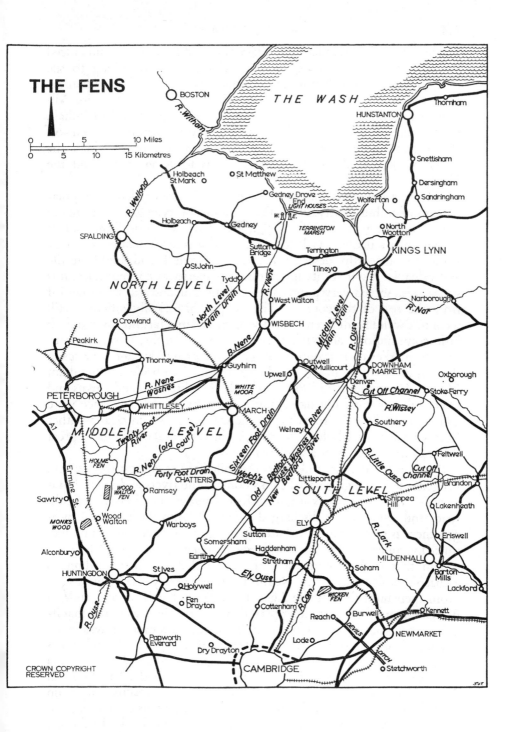

THE FENS

0   5   10 Miles
0 5 10 15 Kilometres

BOSTON

THE WASH

Thornham

HUNSTANTON

R. Witham

Snettisham

Dersingham

Holbeach
St Mark

St Matthew

Sandringham

Gedney Drove
End
LIGHT HOUSES

Wolferton

R. Welland

Holbeach

Gedney

W.R.R.E.

TERRINGTON
MARSH

North
Wootton

SPALDING

Sutton
Bridge

Terrington

KINGS LYNN

St John

Tydd

R. Nene

Tilney

NORTH LEVEL

West Walton

Narborough

R. Nar

Crowland

North Level
Main Drain

WISBECH

Middle Level
Main Drain

R. Ouse

Peakirk

R. Nene

Thorney

Guyhirn

Upwell

Outwell
Mullicourt

DOWNHAM
MARKET

Oxborough

R. Nene
Washes

WHITE
MOOR

Denver

Cut Off Channel

Stoke Ferry

PETERBOROUGH

WHITTLESEY

MARCH

Welney

Bedford River

R. Wissey

Southery

MIDDLE   LEVEL

Twenty Foot
River

R. Nene (old cour?)

Sixteen Foot Drain

Old Bedford River

New Bedford River

Feltwell

Cut Off
Channel

HOLME
FEN

Forty Foot Drain

CHATTERIS

Welch's
Dam

Littleport

SOUTH LEVEL

Brandon

Ermine St.

WOOD
WALTON
FEN

Ramsey

Shippea
Hill

Lakenheath

Sawtry

Wood
Walton

Warboys

ELY

R. Lark

Eriswell

MONKS
WOOD

Somersham

Sutton

Haddenham

MILDENHALL

Alconbury

Earith

Stretham

Soham

Barton
Mills

HUNTINGDON

St Ives

Holywell

Ely Ouse

R. Cam.

WICKEN
FEN

Lackford

R. Ouse

Fen
Drayton

Cottenham

Reach

Burwell

Kennett

Papworth
Everard

Dry Drayton

Lode

DEVILS DYKE

NEWMARKET

CROWN COPYRIGHT
RESERVED

CAMBRIDGE

Stetchworth

The higher land and stone-built villages beyond the railway, and indeed Peterborough and Huntingdon themselves, seem to belong to the East Midlands rather than to East Anglia even though the reorganization of 1974 made them officially part of a larger Cambridgeshire. My southern limits run from St Ives to Cambridge and Mildenhall. From there, a very convenient and significant feature, the cut-off channel, marks the eastern edge to Denver Sluice, from which the lower reaches of the Great Ouse take us to Kings Lynn and the Wash.

The outer boundary, or the Fen edge as it is often called, is irregular in alignment, but clearly discernible for most of its length. From many points, only twenty to fifty feet above fen level, one looks out as though over a flat, empty landscape, but this is today neither a watery waste nor an earthy desert; most of it is Grade I land, highly fertile and valuable. It spite of its agricultural prosperity and importance, it is still an area served very poorly by road and rail, and still seems cut off from the rest of the country. The people, historically different, still seem to dwell in a different world in their isolated farmsteads and drab little communities, although they must come 'ashore' from time to time to market their produce and get their provisions and services in the larger 'border' towns of Kings Lynn, Cambridge, Downham Market, Huntingdon and Peterborough. The little fenland towns and larger villages stand out like island refuges, as indeed they once were and occasionally still are, while in the centre, visible in clear weather from virtually the whole of the Fens, is the cathedral of Ely like a great ship riding at anchor in a wide sea.

Between the islands, and across the miles of flat, almost treeless and hedgeless levels, high parallel banks contain the rivers and main drains in which the water flows at a level feet above the neighbouring fields, roads and dykes, to be discharged eventually into the Wash. How it gets there is something I shall attempt to explain later, but it involves much ingenuity and constant vigilance in operating a complex drainage system that is the culmination of a saga that began, according to archaeological evidence, in Neolithic times, nearly 5,000 years ago. From then until the Middle Ages, the relative levels of land and sea fluctuated and there were long periods when the Fens were uninhabitable, except on the edges and islands. Serious attempts at systematic drainage began with the Romans, traces of whose canals and dykes can still be seen. After the Romans left, neglect and another rise in sea level, caused flooding again, and it was not until the late fifteenth century that large-scale, methodical attempts were resumed to drain the Fens and reclaim land for agriculture. Of what was done then, and in the seventeenth century, much evidence remains in the landscape, and I shall describe those works later, together with the major schemes of the twentieth century. Until these last were carried out, and it is still too soon to be complacent, drainage and flood prevention were vicious problems with self-defeating solutions as with better drainage the level of the peaty land has sunk even farther below that of the rivers and the sea. As a result of the work done, mainly in the last 500 years, this part of East Anglia is today almost entirely the product of man's activity and ingenuity. Hardly anything is as it was. Most of the rivers have been diverted, canalized or abandoned; many new rivers, dykes and relief channels have been created. A completely new pattern has been imposed since the Middle Ages, and the old can be traced only with diligence and difficulty. As in other fields of research, aerial photography has proved invaluable. The famous Cambridge University collection built up by Dr St Joseph, includes pictures on which can be seen the fantastically intricate patterns (rather like the blood system of arteries and capillaries) of the old rivers with their tributary streams and minute watercourses, covering the present-day pattern of rectangular fields bounded by straight dykes. It is remarkable that the old system should have been so intricate, but it is almost incredible that so long after it has disappeared under arable cultivation, it should still be possible to see it all in photographs.

The courses of some of the old, vanished rivers can be seen more easily as raised banks, or 'roddons', winding across peaty fields which have sunk because of better drainage. Some of the roddons are now the sites of elongated villages built on the only firm ground available in the peat fens.

The southern fens, about as far north as March, are mainly of peat; from there to the Wash are the silt fens, laid down by the rivers to levels now a little, but significantly, higher than the peat fens, thus aggravating the drainage problems, and, incidentally causing subtle differences in appearance and character.

It might have seemed obvious for me to split my description of the Fens into peat and silt, but in a sense that would have been an arbitrary division, for all the rivers run from south to north through both, and it is more logical to base my account on the drainage pattern rather than soils. I have therefore taken Vermuyden's main drainage feature, the Bedford Rivers system, as my dividing line. It runs almost as straight as a die from south-west to north-east across the centre of the Fens, and acts as a very real visual and physical barrier between the South Level and the Middle Level.

It might be thought that the engineers and the farmers have reduced the Fens to the ultimate in dullness, but the history and nature of what they have done are of absorbing interest, and the elements have not been entirely mastered. In fine, warm, weather, there is a wonderful feeling of space and exhilaration, but extreme heat can bring the discomfort of the desert and disastrous duststorms. In winter, biting gales and swirling mists, and occasional extensive floods, remind us of the dark ages when the Fens were swampy wastes inhabited by fishermen and wildfowlers.

8

West of the Washes

B ETWEEN Huntingdon and Peterborough, the
main railway line from Kings Cross to Edinburgh runs parallel with, but about two and a
half miles from, the A1, the Great North Road, which follows the
route of the Roman road, Ermine Street, from Alconbury northwards.
Although the railway is by comparison very new, it achieved fame as
the route of the Flying Scotsman, which, until diesel locomotives took
over in 1963, was hauled by the splendid Pacific-type steam engines of
which the Flying Scotsman itself was the best known. Now, in 1978,
the streamlined High Speed Train has been introduced on this line,
and may be seen streaking along the high, ten-mile embankment that,
since the mid-1850s, has been in effect the western border of the Fens.
The natural edge of the limestone hills is fairly high, with peaty tongues
penetrating between the spurs. These tongues have been cut off by the
railway from which generations of travellers have looked out over
the seemingly endless miles of the Middle Level to the east, and
the remnants of the ancient forest on the slopes to the west.

The largest of these remnants is Monks Wood. Although it is just
outside the artificial boundary I have chosen, it is well worth a visit for
its own beauty and interest and because it houses the experimental
station of the Institute of Terrestrial Ecology whose studies have
greatly widened our knowledge and understanding of the Fens. The
modern buildings stand in a woodland clearing on the site of a Romano-
British settlement, and maps in the entrance hall illustrate the shrinkage
of the forest from almost complete cover in A.D. 200, to the scattered
woods we see today. Monks Wood consists of nearly 400 acres of
mainly oak and ash, and is managed by the Nature Conservancy
Council as a National Nature Reserve with a very attractive nature

trail open to the public. This reserve is of outstanding interest to botanists, entomologists and historians, and to the layman who can enjoy, especially in spring and summer, the beauty of the trees, the wild flowers, birds and butterflies.

The road to the east from the experimental station passes between the ancient woodland of Monks Wood and the conifer plantation of Bevills Wood. Here we are on the northern edge of the wide spur of high land (high in relation to the Fens, but in fact only about 100 feet above sea level) which projects between the Middle Level and the Great Ouse eastwards nearly as far as Earith. The road plunges down a steep slope near the east side of Monks Wood, between brown fields, and a side road goes under the railway into Wood Walton village green with its large horse-chestnut trees. A mile to the north the church stands in isolation on a ridge in the open fields, and looks out over the flat peaty fens towards Ramsey and March. In the Middle Level, the fen 'islands' are fewer and lower than those in the South Level beyond the Bedford Rivers, but from Wood Walton the view of typical fenland with long straight dykes is broken in the near distance by the two-miles long rectangular block of fen woodland, now the Wood Walton Fen Nature Reserve, which we shall visit later. The made-up road finishes at the hamlet of Church End where we see the low, grass-covered earthworks of Castle Hill, next to Manor Farm, virtually on the fen edge. Fen Cottage and a notice, Lavenham Fen Farms Ltd, reflect the character of the area, which must always have been remote and lonely, but which has been made even more so by the high barrier of the railway. The road deteriorates into a rough track passing under the railway, back to the west side, to the peaty flatness of Sawtry Fen. Tracks and paths cross the fen by Abbey Farm and the scant remains of the Abbey, and connect with Ermine Street, now the dual carriageway of the A1. Drains and dykes through Sawtry Fen pass under the railway, and one of them, significantly named Monk's Lode, continues north-eastwards to join the old course of the River Nene and the general system of fen waterways.

An historical study of the Huntingdonshire fens, by the Institute of Terrestrial Ecology at Monks Wood in the mid-1970s, has shown that the fenlands of that county were among the last to be effectively drained, and that this was not finally achieved until the second half of the nineteenth century. With improved drainage made possible by steam pumping engines, and the improvement of peatlands by warping (adding clay), landowners and tenants were ready to risk spending capital on large-scale reclamation. Even then it was not practicable to keep the whole area under cultivation and some remained as pasture, particularly in Holme and Wood Walton Fens.

The reclamation destroyed most of the old fenland vegetation and transformed the landscape to the now familiar rectangular, hedgeless fields divided by long, straight dykes. Even Whittlesey Mere, which had been the largest natural lake in southern England—about six miles by three miles—was drained in 1851 and cultivated. Virtually the only areas to retain their old 'natural' features were what later became the nature reserves of Holme Fen and Wood Walton Fen, though, as we shall see when we visit them, they had, like Wicken Fen in the South Level, been modified by man's activities, and are now positively managed, not merely protected, for nature conservation.

At Wood Walton Fen 342 acres were purchased in 1910 by the Hon. Charles Rothschild as a nature reserve and for rough shooting, and further land purchased later by him was added after he had handed the reserve over to the Society for the Promotion of Nature Reserves. Since 1954, the Nature Conservancy have leased Wood Walton from the S.P.N.R., and have designated it as a National Nature Reserve.

It is approached through a hamlet called Ramsey Heights, 13 feet above sea level, on a narrow road which descends to fen level just beyond the warden's house. In his greenhouse he cultivates great water dock, the food plant for the rare large copper butterfly, which is found at Wood Walton Fen but nowhere else in this country. It was reintroduced from Holland in 1927, after becoming extinct in Britain in the nineteenth century. Parts of the fen are managed specially to maintain the plants and to protect the breeding butterflies.

The low stony causeway passes a tiny wooden cottage now derelict, almost invisible under a canopy of brambles and shaded by two huge, old apple trees which were just coming into flower when we saw them. As we walked towards the eastern edge of the reserve we noticed that the black peat fields beside the causeway were several feet below the level of the land in the fen itself. This difference in level, as at Wicken Fen, causes the chief management problem which is to maintain the wet conditions necessary for rare fenland plants including the fen violet. Along the eastern edge of the reserve runs Great Raveley Drain into which flood water is pumped from the dykes draining the arable fields over a wide area around the reserve. In 1978 the drain was being widened and its eastern bank increased in height, as part of a scheme by the Middle Level Commissioners to make greater use of the reserve for storage of flood water, helping at the same time to maintain the desirable wet conditions. The scheme is a complex one and its success will depend on maintaining an effective balance between the interests of land drainage and of nature conservation. Dragline excavators were working and a miniature railway had been laid along the west bank to move the excavated clay. The tiny yellow diesel engines and trucks ran along under the tall willows and poplars that towered high above the alder, willow and birch that screen the interior of the Fen.

Green, spongy droves run alongside the rectangular network of dykes, and give access to the various 'compartments' of woodland, grass and reed bed. Originally, before drainage, the surface was a raised acid bog. Most of the top layer of acid sphagnum peat was removed during the peat-cutting era, and now only the southern part, especially that called the Heath Field, is acid, with plants such as heather and bog myrtle. The rest of the reserve is alkaline because the water drains to it from the limestone hills around Monks Wood.

Near the centre, stands the Bungalow, close to the crossing of two droves, in a lovely setting of fine silver birch and other trees. It is a large, reed-thatched, black weather-boarded building on concrete posts supporting it above flood level. Two of the posts are marked to show 'soil surface' level in 1910 (about 2 feet 6 inches above the present ground level) and 'high water' levels in 1954, 1966 and 1947, about 1, 2 and 3 feet above the present ground surface. Birds are abundant and varied, and the more expert and specialized human visitors will find many plants and insects, some of them very rare.

To get from Wood Walton Fen to Holme Fen, one goes north from Ramsey Heights, on straight roads, bumpy through subsidence, past the site of Ugg Mere, over the old River Nene, on the banks of which stands the lonely brick tower of a former windpump. Near Halfway Farm, south of the Holme Fen birchwoods, is an Ordnance Survey triangulation point marked on the map as "O". The square concrete block just below road level can be seen in the long grass. The black peaty fields on either side of the road had evidently been deep-ploughed recently, as they contained large stacks of black tree trunks, which I assumed had been unearthed from below the peat surface.

The Holme Fen posts stand in a little clearing in the birch woods, and are reached by a wooden footbridge over a narrow, peaty lode. The earlier post, a cast-iron pillar from the Crystal Palace in London was erected in 1851 on the south-west edge of Whittlesey Mere, at the time when the Mere was being drained for cultivation. Replacing a wooden post of 1848 put there to record peat shrinkage caused by drainage, the cast-iron post was put down to the base of buttery clay 22 feet below ground level, and its top was left flush with the ground. Within ten years the ground level had fallen nearly five feet. A second post—a cast-iron lamp post—was erected in 1957, with its top level with the top of the 1851 post. Small plaques on the 1957 post show ground levels at 1848 (13 feet above the present level), and at intervals until 1892 since when the level has sunk only about two feet. The history of changing uses since 1848 is complex, but reflects the age-old problem of the fens in that drainage lowered the levels so that arable use was only short-lived, and the planting of silver birch, bracken and bramble followed soon after 1900 for cover for game, and the birch woods survive in all their glory.

West of the railway are several square miles of fen between the villages of Holme and Yaxley, whence a road runs north-easterly on a ridge giving views to the north-west of the city and cathedral of Peterborough seen behind a multitude of tall, thin brickworks chimneys standing beside enormous clay pits. South-eastwards one looks over seemingly endless miles of peaty fen. From Farcet, where some houses and walls are of grey stone, a road runs down to fen level, and over the old Nene, to cross the peaty fields to the grassy mounds of a Civil War fort at Horsey Hill, which, at 23 feet above sea level, is another example of the importance of the smallest rises in the Fens.

West of Whittlesey are huge claypits and brickworks, some still active, some worked out and derelict. In the Peterborough and Whittlesey area, some derelict pits are being refilled with train loads of ash from Trent Valley power stations, and restored to agriculture, but it seems likely that many years will elapse before most of the areas can be fully restored.

The Fen Causeway, a Roman road, from west to east changes from a green lane to a rough track and then to a made-up road running through Whittlesey north of its centre. A little farther north we come to Morton's Leam, a drainage dyke constructed 500 years ago between Peterborough and Guyhirn, a distance of over twelve miles. In 1728 the River Nene was diverted to an almost dead straight course between the same two places, creating between the new river and Morton's Leam, the Nene Washes, a storage area for flood water comparable with the Ouse Washes between the Old and New Bedford Rivers. The Nene Washes, since the 1950s, have declined in interest as the haunt of wildfowl, and the central section (east of the Thorney road) has mostly been converted to arable. However, the whole of the Nene Washes, including the arable part, are still used as part of the flood control system, and many acres can be seen under water each year. The ditches and drains still contain some rare plants, and many wildfowl are present during floods, but the birdlife then and in the breeding season is thought to be, in effect, an 'overspill' from the extensive nature reserves in the Ouse Washes.

At the east end of the Nene Wash, the river and Morton's Leam join, leaving the peat, to flow through the silt fens to Wisbech, set in the heart of a fruit-growing area famous for strawberries and apples. To the north of the river the pattern of roads is less regular and some of the winding stretches are on the lines of banks marking successive stages of reclamation as the silt, partly from the rivers and partly from the sea, built up and pushed the shoreline of the Wash farther north.

From Guyhirn to Wisbech roads run along the bank on either side, culminating in the North Brink and the South Brink, where splendid three and four-storey houses face each other in Dutch fashion across the narrow tidal river. The North Brink has a long, almost unbroken frontage of large Georgian houses with flat, parapetted fronts mostly of dark red brick, though one or two are of stone. The finest of the red brick houses is Peckover House, owned by the National Trust. One building breaks the long Georgian frontage which is coherent in character though varying in scale. The exception is a large Victorian building, the Friends' Meeting House, of yellowish brick with crow-stepped gables facing the river. It was designed by Algernon Peckover of Peckover House, and Pevsner criticizes it as being completely out of keeping and the designer as having no sympathy with Georgian architecture. However, to me, it is impressive in its sheer boldness and disregard of its more urbane neighbours, and the setting is so spacious that I think the sin was not as serious as our architectural historian suggested. Across the river is a shorter frontage of good Georgian buildings, including the birthplace of Octavia Hill, one of the founder-members of the National Trust. Appreciation of the South Brink is made more difficult because, facing north and fronting a very busy trunk road, it does not enjoy the peace and sunshine that contribute so much to the perfection of the North Brink.

The eastern ends of the Brinks are joined by what was until recent years the only bridge connecting the two parts of the town. On the west side of the river, the massive brick warehouses are in a sad state, since the port activities have moved downstream and a new fixed bridge has made them inaccessible to shipping. The decay of the warehouses has been accelerated by the scouring of the tides and the floods which cause great damage and distress in much of the town from time to time, the most recent and one of the worst occasions being in January 1978.

Bridge Street leads east away from the bridge into Castle Square and the Georgian oval which is the secluded and beautiful heart of the town. The oval, consisting of Union Place, Ely Place and The Crescent, surrounds the site of the late Norman castle, now flattened and occupied by gardens, and an old house, called The Castle, behind high gates with stone piers. The outer edge of the oval, and Castle Square at one end and Museum Square at the other, and Market Street to the north, are lined with unbroken terraces of three-storey, Georgian houses (many of them now offices) of typical local reddish-brown-black bricks with white-painted windows and pedimented doorways. Above the east end rises the fine pinnacled stone tower of the Church of St Peter and St Paul. The whole scene is most satisfying, being well-preserved and peacefully free of through traffic. It is not spoilt by the unashamedly modern county library that occupies part of the curved frontage of Ely Place and harmonizes without copying its Georgian neighbours; the secrets of success are the use of a good brick, conformity of scale and window sizes and levels. The curve of the castle ditch is perpetuated in the alignment of the south side of the Market Place, which must have been much larger before encroachment of buildings during the last few hundred years on the north and east.

The old course of the Nene, having wandered from Peterborough across to Ramsey and March, Upwell and Outwell, approached Wisbech from the south-east. It passed to the east of the town centre but has been cut short and for the last mile and a half has been obliterated by a dual-carriageway relief road, from which we see the rather shabby backs of old buildings, a large, untidy car park and a huge area that has never been properly cleared up since the road was constructed. It is an unsightly approach to a town that has so much well-preserved beauty in its older streets and buildings.

The new quay and the industrial area extend for about a mile along the right bank below the new bridge. Post-war improvements to the port increased the seaborne trade to 210,000 tons in 1973, most of the cargoes being timber, oil and grain. Wisbech has been a port since the foundation of the town in Norman times when it was at the lowest crossing point of the Nene and the Ouse (which joined at Upwell a few miles to the south) and stood at the head of a wide, marshy estuary. The prosperity of the port was affected by the diversion of the Ouse about 1300 to its present outfall at Kings Lynn, and by the continuing problem for several centuries of the Nene becoming silted up below Wisbech. It was not until the 1600s, 1700s and 1800s that the river was converted, in stages, into a long, almost straight, embanked channel for the passage of ships between the town and the Wash. During these three centuries there was progressive reclamation to agriculture of thousands of acres of former marshes between the new channel and the long-established edge of the silt lands believed to have been enclosed in the second and third centuries. Most of the west side was reclaimed during the seventeenth and eighteenth centuries very nearly as far north as the present river mouth; progress was slower on the east side and did not reach the same latitude until 1951.

A few miles below Wisbech the river crosses into Lincolnshire, but I feel justified in straying across the county boundary to the shores of the Wash. By 1850, reclamation had reached a point about seven miles below Wisbech and a new road on a causeway was constructed from east to west, crossing the river at what became Sutton Bridge, later replaced by a combined road and rail bridge. In 1881 docks were built on the west side of the river a little downstream of the bridge, and, had the sides of the docks not collapsed within a few weeks of completion, they would have been a serious threat to the future of the port of Wisbech.

A riverside quay, and the swing bridge survive, but the docks are now just large, grassy hollows in a golf course. From the north end of the golf course a narrow road follows the demarcation line between land reclaimed in the seventeenth century and the eighteenth century, but most of the farmhouses seem to have been built during the following 200 years. At King John's Farm, built in 1878 (I wonder if the farmer has searched for buried treasure!), a road leads past Curlew Lodge—another evocative name—to the river bank. When we were there in September 1975 a very high tide was just beginning to ebb silently and smoothly between the long, straight, grassy banks to the river mouth now about half a mile beyond the old, twin, white-painted lighthouses. The tall roadside trees, beech, chestnut and sycamore continue just behind the river wall as far as the lighthouse on the west side, but stop short on the east side at the 1867 bank line. North of that, the areas reclaimed later are devoid of trees.

Before the brickwork was covered with white paint, the two tapering, four-storey buildings must have looked more like windmills without sails than conventional lighthouses. I have borrowed that description from Peter Scott who took a lease in 1933 of the already disused East Lighthouse. During his schooldays at Oundle he had spent holidays at Hickling Broad, and while he was at Trinity College, Cambridge, he escaped when he could from his academic studies of the natural sciences, to go wildfowling in the Ouse Washes and on Terrington saltmarsh between the mouths of the Nene and the Great Ouse. During the late 1920s he started painting pictures of wildfowl in their natural, marshland settings, and developed the interests which were to occupy him for the next fifty or more years.

He lived in the East Lighthouse until 1939, and during those six years he was able to study and paint the coastal wildlife at close quarters, and his interest in shooting steadily declined. He became a pioneer in netting and ringing geese as an effective way of learning about migration, and at a decoy not far away he built the prototype of many later observation hides that could be entered by watchers without being seen by the birds.

With the approach of the war in 1939, his collection of geese and duck at the lighthouse had to be dispersed to friends with similar interests at Holbeach in the fens and Horsey Island in the Walton Backwaters of Essex. Peter Scott served with distinction in the Royal Navy, mostly in 'little ships', during the war years, when his shooting was almost exclusively directed at the enemy.

At the end of 1945 he found the farm and the marshes at The New Grounds, Slimbridge in Gloucestershire, and during the following

Terrington St Clement Church

Wisbech—Ely Place, Library and Church

River Nene—East Lighthouse and Wisbech Pilot

Denver Sluice and New Bedford River

Mullicourt Aqueduct, Outwell

Ouse Washes looking north-east from Coveney

Whitemoor Up Yard, March, from Control Tower

Ely Maltings and Cathedral

Little Ouse joining Great Ouse, Brandon Creek

Wicken Fen Windpump

Kings Lynn Custom House

Santon Downham forestry village

Forest Walk, Santon Downham

year the Wildfowl Trust was formed. Peter Scott and his friends and associates were embarked on what became one of the most important conservation bodies with world-wide connections. It is gratifying that one of the best known and respected international naturalists of the century acquired and developed his interests in the Fens and on the coast of East Anglia and that the trust is very active in the region. Their collection at Peakirk near Peterborough is complementary to Slimbridge, and they use for study and ringing wildfowl the Borough Fen Decoy where Peter Scott in the early 1930s learned how to use a decoy for its original purpose. In the Ouse Washes, between the Bedford Rivers, thousands of wigeon and other duck, and many whooper and Bewick swans, spend their winters on the waters of the trust's Welney Reserve.

Since 1950, further reclamation of the saltings has left the East Lighthouse about three quarters of a mile from the river mouth, and new, embanked fields, bare of trees and buildings, stretch for seven miles eastwards, including what was Peter Scott's beloved Terrington saltmarsh, to the mouth of the Great Ouse. The advanced stage of the saltings west of the Nene, makes it seem likely that they will soon be ripe for reclamation as an extension of the land that was enclosed in 1950 just east of the mouth of the Welland. New saltings soon form just outside the sea walls, with the growth of maritime plants such as sea purslane, saltmarsh grass, glasswort and sea aster, accelerating the silting up process.

Beyond the saltings are vast areas, totalling about 100 square miles of mud flats and sand flats intersected at low tide by narrow, winding creeks and the dredged outfall channels from the four main rivers that flow into the open waters beyond. The intertidal mud and sand flats, containing innumerable invertebrate creatures—snails, shellfish and marine worms—make the Wash one of the most extensive and valuable feeding and wintering areas for thousand of wading birds, ducks and geese. Wildfowling continues in unprotected areas, and cockles, shrimps and mussels are gathered by fishermen based at Boston, Fosdyke and Kings Lynn; lugworms are dug from the mud for use by anglers as bait. Common seals breed in the Wash and haul out on the sand banks, where by licence some are hunted and killed for their fur. The richness of the wild life, and the fact that some local people depend on it for their living, creates a continuing conflict of interests which it may never be possible to resolve to everyone's satisfaction. Without doubt, the tremendous amount of research in recent years with participation by the many bodies involved, has created a store of positive information on which to base action affecting commerce and conservation.

The research has been accelerated, and its scope widened since 1966 by more positive consideration of suggestions, first made many years ago, that the shortage of water supplies in East Anglia and south-east England could be solved by putting a barrage across the Wash and using it as a vast reservoir.

In 1970 the government published *The Wash: Estuary Storage*, the Water Resources Board's report on a 'desk study' by consulting engineers who had been asked, without extensive field and laboratory investigation, to report on the scope for water conservation in the Wash. Views were obtained from local authorities and official bodies concerned with navigation, water supply and drainage, agriculture, fishery, transport and nature conservation. The consultants concluded that embanked reservoirs about half-a-mile offshore, between the Great Ouse and the Nene, and later between the Nene and the Welland, would be more practicable and less damaging to other interests (especially to the ports and nature conservation) than a continuous east-west barrage across the Wash. The report acknowledged that adverse effects on the wild life, especially birds and seals, would result, and that the degree of harm would vary according to the details and extent of any scheme that might be implemented. The evidence received and considered by the Water Resources Board included a report by the Nature Conservancy on *The Ecology of the Wash and the Implications of the Proposed Barrage Scheme*. The title may deter the general reader, but anyone interested in natural history will be rewarded by the wealth of information about present conditions and wildlife of all kinds and the assessment of the effects of various possible schemes. It is especially interesting to note that the national and international importance of the Wash has increased considerably in post-war years because of the large-scale destruction of similar habitats through continuing land reclamation in Holland. Schemes were being considered for water storage covering large areas in Morecambe Bay and the Dee and Severn estuaries; the airport site at Foulness and Maplin Sands was mentioned, but that particular threat seems to have disappeared, at least temporarily.

The desk study was followed by a feasibility study, the results of which were published in 1976, after detailed survey work and site investigations in and around the Wash, and the construction and study of a physical model at the Hydraulics Research Station at Wallingford in Berkshire. All other aspects were studied in greater detail than before, and local research continued on natural history and fisheries. All this may seem academic in view of the conclusions reached that, while it would be possible to build reservoirs on the foreshore, they were not likely to be economic or necessary during this century, particularly as more water could be taken from the Great Ouse and the Nene at lower cost. However, the engineers who carried out the feasibility study have left two visible features proving that their work was not

confined to the office and the laboratory. Two trial banks, each about
200 yards in diameter and about twelve yards high, have been constructed, one just beyond the edge of the Terrington saltmarsh, and the
other about two miles offshore, north-east of the mouth of the Nene.
They are on the suggested inner and outer edges of the site of a full-
scale reservoir (if one were to be built) and have been constructed by
using sand from the tidal flats, strengthened with rock for wave
protection. The inshore bank, constructed in 1972, has suffered some
damage, particularly in the exceptional storm of 11th January 1978
which flooded Wisbech and Kings Lynn, but the stronger offshore
bank survived undamaged.

At the time of our visit in the autumn of 1975, we could see excavators and cranes putting the finishing touches to the offshore trial
bank. Our viewpoint near Gedney Drove End, west of the Nene, was
at the head of a little inlet on the bank of which, like a stranded whale,
lay a small hovercraft, used for taking workers to and from their site
out in the Wash. As we watched, a dozen men went aboard. The
powerful engines started up, and as the 'skirt' filled with air, the craft
slowly raised itself off the ground and slid gently into the water. It
turned, and its overhead propeller spun faster with a roar like an
aeroplane, to take it smoothly over a low mudbank, the tide having
recently started to ebb. Once in the main creek, the hovercraft quickly
gathered speed, passing between lines of marker posts and across the
very shallow, open water to the dish-shaped 'island' which was
eventually to be filled with sea water as part of the feasibility study.

This landmark—or seamark—will remain as a fairly unobtrusive
feature, and, with the indefinite postponement of full-scale reservoirs,
we should be able to enjoy for many years to come the marvellous
spectacles of thousands of waders—dunlin, knot, godwits and others—
feeding on the mud and sand flats, and flying and wheeling in smoke-
like clouds, both in winter and summer. The wintering geese and duck
will still come and go, flying over in skeins and 'vees', and the flocks
of finches, buntings (including snow buntings and Lapland buntings)
and larks, will feed on the seeds of saltmarsh plants. There remains a
vast area for the birds and seals, but remembering the tens of thousands
of acres that have been reclaimed since Roman times, and the continuing
large-scale reclamation in the present century, we can understand why
naturalists are still apprehensive.

Turning inland from the Lincolnshire side of the mouth of the Nene,
we go back in history from the edge of the present saltmarshes, across
the land reclaimed in the 300 years preceding 1900, crossing or running
along the raised banks that, so to speak, separate the centuries. In
Victorian times, small, new villages were built at Gedney Drove End,
and Holbeach St Matthew, St Mark and St Luke, each with small

brick churches designed by Ewan Christian. East of the Nene the land on the same latitude was reclaimed much later and has only scattered farms and houses on the banks between large rectangular areas successively enclosed during the past hundred years.

Along the southern edge of the seventeenth-century land runs the Sea Bank, sometimes called the Roman Bank, though it is now thought to have been constructed in late Saxon times. It marked for hundreds of years the rather precarious coastline of the Wash. Along that old coast, from Spalding to Wisbech and Kings Lynn, liable to sea flooding in olden times, stood, and still stands (though now five or six miles from the coast) a line of villages. Each has its splendid church of stone from Barnack in Northamptonshire. The tall towers and spires, in five cases detached from the bodies of their churches, of Holbeach, Fleet, Gedney, Long Sutton, the Tydds, Walsoken, West Walton, the Walpoles and the Terringtons, are most impressive landmarks indicating the location of the famous Marshland churches, seen across the flat landscape. They were mostly built between 1100 and 1400 and in architectural books their descriptions abound in superlatives. It seems surprising that so many magnificent churches were built here, but they are attributed to the prosperity resulting from a period of active draining, reclamation and cultivation of rich land over a very large area of silt fen.

Having visited the southern shores of the Wash, and the Marshland churches, we return to Wisbech and set out on the last leg of our tour of the western Fens. The main road going south-east out of the town follows the Wisbech Canal to Outwell, whence Well Creek continues to Nordelph and joins the Great Ouse at Salter's Lode, just below Denver Sluice. These canals were important commercial waterways until the early years of the present century, but are now used only by pleasure craft and anglers. Between Outwell and Nordelph, Well Creek which dates from the 1200s or possibly much earlier, passes over the Middle Level Main Drain by means of a navigable, iron, aqueduct, built in 1848 and named after the former Mullicourt Priory on a neighbouring site. The Main Drain, a wide extension of Vermuyden's Sixteen-Foot Drain of 1651, goes under the aqueduct and the main road, and runs dead straight for over seven miles to the north-east to discharge into the Great Ouse three miles above Kings Lynn. The history of the Mullicourt Aqueduct is explained on a notice board erected by the Norfolk Museums Service at the south end of the little white-railed road bridge a few yards away. The details are reproduced on an illustrated card, one of an excellent series on Water Transport in Norfolk.

As we turn back along the minor road beside Well Creek, it is amusing to remember the people of Nordelph, before their own church was built in 1865, travelling in a horse-drawn barge along Well Creek to church at Upwell (according to the card, but perhaps some went to Outwell church which they would have reached first). The two villages run without a break along the old Nene and the Wisbech Canal. The houses on either side face each other across the boundary between Norfolk and Cambridgeshire, and remind us of the North and South Brinks. Though the houses are not so large as at Wisbech, the effect is very pleasing and both villages have fine churches of Barnack stone.

From 1883, Outwell was served by another means of transport, which, in the following year was extended to Upwell. The Wisbech and Upwell Tramway, built by the Great Eastern Railway, was a standard gauge light railway running south-east from Wisbech East Station. The track ran alongside the main road, and was not fenced off; indeed it crossed the road at several points, and in part ran along the bank of the Wisbech Canal. It was just under eight miles long and the maximum permitted speed was 8 m.p.h. The small flat-roofed coaches were hauled by four-wheeled, wooden-bodied steam engines, with protective side plates and 'cow-catchers' fore and aft. Freight trains carried local horticultural produce and took coal to the villages *en route*, and to a quay on the canal at Outwell, where it was loaded into barges and taken by water to steam pumping engines in various parts of the Fens. Proposals to extend the tramway to Friday Bridge and Welney were dropped, but the original line continued in use for goods traffic until 1966. The old, wooden-bodied steam engines bore successively the initials of the Great Eastern Railway, the London and North Eastern Railway and British Railways, and were finally superseded in 1953 by diesel shunting engines (also specially fitted with side plates and cow-catchers). The passenger service had been discontinued at the end of 1927 and some of the coaches were then transferred to the Thaxted branch line in Essex where I saw them in my schooldays in the 1930s. The Wisbech and Upwell Tramway was well known to the Rev. W. Awdry who produced the famous illustrated *Railway Series* of little books for children. No. 7, *Toby The Tram Engine*, was first published in 1952. Perhaps it is not too irreverent to suggest that its author may have regarded the opportunity to move to Emneth parish (between Wisbech and Outwell) in 1953 as a 'godsend'; at any rate he was delighted to be there and soon became friendly with the tramway staff!

Where the tramway ran alongside the road, wide verges remain in front of the houses that have built along what was a quiet, tree-lined country road in the 1880s. Tangible traces are few, but one can still see where the line crossed a road diagonally near the school at Upwell. The Wisbech Canal was filled in, and between the outskirts of the town and Upwell, one sees a wide grassy strip flanked by roads and houses.

At the south end of Upwell, a road running on the roddon of the long 'extinct' Old Croft River (which wound its way across from Littleport and is still commemorated for much of its length as an old county boundary) converges on the old River Nene flowing from the west through Ramsey and March.

From Upwell, for about nine miles, an almost dead straight road runs alongside Vermuyden's Sixteen-Foot Drain of 1651, now in 1978 being dredged and widened to about sixty feet. Pumping stations large and small, public and private, lift the water from lateral dykes draining the lower fields on either side. On this section, heading south-west, parallel with the Bedford Rivers, we pass from the silt fens to the peat, near Stonea, where grassy earthworks of an Iron Age settlement survive on a small area of higher land not far from the railway on its long straight run from Ely in the South Level, across the Ouse Washes, into the Middle Level.

At the north-west end of the fifteen-mile straight, trains come to March, which became an important railway junction in the middle of the nineteenth century. The station, the locomotive depot and the goods yard were developed on poor land well to the north of the old town, and the intervening land became built up as railway activities increased. In the early 1930s, two huge marshalling yards at Whitemoor, on either side of the main line to Spalding, were added to the existing installations, to form what was for many years the biggest complex of its kind in Britain. The site lay conveniently between the mining and industrial areas of the north and the agricultural land of East Anglia. Freight trains from the north and south were 'broken up' and re-assembled to form new trains for various destinations. This was done by pushing the wagons over humps from which they rolled down gradients of 1 in 18 into chosen tracks fanning out from the foot of the humps into miles of parallel sidings.

The yards and humps are still there, extending for nearly two miles from Vermuyden's Twenty-Foot River of 1651 to March junction. The hexagonal control towers, looking rather shabby after forty years, are still used, with the original hydraulic braking controls, but with newer electrical controls for the complex system of points and crossings. With the changed pattern of traffic and the post-war contraction of the national railway system, the 'down' marshalling yard is now used only for storage of rolling stock, adjoining the locomotive depot, and only the 'up' yard is still used for the 'sorting' and despatch of freight trains. About halfway along the yard, an insignificant Portakabin office houses a sophisticated computer installation, linked with other parts of the country, which records the location, contents and destination of all freight wagons, empty or full, stationary or in transit.

Having the privilege of visiting the 'up' yard control tower, I found it fascinating, from the comparatively high vantage point, to look around and reflect on the changes in the prosperity and technology of the railway during the past century, and the infinitely longer history of the area in which this huge network of sidings is located. The tower stands roughly on the boundary between the silt and the peat fens, and close to the east-west line of the Roman Fen Causeway which we saw at Whittlesey. To the west and east respectively are Westry and Estover Farms with documented histories going back to 1221. To the south is the tall spire of the parish church, inexplicably located over half-a-mile beyond the town centre which grew steadily on the riverside as a market and small port from medieval times until the coming of the railway which expedited the growth of the town and the decline of waterborne traffic. This is an interesting town which deserves more study than it appears to have received, bearing in mind the many aspects of its very long and varied history on the northern tip of a long, irregularly shaped 'fen island'. The road southwards winds its way on the low ridge, with wide views across the peaty fields to east and west, through the ancient villages of Doddington and Wimblington, to Chatteris, just beyond the Forty-Foot Drain.

South of Chatteris, the road to Somersham runs on a low, winding ridge, which for several miles was the boundary between the counties of Huntingdon and Cambridge. Its route seems to have been determined by the course of an old river which in its turn was, at least in part, the successor to the Roman Car Dyke that ran across the Fens from Cambridge to Lincoln. Where the road turns south-west about a mile and a half short of Somersham church, the county boundary bears to the south-east along a drain on the line of the Car Dyke. The Roman canal was cut by the construction of the Old Bedford River in 1637, at a point which, over three hundred years later, became the scene of a unique, but short-lived enterprise.

In 1967, the National Research Development Corporation announced their intention to finance the construction of an 18-mile concrete track for developing and testing 'hovertrains'. The 4-foot high track was to run parallel with and just west of the Old Bedford River all the way from Earith to Denver. By the spring of 1971 the first mile, starting at Earith, had been built 10 feet above the ground and a start had been made on a further two miles at a height of 25 feet. By then the engineers had presumably realized the need to go over the top of the farm tracks and roads crossing the route. The track consisted of a concrete beam on which trains powered by linear induction motors would rush along on a cushion of air at speeds of up to 300 m.p.h. The designers claimed that there would be no pollution or disturbance and hardly any noise. Britain's first hovertrain RTV 31 had its maiden run on 10th December 1971 at 20 m.p.h., but it was not thought possible to exceed 90 m.p.h. until the track could be extended to seven or eight miles. Tracked Hovercraft Ltd were hoping the system, possibly with magnetic suspension instead of air, would be used eventually for high-speed travel between London and the proposed Maplin airport, and for intercity services at speeds that they claimed would have brought the whole of East Anglia well within commuting range of London. Rather naïvely, the company did not seem to see that as anything but a benefit, nor did they see (or admit) any difficulty in building long distance tracks quickly and cheaply. On the latter point one cannot help reflecting on the fact that they had to scour the country to find a site for a test track a mere 18 miles long which was not without fairly formidable snags.

However, the line of pre-cast concrete beams on their concrete pillars, ran alongside Vermuyden's grassy bank for three miles, but only for three years before the whole system was dismantled after the government's decision not to provide any more money. The decision, strongly criticized by a House of Commons Select Committee, was apparently influenced by current development by British Rail of their High Speed Train (which we now see running along the western edge of the Fens) and the even faster Advanced Passenger Train which is still being developed in the late 1970s.

The saga of the hovertrack in this historical corner of the Middle Level caused much concern to conservationists during a period when the Royal Society for the Protection of Birds, the Wildfowl Trust and the Cambridgeshire and Isle of Ely Naturalists' Trust were acquiring land in the Ouse Washes. It was not surprising that they were alarmed at the disturbance and danger likely to be caused to birds and other wildlife by streamlined vehicles hurtling at 300 m.p.h. along the side of the Washes from end to end. All that now remains of the project are a workshop building and a gantry crane, now used by another engineering firm, just on the outskirts of Earith. The concrete pillars and beams of the track that ran to the north-east, have been removed, and cattle graze peacefully in the lush grassy meadows below the outer bank of the Old Bedford River.

9

Ouse Washes and South Level

BY the time the Great Ouse enters the Fens at Holywell, it has already flowed for about a hundred miles, and has another sixty miles to run before discharging its waters into the Wash. On its long, winding way from its source near Brackley in Northamptonshire, through Buckingham, Bedford and St Neots, it is a delightful river, particularly in Bedfordshire and Huntingdonshire. In those counties, as far down as St Ives, it is a typically pastoral river meandering through lush water meadows, past picturesque villages and small towns with watermills and tall church spires. The narrow gap where the river flows between Godmanchester and Huntingdon, and the extensive old water meadows west of the ancient bridges on Ermine Street, have been devastated by a new, wide, bypass road on a high embankment and viaduct. However, the river has kept much of its tranquil beauty below Huntingdon, with the villages of Wyton and Houghton (noted for its huge brick and weather-boarded watermill) on the north side and the Hemingfords on the south; all four with spired, stone churches close to the river. Seen from across the broad, green water-meadows, St Ives looks very attractive, with its tall church spire, old houses and public gardens overlooking the tree-lined backwater that flows by the west end of the little town. The east end has a superb, early fifteenth-century stone bridge, with a little central chapel of 1426 on the downstream side; the bridge is so narrow that it can take only one line of traffic, and pedestrians still have to take refuge in the little triangular spaces above the 'cutwaters' between the arches. The best views of the bridge are from the river, or from the quay on the north bank just downstream.

The pleasure and hopes raised by these western and eastern extremities of the riverside, are rather dashed by the drab, run-down nature of the town centre and the inaccessibility of the river from it. Old buildings and back-yards, and one or two long, narrow and neglected lanes lead to the river bank, but have long ceased to serve any useful or pleasurable purpose except that of access to the backs of shops and to a few small houses. The present market place, east of the bridge, is wide, but undistinguished except for the statue of Oliver Cromwell and an exceptionally fine stone non-conformist church built in Victorian times and having a spire almost equalling that of the medieval parish church a quarter of a mile away. I think the market place must originally have extended west of Bridge Street but there a block of buildings leaves only a narrow lane on each side, and a wide main street beyond tapering westwards towards the fine old house standing at right-angles to the river in front of the church. In the autumn of 1977 that house, with a grey brick Georgian-style façade undoubtedly concealing a much older building, was apparently empty and the ground-floor windows were boarded up.

Below the medieval bridge, the gentle slopes on which the town stands draw back from the broad river, and soon give way to the beginning of the Fens at a point overlooked on the north side by the delightful little village of Holywell which stands on a low rise beside a little tributary. It has an old, stone church and rectory at one end and Ye Olde Ferry Boat Inn at the other. In front of the inn, a white thatched building enlarged in recent years, is a green beside the river where it is joined by the tributary that has flowed past the church and the site of the Holy Well. Pretty thatched cottages face across the road and look out over the green water meadows. This is the point where the Great Ouse changes its character from a natural river to a fenland river. The villages on the other side, Fen Stanton and Fen Drayton (the names are significant of the change), Swavesey and Over, stand well back on firmer, slightly higher ground.

Below Holywell and Fen Stanton the Great Ouse runs between banks artificially raised to protect the dyke-drained fen meadows behind them. At Brownshill Staunch, a lock marks the upper limits of the tides, and two miles farther down at Earith we come to the sluices and locks which control the flow of the Great Ouse, and the flood waters from its very extensive basin, into the twenty-mile straight courses of the Old and New Bedford Rivers and the long winding loop of the 'Old West River' through Ely and Littleport; all converging again on the sluices and outfalls at Denver.

The broad, tree-lined river that skirts the southern edge of Earith, then splits into three. The main tidal river continues unimpeded in its flow but changed in direction and name to the New Bedford River or Hundred-Foot Drain. This artificial channel was constructed by Vermuyden in 1651 after the discovery that the Old Bedford River had not solved the flooding problems, and runs as straight as it can between high banks for twenty miles to Denver. The Old Bedford River, constructed fourteen years before, runs on an even straighter course from Earith to Denver. Its western bank is higher than the eastern so that flood water, some diverted through the sluice from the main river at Earith and some pumped in from the Middle Level, especially via Vermuyden's Forty-Foot Drain at Welches Dam, can spill into the meadows between the Old and New Bedford Rivers which run parallel about half-a-mile apart for most of their length. These meadows are the Ouse Washes and in most winters for shorter or longer periods are flooded from end to end. The flood waters are prevented from reaching too high a level by sluices at the Denver end discharging into the tidal river. I will attempt later to explain the system as it is today with Denver as the key point in the massive and complex flood-protection scheme that was completed in 1964. But Vermuyden in the 1600s created what was then an entirely new pattern, with profound effects on the landscape, including radical changes in the courses of old rivers. His system was remarkably effective for much of the time, but was never adequate to prevent extensive flooding in extreme conditions, and much of what he, and indeed some of his successors, did, adversely affected the interests of navigation on old waterways. Many of these problems have been largely solved in recent times, by co-operation, sometimes preceded by bitter controversy, between conflicting interests.

All the work that has been done since the creation of the Bedford Rivers system over 300 years ago has left virtually unchanged its effect as a complete south-west to north-east barrier across the Cambridgeshire fens. Its high outer banks preclude visibility between the South and Middle Levels, except from a few fen 'islands' on either side, and very few roads cross the Washes. Between the banks is a unique, long narrow area cut off and utterly different from the thousands of acres of cultivated land outside. Even if we know what to expect, it is still exciting, after travelling across mile after mile of intensely black farmland to climb up over the high banks of the New Bedford River and drop down into the Washes. These hundreds of acres of grazing meadows—for regular flooding precludes their cultivation—make up a strange, enclosed and secret world seen only fleetingly by the passing motorist on the Littleport to Welney road or the passenger in the train rumbling over the viaducts at Manea.

In summer, the Washes serve as grazing land for cattle, and in favourable seasons crops of hay may be taken. To the casual observer this is a pleasant, pastoral scene, admittedly contrasting strangely in shape with the water meadows beside the Great Ouse in Bedfordshire, but a welcome relief from the apparent dullness of the neighbouring farmland. He may not know that in summer, the Washes attract many interesting and unusual breeding birds, but in winter, even from a train he would be almost certain to notice the many thousands of wildfowl on the floodwaters. Almost the whole of the twenty-mile strip contained between the Old and New Bedford Rivers has been acquired or leased from 1964 onwards by the Royal Society for the Protection of Birds, the Wildfowl Trust and the Cambridgeshire and Isle of Ely Naturalists' Trust. The Ouse Washes are in fact one of the most important and interesting nature reserves in Britain, and indeed are of international importance because of the large numbers of wild duck, geese and swans that are winter visitors from northern Europe and Russia. The fact that much of the area is now controlled by conservation bodies has naturally curtailed the centuries-old sport of wildfowling, and some management and maintenance of internal drainage dykes is done, but the suitability of the Washes for the special breeding birds in summer, and the vast wintering population, is due mainly to the perpetuation of the old regime of summer grazing and winter flooding. There is also a remarkable variety of plants, many of which are not found in the drained, arable land outside.

The importance and interest of the Ouse Washes for wildlife depends mainly on their being the biggest single area of regularly flooded fresh grazing marshland in England and Wales. The long, continuous strip, totalling over 5000 acres, may appear at first glance monotonously uniform, but the rivers on either side, their raised banks, the grazing meadows and the ditches that divide them and the osier beds, provide a great variety of habitats which is enhanced in its attraction for wildlife by the seasonal changes.

In late spring and early summer, unless wet weather has continued much later than usual, the meadows are free of surface water, but the winter flooding has left the ground soft enough to attract wading birds which feed mainly by probing into mud or soft earth. From the hides we can see the long-legged, long-billed, black-tailed godwit nesting and feeding among the slow-moving cattle. The nesting of godwits was first noticed in 1952, and their numbers have since increased gradually; if and when they nested here before 1952 is not positively known, but the discovery in the peat of bones of this and other species at least proves that they were in this part of the fens long ago. Ruffs and reeves, curious in appearance and behaviour, also breed here but in very few other parts of Britain. Commoner birds such as lapwing, mute swans, and ducks, and the many warblers and other small birds that frequent the osiers, all add interest to a summer visit.

Other things go on, mostly outside the breeding season, to remind us of earlier times and of the fact that even now the protection and encouragement of birds is not the only purpose of the Washes. Osiers

are cut and tied into long bundles, woven into great mattresses, and
laid along the edges of the rivers to protect the banks from erosion by
flood water. Water Authority dragline excavators restore and raise
damaged banks and deepen channels; pumping stations, sluices and
dykes have to be maintained. These activities were included in a
splendid film, *The Lonely Level*, made by the R.S.P.B. in about 1970.
It condensed the year into a fascinating sequence of the seasons, showing
the almost incredible changes in the scene and conditions and the
equally spectacular changes in the numbers and kinds of birds. The
film showed the River Authority's official mole-catcher, with his two
black dogs, and his tubular traps which he sets below ground level in
the mole tunnels. The moles evidently do a great deal of damage by
tunnelling in the river banks especially when flood waters force small
animals into closer concentrations on the higher ground. There was
also the old punt-gunner, with his long, narrow, grey punt, pushing
out into the wintry waters to discharge his enormous gun with a one-
inch bore and ¾lb of shot. A dying profession, lamented by some such
as James Wentworth Day who saw much that was romantic in those
tough, weather-beaten characters who went out at dawn and dusk
in the bitterest days of winter to pit their wits and their guns against
the wildfowl on the fens and on the coastal marshes of East Anglia.
Some wildfowling continues in limited areas under concessions which
the conservation bodies undoubtedly had to make in order to obtain
control over the majority of the Washes for the protection of birds.

The film very fairly showed all these aspects and is, I think, one of
the best bird films ever made, but there is no real substitute for a
personal visit, preferably in winter. If the date has to be fixed in advance,
the weather conditions will be unpredictable, but the effort will be
richly rewarded. We went on a Sunday in early January, 1971, a day
on which B.B.C. Radio was broadcasting a recording of a 'radio
nature trail'. As we learnt a few days later by listening to a repeat of
the programme, their visit was about a week before ours. They described the beauty of the hoar frost on the teasels and osiers, following
a spell of snow, fog and frost. By the time we went this had all gone.
The morning was warm and sunny, indeed the sun shone brightly all
day in a blue sky with a little wispy cloud, and in the afternoon the
temperature reached 60°F!

We approached along the main road from Littleport and as we
drove up the bank and over the New Bedford River, we noticed just
to the north the long, footbridge which the Royal Engineers had put
across the river to the Wildfowl Trust's splendid hide on the west
bank. The main road winds between hedges and trees on the course
of the Old Croft River, crosses Delph Bridge into Welney and on into
the western Fens. But we stopped at the bridge and walked northwards

along the green track between the Old Bedford River and the River Delph which run close and parallel, but at different levels along the west side of the Washes for all the twenty miles from Earith to Denver.

We noticed the so-called 'tide-line' of vegetation and seeds left on the green, grassy bank of the River Delph when the flood level recedes. Many small birds were feeding there, including redwings, fieldfares and goldfinches. But as we walked on all our attention was drawn to the far side of the river; to the east were large lagoons of shallow blue water between us and the Wildfowl Trust's hide. We heard the strange call of the Bewick swans, rather like the call of hounds, and the whistle of wigeon in flight. Sometimes a party of swans would take off and circle round majestically, gleaming white in the brilliant sunshine, and land again with a powerful surge. They seemed to call both when on the water and in flight, when we were near them. All three kinds of swans, many Bewicks and a few whoopers and mute swans, were altogether on one lagoon. Every now and then a cloud of duck, mostly wigeon, would rise into the sky and fly round before settling again on the shallow water. After walking for a mile or so we turned back. The sun was sinking lower and the distance was getting hazy to the north and south along the Washes. Several small flocks of duck flew quite high overhead, evidently making for the Washes farther south, perhaps to the R.S.P.B. Reserve near Welches Dam. Quite clearly they were going somewhere, flying as they were in V-formation or in echelon, and not in dense clouds like those that had earlier circled round after being disturbed, before settling down again quite near. At the end of an incredibly warm and sunny day for January, we made for home and enjoyed a glorious sunset with gold and pink belted clouds and the pines and oaks and elms of the Lark valley beautifully silhouetted against the western sky. A week or two later the main road across the Washes to Welney was under three feet of flood water.

To sum up my impressions, I think everyone interested in nature conservation is delighted that so much of the Ouse Washes is now protected as a wonderful oasis for wildlife between vast areas of intensely cultivated land. There are still problems, and worries about the future. Fenland farmers are naturally concerned about the increasing numbers of wintering wildfowl that graze on the fields of winter wheat. Arrangements exist for liaison between all the various interests, and with understanding and some give and take, they can exist together without too much conflict. The threat of disturbance from the experimental hovertrain track has gone with the dismantling of the short section that had been constructed, and it seems very unlikely that the project will be revived. The most serious question for the conservationists is whether the major drainage and water supply schemes, which I shall describe later, will adversely affect the Washes by reducing the

amount of flood water that has to be spilled into them in winter. Up
to date there has been no such set-back and the Ouse Washes remain,
in the words of David Lea of the R.S.P.B. "as one of the few places in
southern England where a true feeling of wildness can be obtained.
Here one can really enjoy wild birds in wild places—whether it is the
thrilling sights and sounds of the godwits calling and displaying over
their breeding meadows or the magnificent music of the Bewick swans
in winter ringing across the flooded marshes".

At the north end of the Ouse Washes the Old and New Bedford Rivers
converge on the sluices and locks of Salters Lode and Denver which
together form the focal point for the drainage system of about half of
the East Anglian fens. From the west, to Salter's Lode, runs Popham's
Eau constructed in 1605, and from the south-east the Denver Sluice
complex receives the waters of the Ely Ouse (or 'Ten-Mile River'),
and of the cut-off channel of 1964.

The whole of the South Level and the eastern part of the Middle
Level discharge their surplus water through this key point. The
technical complexities are formidable but I will try to describe the
system which I can understand much better after a visit to the area.
At Salter's Lode, just north-west of Denver, the Old Bedford River
discharges through a lock into the broad Great Ouse, which is tidal
back as far as Brownshill Staunch above Earith and from which it
runs to Denver as the New Bedford River. The discharge from the
fresh-water loop of the Great Ouse, after flowing on the course to
which it was diverted in 1827, north of Ely, is controlled by sluices at
Denver which regulate the volumes in the tidal section flowing down
to Kings Lynn or the eleven-mile relief channel which discharges into
the river a mile above Kings Lynn. The remaining key feature is the
cut-off channel which reaches Denver after running for twenty-seven
miles round the eastern side of the Fens. It starts at Barton Mills where
a sluice enables the waters of the Lark to be diverted when necessary,
and crosses the Little Ouse and Wissey (it passes under them in concrete
syphons) whose flows can in time of flood be similarly diverted. The
relative flows and levels and discharges of the various rivers converging
on Denver are regulated by the sluices we see spanning the rivers. The
sluice across the cut-off channel is an 'impounding sluice' with the
additional function of holding back water in the channel for transfer
to Essex under the Ely Ouse/Essex Water Scheme. Water is taken out
about fifteen miles back near Lakenheath at the Blackdyke Farm
pumping station which I have described in the chapter on the East
Anglian Heights.

The wide, straight rivers with their massive, grassy banks high above
the fenland fields, and the sluice structures spanning the channels,
make an impressive sight even in calm, summer weather, but in winter

when the Ouse Washes are flooded, and the sluices are discharging vast
volumes of turbulent water into the tidal river and the relief channel,
the scene is an awesome one. Then one realizes the magnitude of the
job of getting the enormous amount of water from the Great Ouse
Basin safely through the Fens without endangering life and property
by flooding the thousands of acres of first-class farmland below the
level of the rivers

The centuries-old danger of flooding in the South and Middle
Levels seems to have become very remote since the major works were
carried out after the last war, about 300 years after the main pattern
had been created by Vermuyden. I have covered very briefly elsewhere the problems and history of the drainage of the Fens since the
earliest times, and will now confine myself to a description of the
recent works which are on a scale comparable to those of the seventeenth century, and which appear to have removed the risk of flooding
over a very large area, though they have not solved the problems of
the shrinkage and disappearance of the peaty soils.

The post-war works were based on recommendations in a report in
1940 by consultants who had been engaged by the Great Ouse Catchment Board soon after serious flooding in 1936 and 1937. The main
works had to be delayed because of the war, but the raising of flood
banks along rivers continued, and working drawings were prepared for
execution when it was possible to proceed. The worst recorded flood
put 37,000 acres under water in March 1947. Considerable damage
was done to the banks, and it took until June to pump the Fens dry and
until the end of the year to repair the banks. The implementation of
the scheme was further delayed by strong opposition from the Kings
Lynn Conservancy Board and shipping interests who feared adverse
effects on the port and shipping channel. Nearly four years of negotiations took place after the Bill receiving Royal Assent, and work did not
start until June 1954. The long delay was, however, not entirely
disadvantageous. In fact, as W. E. Doran, who was then Engineer to
the Great Ouse Catchment Board, wrote in 1965, "it was certainly a
most fortunate and extraordinary coincidence that the highest recorded
fluvial flood of 1947 should have happened in time to enable the
original scheme to be completely modified, and that the highest known
tidal surge (on the night of 31st January 1953) should have occurred
shortly before the commencement of the work on the Relief Channel
so that the spoil from the new channel excavation could be used to
raise the tidal river banks."

The work started then in June 1954 and was done in three parts.
The relief channel, from Denver to St Germans, just above Kings
Lynn, was completed in 1959. About 12 million cubic yards were
excavated to make it; some of the material was used to raise the banks

of the tidal Great Ouse and some to create the high, grassy banks we now see on either side of the wide, straight new river, 11 miles long, which is 80 yards wide at Denver and 150 at the Kings Lynn end where an automatic tail sluice enables flood water to be discharged when the tide is low.

The second part, started in 1957 and finished in 1961, involved the widening and deepening of 19 miles of the Ely Ouse from the mouth of the Cam, at Stretham, down to Denver. This difficult task included setting back the existing flood banks and making new roads where old ones had to be buried. The normal water level was 6-8 feet above the level of the fens behind the banks. The results of this part of the scheme are not so obvious in the landscape, unless one remembers the former, narrower river, but the banks are higher, the river wider, and there are many new bridges and new lengths of road.

The third part, constructed between 1960 and 1964, was the cut-off channel. Much of it runs between raised, grassy banks, and it widens gradually from about fifteen yards at the start at Barton Mills to about fifty yards at Denver. Already it attracts many water birds and fishermen, and in places, as at Hilgay, it is lined with belts of tall poplars and has a pleasing Continental character.

The remaining vital works were for the protection of the shipping channel and were of no direct benefit to the Fens. They cost nearly £1 million and included the construction of new and the improvement of the old training walls taking the channel through the mudflats between the port of Kings Lynn and the open waters of the Wash. The three main contracts for the actual Flood Protection Scheme cost over £9 million and the overall total was about £10½ million.

Apart from these vital, major works, improvement and maintenance of all the dykes and larger waterways are never-ending tasks, and there is an intricate system of pumping and draining, all focusing on the key point at Denver.

There, the creation of the flood protection and water conservation works is recorded in commemorative tablets. The head sluice was opened by Mrs Christopher Soames, on behalf of her husband who was then Minister of Agriculture, on completion of the Flood Relief Scheme in 1964, and was named the A. G. Wright Sluice in appreciation of the work of the Chairman of the Flood Protection Scheme Committee from 1954 to 1964. Nearby, a plaque on a modern flat-roofed building records the completion in 1971 of 'Control Structures' for the Ely Ouse/Essex Water Scheme; here is the northern end of that scheme, about forty miles from the Wixoe pumping station in the upper Stour Valley.

Before the construction of the Old and New Bedford Rivers, the Great Ouse followed a long, winding arc eastwards from Earith to

Stretham and then northwards past Ely and Littleport to Denver. That is an over-simplification of its history which is but a part of the many changes since Roman times, but a journey along what can now conveniently be called the old course of the river, shows us some interesting features. At Earith, the new Hermitage Lock replaces earlier sluices and locks at the entrance to the 'Old West River' which is in normal conditions a fairly static 11-mile backwater from here to its meeting with the Cam just beyond Stretham. A new yacht basin beside Hermitage Lock reminds us that, while commercial navigation is almost extinct except at the Wash ports, large numbers of pleasure boats use the fenland rivers; in the late 1960s and early 1970s about 3,000 per year passed through this lock.

North and south from the high banks, one looks out over the peaty fields to some of the more prominent fen 'islands'. Over, Willingham and Cottenham to the south do not rise beyond fifty feet above sea level, but the Wilburton-Haddenham ridge rises to over a hundred feet, ending at the west end in a bare, rounded, grassy promontory where sheep graze on the skyline. A little farther to the north again, the large village of Sutton along the ridge and southern slopes, with its tall stone church tower at the east end can look almost Italian when seen on a bright summer day with a slight heat haze under the blue sky.

The Old West is a typical fenland river, between artificial raised banks set back so as to contain flood water when necessary. Little can be seen from a small boat except for the occasional farm and bridge and riverside inn. For its first five miles east of Earith it seems likely that the river is approximately on the course of a canal constructed by the Romans to link Cambridge and Lincoln; parts of the Car Dyke can still be traced as banks and ditches. Until well into the nineteenth century the scene must have been enlivened by the many windmills which drove large scoop-wheels to lift the water from the field drains into the rivers. In the 1800s they were superseded rapidly by steam pumping engines, of which very few remain today for they have given way to electric and diesel driven pumps.

Fortunately the Stretham Engine has been preserved. It stands just below the bank at the north end of Engine Drain, a rather insignificant-looking ditch which brings water from the Waterbeach Levels. The Engine House, built in 1831 of grey brick with a slated roof, is plainly functional almost to the point of ugliness. The coal yard and tall chimney are still there, and at one side is a rather crude extension built to house the diesel engine which took over in 1925 from the steam engine which was, however, still used from time to time until 1941.

The building and the machinery were restored in the 1960s and are now beautifully maintained by the Stretham Engine Preservation Trust. The arrangement and design of the engine, boilers and scoop wheel are a joy to behold. The presence of the tools and other relics, such as long-handled spanners, oil cans, glass oil 'drip-feeds', and the splendid condition of all the equipment, make one feel that it could all be set in motion again with very little effort. The boiler house contains three boilers (one of them now used to store oil for the diesel-engined pump) which produced the steam to drive the massive beam-engine in the actual engine house, a building about fifty feet high. The shaft from the overhead rocker beam turned a 24-foot flywheel geared to the scoop-wheel 37 feet in diameter housed in the adjoining part of the building. The history and workings are admirably described in Mr R. L. Hill's leaflet published by the Trust and illustrated in separate drawings by Mr P. G. Norman. Perhaps I will be forgiven for lapsing into guide-book jargon if I suggest that no tour of the Fens is complete without a visit to the Stretham Engine.

Half a mile downstream the road from Stretham to Wicken bridges the river at a point where there was only a ford until after the First World War. The bridge was built, I believe, in the early 1930s when a new road was constructed across the low-lying site of Stretham Mere to the Cam which previously was crossed by a ferry. This illustrates how poor road communications were in the Fens until quite recently and they are still far from ideal for the long-distance traveller. Access to outlying farms was improved greatly during the Second World War when the Ministry of Agriculture initiated the construction of many miles of concrete roads in place of the unmade droves that were almost impassable in wet weather.

On joining the Cam, the Old West River changes its name to the Ely Ouse until Littleport whence it continues as the Ten-Mile River to Denver. Between 1957 and 1961, the whole of the 19 miles from Stretham to Denver was widened and deepened as Part II of the great flood protection scheme. It is now a broad river with long straight reaches between high banks which conceal it from the roads that run alongside and below them on the outer side for many miles beyond Ely.

The town stands at the eastern end of one of the larger and higher fen 'islands', and slopes down to the river. For long periods in its early history, which is thought to have started with an early Saxon settlement in the sixth or seventh century, it was a true island surrounded by water and swamps and accessible from elsewhere only by boat. The cathedral was built on the highest point of the town as it then was, and has ever since remained a splendid focal point in the landscape, seen from all round across mile after mile of flat fenland and indeed, in clear weather, from high ground beyond the Fens. It is one of the largest and most magnificent of English catherals and has the unique feature of the central octagonal lantern tower that was built after the original Norman tower collapsed in 1322. The structure of the lantern includes in each corner an oak pillar 63 feet in height and nearly four feet in diameter. It would be difficult, today, in this country to find oaks large and tall enough to supply such a need.

The cathedral is so well known that there seems no point in my describing it in any more detail, but it is worthwhile taking a little time to explore other features of Ely's history and townscape. The cathedral and its precincts, the green slopes of the Abbey Park and the earthworks of the castle, occupy a large block of land south of the Market Place. The backs of the ancient precinct buildings north of the cathedral line the narrow High Street beyond which a network of narrower lanes and alleys lead one through to Market Street. This suggests that the Market Place, as in many other old towns, was originally much more extensive and was gradually encroached on by buildings in the late Middle Ages. The west front and tower of the cathedral face across a delightful triangular remnant of the once larger Palace Green, flanked now by fine old houses. Next to one of the finest, a beautiful house with a Georgian red brick front, on the north side of the green, and just across the road diagonally from the cathedral, is an uncompromisingly modern but remarkably civilized library built in recent years by the County Council. The King's School and other old buildings in the town centre are of great interest, but it is well worthwhile to make time to see the lower part of the town.

The river's old course apparently bypassed the town, and flowed through the marshes about half a mile to the east, but it was diverted in the eighteenth century to pass along the edge of the slopes. This helped the development of the town as an inland port with small dock basins constructed later in association with the railway. The inter-war building of the large beet sugar factory revived the commercial use of the fen waterways, as beet from farms over a wide area was brought by barge to the factory. Water-borne trade has since virtually ceased with the increased use of lorries and the improvement of farm roads, but Ely is now a very popular centre for fenland pleasures boats, the increase of which may well be due partly to the serious congestion on the Norfolk Broads in the height of the season. Near the riverside, a very fine range of maltings have been restored and are now used for concerts and other public functions.

Finally, Ely has something to interest the naturalist. Between the town and the sugar factory are large lakes formed by the excavation of clay for the maintenance of river banks. Part is still being excavated by the Water Authority, but most of the 80 acres now form a nature reserve managed by the County Trust. One large lake is used by a sailing club and there is some fishing, but the whole area has a very interesting variety of birds and plants in the scrub, woodland, reed beds, open water and damp meadows, much of which can be seen from public paths.

The Jurassic clay which forms the bulk of the fen 'islands' joins the peat at fen level, but as the peat has become lower with shrinking and by windblow, it has also receded from the edges of the islands and more clay is exposed, to the detriment of farming interests. Maps produced in 1965 as part of a British Association treatise on *The Cambridge Region* suggested that a further wastage of 2 feet of peat would see the disappearance of virtually all the rich soil of the peat fens!

The river north of Ely passes through these peat fens on the way to Denver, and is joined by three similarly embanked rivers, the Lark, Little Ouse and Wissey, crossing the South Level from Suffolk and Norfolk. From Denver to Kings Lynn the tidal Great Ouse runs between raised banks parallel with and a little west of the Relief Channel. This section of the river was until 1821 a wide, winding, shallow estuary. It was then straightened, banked and deepened, and these improvements for navigation were followed by a major straightening and diversion (in a north-westerly direction) of the channel from the town through the shoals of the southern Wash to the open sea beyond.

Later, the riverside quays were straightened and improved, and enclosed docks named Alexander and Bentinck were constructed in the late 1800s on the northern fringe of the old town. Between the two docks, the former mouth of the Gaywood River was left to accommodate the 'fisher fleet' of small sailing craft used by local fishermen in the Wash. The boats are now diesel-engined and there are still valuable landings of shrimps, cockles and mussels.

To the north, saltings built up from the old coastline between the town and Snettisham, and in the century following 1865, about twelve square miles were progressively reclaimed for agriculture adjoining the south-eastern corner of the Wash.

Just west of the disused railway station and level crossing at North Wootton is an area of bumpy land, partly grass, partly arable, just above marsh level, and beyond the bumps are the dead flat acres of reclaimed marsh. Long straight roads on low embankments run through the land reclaimed in 1858, 1861 and 1866, brown, fertile alluvium, growing beet, corn, potatoes and onions. The farmhouses and cottages are Victorian and drab, one bearing the date 1899; asbestos-clad barns have been added recently. Looking west one sees a high north-south bank beyond which the twentieth-century reclamation took place more positively and methodically in neat rectangles, from 1904 to 1933, and beyond that again yet more was enclosed during the 1950s and 1960s, up to the edge of the present saltings and mudflats.

From South Wootton a broad new road runs west and south-west across land reclaimed in 1873, where overspill houses now stand, to the factories, oil storage tanks and the docks on land reclaimed in 1865.

In spite of modern growth and redevelopment, not all of it as sensitive as such a splendid historic town deserved, it is still possible to trace the pattern of the original town established in the late eleventh century between two parallel streams, Purfleet and Millfleet. The delightful seventeenth-century Custom House, looking as though inspired by Christopher Wren, stands beside the muddy outfall of Purfleet. The importance of the riverside quays has tended to decrease since the opening of the enclosed docks—circumstances opposite to those in the port of Ipswich—and there is a rather sad mixture of dereliction and preservation. But the limits of the original town still contain some wonderful buildings including the beautiful twin-towered church of St Margaret which faces the Trinity Guidhall of 1423 with its impressive chequered front of white stone and black flint. Another Guildhall—St George's—of the same period but completely different in character, stands between the famous Tuesday Market Place and the river. It belongs to the National Trust and is used for concerts and for the annual Festival of the Arts.

The improvements of 1821 to the estuary and the river, enabled Kings Lynn to recover its centuries-old prosperity as a port, which indeed increased in the succeeding 150 years to an annual trade of over 1 million tons. The river works and fen drainage did not however make the town immune from tidal flooding and it suffered very severely in the North Sea coast floods of January 1953 and again almost exactly twenty-five years later.

Contrasting utterly with the large tidal ports of Wisbech and Kings Lynn, are the many ancient village ports around the fringe of the Fens. These were part of the comprehensive and historical but frequently modified network of waterways on which goods were transported from place to place across the vast low-lying areas where roads were poor or non-existent. Goods such as coal, wine and timber, imported from other countries, were transhipped into barges at Wisbech and Kings Lynn for distribution inland. Northamptonshire stone for church building was brought across the Fens by water, and local agricultural produce, and peat and reeds, were distributed by similar means. Most of the internal movement of commerce on the fenland waterways was unable to compete with the coming of the railways, and the small amount of water-borne trade that lingered into the twentieth century was finally killed off by the growth of road transport. However, many traces are still to be seen in villages that once served as local ports. The most interesting group lies along the south-eastern edge of the Fens, where the Romans constructed long,

straight lodes, or canals, from the River Cam to Bottisham, Swaffham
Bulbeck and Reach, with a later branch from Reach Lode to Burwell.

The Devil's Dyke or Ditch runs almost dead straight for 7 miles
down from the chalk hills to end in the centre of the village of Reach
so that the Dyke and the Lode formed a continuous line of defence.
There are still little dock basins now silted up, off the main watercourses on either side of the central hythe, a little promontory projecting into the fen. Reach was an important local port from very early
times, but Burwell and Swaffham Bulbeck prospered later when Reach
declined. They both grew extensively northwards, away from the old
village centres; Swaffham Bulbeck's Commercial End and Burwell's
North Street. At Swaffham, one firm developed in the eighteenth and
early nineteenth centuries a large and varied trade, and many of their
houses and buildings, backing on to the remaining old wharves and
'docks' and the Lode, can still be seen.

At Burwell the end of the Lode divided to serve many private
basins and short canals at the rear of the merchants' houses on the west
side of the street for about a third of a mile to the north and south of
Anchor Lane. Most of the houses are narrow and at right-angles to the
street, on long plots ending at the water's edge. Some of the basins
are silted up and overgrown with grass and reeds, but a dozen or more
are still easily recognizable for what they were, and a few have wooden
boathouses. The approach by boat is the best way to appreciate the
atmosphere and history of this little, ancient port.

Coming from the east up Burwell Lode, one passes a rather dilapidated building that is now a fertilizer store. It was built as a fertilizer
factory in the early 1900s and received imported phosphates by water
from Kings Lynn. Other ingredients came from the gault pits in Little
Fen just to the north, and the 1930 Ordnance Survey map shows a
'mineral railway' running from the pits into the factory; the rails can
still be seen crossing the road. The pale Burwell bricks were also made
by the same firm from the gault dug here and the products of the brick
and fertilizer factories were, it seems, distributed locally, and more
widely, by road, by barge from the quay, and on a mineral railway
that connected with the Newmarket to Ely line. The hard chalk, or
clunch, quarried on the higher ground at Reach and Burwell, and used
there in many buildings, was also carried away by barge. The 1930 map
shows towing paths on either side of Reach and Burwell Lodes.

From Hythe Bridge, Burwell, a narrow, winding road follows the
course of the dyke known as the Weirs, along the edge of the Fens.
Moorhen and duck paddle, and a grey heron stands, in the water just
opposite the huge transformer station from which tall pylons radiate
in long lines to north, south and west. The road curves round, back
towards the site of the railway station where there now stands a huge,

modern factory looking over the meadows to the grassy earthworks
which are the remains of the castle, on a Roman site, just below the
tall tower of the church. Thus at Burwell we have visible evidence of
features and activities covering the last 2000 years in the life of a
fascinating fen-edge settlement.

I must end my account of the Fens, which in spite of its length, has
far too many omissions and inadequacies, with a brief survey of the
South Level between the Ely Ouse and the Breckland. Here we have
one of the largest and most typical areas of peat fen, wide and open,
green in summer, black in winter. The feeling of almost unlimited
space has, however, become increasingly spoilt by wooden poles and
overhead wires, and by the seemingly endless lines of 180-foot pylons
here in the south-eastern fens and marching from north to south on
the far side of the Ouse Washes. More intimate details are noticed as
we travel on long straight roads made humpy by subsidence, and pass
isolated and sometimes tilted houses with their front doors left several
feet up by the shrinkage of the peat. Some buildings, such as the Shippea
Hill signal box when I saw it a few years ago, have had to be shored
up to prevent their total collapse.

Between Burwell and Denver there are very few 'islands' or 'high'
ground to interrupt the view or to provide viewpoints. An exception
is found between Soham and Wicken, in a low ridge from which
there are distant views of Ely cathedral to the north and the chalk hills
far to the south.

A narrow lane off the village street leads to the head of Wicken
Lode and to Wicken Sedge Fen. I think the long-lived fallacy that this
is a relic of natural, ancient fenland has just about been finally buried,
but it is perhaps worth quoting a few authoritative words on the subject.
The National Trust tell us that Wicken Fen, acquired by them mainly
between 1899 and 1911, "includes almost all that is left undrained of the
once extensive fens of the Great Level. Much of the land was in former
times privately owned on a strip system by the inhabitants of Wicken
village. These strips were a source of sedge for thatching, etc., and
were in some parts dug for peat." I am sure "Great Level" here means
the South Level, bearing in mind the continued existence of Holme
Fen and Wood Walton Fen on the far side of the Middle Level.

One walks westwards along the bank from the village end of the
Lode, where sedge and reed cut in the reserve, are still stacked, as in
the old days when water transport was used. Droves and dykes are
kept open between the natural encroaching growth of willow and alder
that would, if unchecked, cover the whole area to the north. Management as a nature reserve is designed to improve and maintain habitats
for a fascinating variety of common and rare plants, insects and birds,
and to enable visitors to see traces of the old fenland activities of

sedge, reed and peat cutting and brickmaking, the last deriving from gault dug from pits in the north-east corner. This is certainly a naturalist's paradise and has been studied intensely for a century, but it provides great interest and enjoyment to the amateur also, in the wonderful seasonal variety of wild flowers and butterflies. Bird life is abundant both in the wooded area north of the Lode, and on the mere (seen from a high-level hide) created in 1954–55 when Adventurers' Fen to the south was returned to the Trust after agricultural use during the war. Just after the mere was made, the little windpump that had stood in Adventurers' Fen since 1908, was moved to the east end of the Sedge Fen, near the head of Wicken Lode. It is a small, black, weather-boarded smock mill, square in section, with its sails mounted on a boat-shaped cap turned into the wind by a long, braced tailpole reaching to the ground. Since its transfer to its present site its role has in effect been reversed. It has been used to lift water into the Reserve where maintenance of damp conditions is so vital and so difficult because the cultivated and drained fields all around have shrunk to a much lower level.

A less well known, but very interesting feature, exists between Wicken Fen Reserve and the River Cam to the west. The Upware Reef is a belt—it hardly rises high enough to be called an outcrop—of corallian limestone just below the surface soil over an area about three miles by one mile running north and south just on the Wicken side of the Cam. The rock is, as its name implies, marine in origin, and is creamy in colour and quite hard. It has been quarried for many years as an ingredient in road-making materials.

Between Wicken and Denver, the South Level is crossed by the Lark and the Little Ouse, flowing between high banks, above field levels, on the straight courses to which they were diverted centuries ago to join the Ely Ouse and the Ten-Mile River respectively. Their old courses can still be detected in parts at least as parish and county boundaries, roads and winding, narrow dykes. Of the three rivers flowing westwards out of Suffolk and Norfolk, only the Wissey still follows its old course, although for its last ten miles it flows between high, artificial banks. Like the other two, however, it is crossed and controlled by the cut-off channel which now forms a very definite barrier and boundary between the Fens and the Breckland.

10

Forest and Breck

HARD against the eastern border of the Fens, and seen from afar across its open levels, lies the forest. Here together in East Anglia are two vast areas contrasting dramatically with each other. They adjoin but they are worlds apart, the one wet and the other dry, the one open and almost treeless and the other clothed in dense, black pine forests. Just as flooding had been a perpetual worry in the Fens, so fire has become the bogey of the forest. The farmers prayed for rain to stop; the foresters for it to come. The Fens had their windpumps, and later their steam and diesel engines, to get the water away; the forests have their tall watch-towers to spy out distant fires, and their static tanks of water in a land having very few streams and rivers.

The forest all around Thetford, and across the borders of Norfolk and Suffolk, is one of the largest in Britain and certainly the largest in the lowlands. The fact that even into the late 1930s topographical writers described the area as the Breckland illustrates what is probably the most rapid, dramatic and large-scale change ever to come about in our region.

Thetford Forest as it is called, had its origins less than sixty years ago, in the early 1920s, and has thus wrought a profound transformation of the landscape within living memory. It has been planted over a large part of the Breckland, the ancient stony waste between the Fens in the west and the heavy land in the east that bore the old oak forests and later became the main arable belt of East Anglia. The Breckland, as related in my first chapter, has a history as long as any part of Britain. Being dry and lying between swamps and forests, it served as an extension of the south-west to north-east corridor of the chalk hills. It is rich in the relics and traces of our earliest inhabitants. There are many ancient tracks, burial mounds, defence dykes, castle mounds and ancient manor houses, and the underground flint workings of Neolithic times at Grimes Graves near Brandon. But before going on to describe the forest, I must record briefly my own earliest remembered acquaintance with the area.

In the early 1930s, I cycled out of Bury St Edmunds in search of the Hill of Health, which I had spotted on a map. It was a tumulus or burial mound, beside a track just beyond the village of Culford, but I did not then realize its significance. From higher ground a little farther on was a wide view north-west over miles of gently rolling heathland with scattered clumps of Scots pine and silver birch—a beautiful, open countryside, shimmering in the summer sun, exhilarating but somehow mysterious. It was one of the largest remaining open parts of the Breckland, once a great, sandy, stony, barren waste of 400 square miles, stretching from Bury St Edmunds in the south to beyond Swaffham in the north, and from the edge of the Fens in the west to Garboldisham and Watton in the east. Would that I had looked more closely and remembered more clearly that summer view of 1932! Already the Forestry Commission had been planting pines over thousands of acres between Thetford and Brandon and Swaffham; and within three years they were to start planting the King's Forest between Culford and Elveden, thus destroying a large area of open 'breck' lying astride the Icknield Way.

The word 'breck' indicates that much of this dry, stony part of the country was broken up and cultivated from time to time over the centuries, but old methods and the activities of countless rabbits made agriculture a very desultory and unprofitable occupation. Although the area was from prehistoric times quite well populated, as evidenced by the many ancient roadways, barrows, flint mines and other remains, it was always arid and infertile, and always mysterious, even eerie, and different and separate from the surrounding countryside.

More serious attempts were made in the eighteenth century and early nineteenth century to convert some of the Breckland into arable, but with varying success owing to the nature of the ground and the fluctuations of the national agricultural economy. Naturally, poor land with low productivity, went out of cultivation in times of low prices. It continued, however, to flourish as a great sporting area in which rabbits by tens of thousands played a considerable part in the economy, but as time went on the more sophisticated sport of pheasant shooting developed as a major attraction for a very strange mixture of high society. The 'sporting', a much more profitable enterprise than farming in such country, was at its height in the days of Edward as Prince of Wales in the latter years of the nineteenth century, and as King Edward VII in the early twentieth century. While this may be social history, it had a profound effect on the landscape as the agriculture was entirely ancillary to the 'sporting', and the effects included the planting of belts and clumps of pines for cover for the game. But even while the great age of social splendour associated with aristocratic guns still flourished, the agricultural revolution was already under way, especially on the huge Elveden estate.

Fortunately for those interested in the past, the landscape of Breckland, its mystery and atmosphere, its specialized flora and fauna, and its long and fascinating history, were recorded in the early 1900s by W. G. Clarke who coined the name Breckland. His book *In Breckland Wilds* was published in 1925, so he had in fact seen the beginning of the Forestry Commission's work, but the effects were to be more fully described in the revision of the book undertaken by R. Rainbird Clarke and published in 1937. So rapid is the growth of a pine forest, even in such a dry climate and on such poor land, that it was possible, only fifteen years after the first tree was planted, to see and analyse the effects on the landscape, and on the highly specialized habitats and plant and animal life of the Breckland.

The two Clarkes, who I believe were not related, described the area in detail, both being extremely knowledgeable about its ancient history and present wildlife, but the books include memorable romantic descriptions of the scenery and atmosphere and the strong, indefinable fascination of one of the most interesting of lowland Britain's wildernesses. Such descriptions, rare in primarily scientific books, originated in W. G. Clarke's book of 1925, but were preserved in Rainbird Clarke's revision and rewriting of 1937, the later writer recognizing the long-term value and interest of what he called sections of a subjective and personal nature. The earlier author referred only very briefly to the effects that afforestation and agricultural reclamation were likely to have on the rare plants and bird life; most of his book had been written before the Forestry Commission started work. By 1937 they had acquired most of the land that was to be planted and indeed had already planted trees on most of it; and much new arable and grazing had been created on former heathland, especially on the Elveden estate. Rainbird Clarke wrote surprisingly little about the agricultural aspects, but gave a very balanced and forward-looking assessment of the probable effects of afforestation. He referred to the criticisms voiced by naturalists, archaeologists, historians, economists, students of social welfare, sportsmen and amateurs of the old Breckland scenery, all of whom feared that the spread of the forests would harm their particular interests. Rainbird Clarke, however, perceived with considerable acumen, that "though some rare species may perish, there is no reason to fear the ultimate extinction of the characteristic wild life and vegetation, provided that some suitable tracts remain unplanted", and he pointed out that some species such as crossbill and roe deer were likely to increase. He recommended the urgent establishment of "a nature reserve" and of a National Park, and called on the scientist to appreciate the unequalled opportunities for studying a forest in the making.

Throughout this century and even before, the Breckland and latterly the forest, have been intensively studied because of the unique character and long history of the area. Its interest and changes derive primarily from geology and climate. Early man settled because of the light, well-drained land, with small streams and rivers, the relative ease of movement and the lightness of the tree cover which could be cleared much more easily than the clay land forests to the east and the marshy swamps to the west. The nature of the land and the continental climate, very dry with extremes of heat and cold (summer temperatures are higher than in the neighbouring areas, and ground frost is recorded on more than half the days of the year), have fostered the unusual tundra-style flora, and encouraged the nesting of the stone curlew and ringed plover. These conditions have been inimical to farming, which never flourished for long at a time until the long, determined and well-planned operations in this century of a few large, wealthy landowners. In earlier centuries the changing prosperity of the country and of farming was reflected in the intermittent cultivation and abandonment of marginal land as in the 'brecks', and evidence survives of many deserted villages. W. G. Hoskins refers to twenty-eight on and around the edges of the Breckland in some of which one sees now only the derelict remains of a medieval church or the dry moat of an ancient farm site.

The climate and ground conditions made the Breckland an inevitable choice for large-scale afforestation by the Forestry Commission, established by the government in 1919, with the object of replacing and creating strategic reserves of timber and reducing the country's dependence on imports. They began acquiring land and planting trees in the Breckland in 1922. There was a general agricultural depression in those years after the first World War, and there were huge areas of waste land, some of which had once been cultivated. The larger and wealthier estates, notably at Elveden, were in fact reclaiming land for agriculture and had their own forestry organization. They were naturally reluctant to part with land, but less fortunate landowners willingly sold or leased land to the Commission who rapidly created a forest on about 95% of the 51,000 acres that came under their control. All this happened during the years when Lord Iveagh was systematically improving the Elveden estate, as I shall tell later, by bringing into grazing and cultivation large areas of formerly barren wasteland. This fact no doubt inspired the observation made by George Backhouse, the recently retired Conservator of Forests for East England, in the 1972 guide to *East Anglian Forests*. Referring to the prosperity which followed the depression in agriculture in the early 1920s he wrote: "New techniques of managing the light land, together with the breeding of new strains of corn, have revolutionized farming in the region and there is little doubt that but for the existence of the forest today the whole area would be under agricultural crops. This is a sobering thought for all who, quite understandably, regret the disappearance of so much of the old brecks or heaths."

One suspects that the converse would have happened if the larger estate owners, again especially the Elveden estate, had not resisted the Forestry Commission's advances, and insisted on pursuing their own agricultural plans. The whole of Breckland, except for the Stanford Battle Area and the military airfields, might have been covered with conifers!

Even where the land could be acquired easily, the Forestry Commission did not have an easy task in creating the forest. Areas to be planted had to be fenced and cleared of rabbits, which were still present in vast numbers in the 1920s. The young trees, raised in the Commission's own nurseries, were planted out and protected until they were large enough to look after themselves. During their early years they had many enemies; weeds might smother them if not controlled, rabbits and deer would eat them if not excluded, insect pests and fungi would kill or deform them if not prevented or treated. If they survived all these, there was throughout their lives the very serious risk of fire, reduced a little in recent years by the disappearance of steam locomotives but increased no doubt by the much greater use of the forest by the public seeking recreation.

During the Second World War some forest land was taken over for military purposes, such as battle and tank training, and huge airfields were created on the fringes. These too changed the landscape considerably, and the airfields in particular, and all that goes with them in the form of traffic and noise, remain with us in the 1970s. On the border of the forest and the fen, drainage works, especially the cut-off-channel, have also changed the scene and affected its present and future evolution.

Despite all the 'enemies' and risks, the forest in general flourished and grew to its present extent. Its effect on the landscape has been and still is criticized by some who dislike conifers in vast numbers and others who mourn the disappearance of much of the beauty and interest of the old Breckland and of its specialized flora and fauna. I will describe later some particular parts of the forest and the intervening open country, but here I can only admit the tremendous effect of the change to a closed and densely planted forest mostly of Scots and Corsican pines. One passes through mile after mile with only the regular rides affording any gaps in the ranks of trees. Wide panoramas of the forest are few because of the relatively flat terrain, but from Gallows Hill, a high part on the main road north-west of Thetford, one can look over the Little Ouse valley and see nothing but forest for miles. The overall effect for the traveller along the roads through the forest is softened very much by the many deciduous trees that line the roadsides. There are avenues of chestnut and lime, and mixed edges of silver birch, oak, wild cherry, red oak and beech, and the pine woods themselves seem much less black and monotonous when the trees have grown bigger and when thinning has let in some light.

Once the forest was well established, a methodical programme for thinning, felling and replanting, was put into practice, and in various areas one can now see forestry in all its stages, and the effects on the environment. In recent years the Forestry Commission, following Government policy, have done a great deal to encourage people to visit and use the forest for recreation. Picnic sites, forest walks and horse riding trails have been created; there are information centres at Santon Downham and West Stow and an arboretum at Lynford Hall. Management takes heed of nature conservation, but some control of the numbers of deer is necessary. All in all the forest increases in beauty and interest year by year and so do the opportunies for recreation by more visitors.

Turning now from afforestation to agricultural reclamation we find that by 1937 when W. G. Clarke's book was revised, ten years had elapsed since Rupert Guinness, Lord Elveden, had succeeded his father as the Earl of Iveagh and inherited the vast Elveden estate. He was to develop the estate methodically and scientifically as a culmination of the efforts of various owners, including his father, during a century and a half of fluctuating agricultural fortunes in Britain. In the late eighteenth century the work of Townshend and Coke in Norfolk inspired their contemporaries and followers. Lord Albemarle, a friend of Coke, took over Elveden in 1786, and at the turn of the century he took in hand "the barren, windswept, rabbit-infested estate" of 4000 acres. His efforts and methods were described by Arthur Young in *General View of the Agriculture of the County of Suffolk* (1804):

Sainfoin and lucerne valuable crops in helping fertility and smothering weeds. Turnips, barley, oats, wheat, rye, sheep (changed from Norfolks to South Downs). Land was extensively marled and manured.

Lord Albemarle promises to be a very active and experimental farmer; and will by improving and planting change the face of the desert that surrounds him.

These are words which could well have been written of the Earl of Iveagh in the late 1920s.

Lord Albemarle also introduced Devon cattle and planted many trees. He was a disciple of Coke, but Elveden was a tougher proposition than Holkham. He sold Elveden in 1813 at the beginning of a bad agricultural depression following the prolonged Napoleonic war. The new owner, William Newton, a wealthy West Indies merchant, bought the estate for the 'sporting', and lived there until he died in 1862. He enlarged the plantations and the house, built roads, made other improvements and continued to farm part of the estate. After him came the Maharajah Duleep Singh of Lahore, who had been exiled from his homeland when a child. In compensation, the British Government gave a large sum to trustees who bought the estate and land at Eriswell for him. According to George Martelli in *The Elveden Enterprise*, the 'Black Prince' as he was known locally, was a good and generous landlord and a keen sportsman. He carried out considerable extensions and alterations to the house, turning it into "an Oriental extravaganza unparalleled in England"; and the old village church was enlarged before he left England in 1885 for India. However he was turned back and spent the rest of his life in Paris where he died in 1893. In the churchyard at Elveden, close to the busy A11 but not seen from it, are three white tombstones, of the Maharajah, his wife the Maharanee, and their son who died at the age of thirteen in the same year as his father.

The estate had declined in another agricultural depression, but was rescued by the first Earl of Iveagh of the Guinness dynasty. He bought it in 1894 and added land at Icklingham in 1898, to make a total of 23,000 acres. Then followed what Martelli described as 'the golden age'. The Earl doubled the size of the mansion and added other buildings, including a water tower "the size of Big Ben", and vast stables. The village was rebuilt, six miles of estate roads constructed, and the church transformed so that little but the old tower is recognizable of the original building. A new nave and chancel were added and later connected by a cloister-walk to a grand new bell tower. All the work was done to a very high standard with very fine faced flintwork and stone carving.

The estate at that time was managed mainly for the sporting, and farming was still subsidiary. Regular visitors included those who later became King Edward VII and King George V, and there was elaborate ritual with lavish entertaining. Farming generally declined until 1906 but then picked up and was further stimulated by the first World War. At Elveden much game land was ploughed and agricultural prosperity continued until 1921 after which political and international factors caused another slump lasting for some years. However, possessing wealth, knowledge and optimism, Lord Iveagh saw the need for better agricultural education and founded the Chadacre Institute in 1921. He died in 1927 and his son, Rupert succeeded to the title and the estate. The heir had strong practical interests in social welfare and science, especially as applied to agriculture, and brought to Elveden years of valuable experience of farming at Pyrford in Surrey. There he trained emigrants for life in Canada, and developed methods of producing pure milk.

Financial crises and ensuing tax increases in 1931 caused even the wealthy to consider economies. At Elveden, the emphasis was changed from sporting (though some was retained) to farming. The number of cattle was increased to enrich the land, and sheep were reduced. T.T. herds were created, and Lord Iveagh was a great pioneer in this. By 1933 he had a large surplus of milk and had to find markets farther afield. He continued to grow lucerne both to increase fertility and for cattle food, and was able to increase the acreage of wheat and of other cereals and root crops, including sugar beet. Mobile milking parlours were introduced, enabling the cattle to stay on the land where they were needed to enrich it. Other forms of mechanization proceeded, and the number of horses, mostly Suffolk Punches, went down from over 200 in 1932 to 100 in 1939. During the years leading up to the war in 1939, the development of the estate farms proceeded in a positive way and according to detailed plans of campaign, which, however, were adapted from time to time. When the war started the government brought into operation their plans to increase food production and thus to reduce the need for imports. The sporting at Elveden became much less important, and the additional 600 acres ploughed up included 200 acres of lucerne leys and old game lands. In 1940, 1000 acres of old sheep walks were ploughed up. All this reclaimed land had to be fenced against rabbits. There was a set-back to progress with the establishment of a tank training ground on a large area of the estate, and considerable damage was done in spite of Lord Iveagh's protests.

Nevertheless, during the war the development of the farming estate continued, and the scientific methods and increased mechanization gave a lead to farmers elsewhere. Even after the war the government continued to encourage agriculture, and on the Elveden estate more and more heathland was brought into production. Between 1939 and 1950 the farm land on the estate was increased by 60%, involving the reclamation of nearly 3000 acres of waste land. Not only acreages, but yields of crops, meat and milk, had been greatly increased, and all this on land previously rated in the lowest category and officially considered only fit for afforestation. In 1950, with more than 8000 acres under cultivation and managed as a single unit, Elveden was the largest arable farm in England. The 1951 programme for the area of 8199 acres showed just over 3000 acres for cash crops for sale, the rest for food for livestock and for increasing the fertility of the land. The policy was to continue to farm as economically as possible and to maintain and increase fertility, cattle and lucerne being the 'twin pillars of the system'. It was all done by careful programming, with an involved regulated rotation, and yet more land was to be brought into production. The farm estate consisted of twelve farms in three groups—Home, Eriswell and Icklingham—but the buying and distribution of foodstuffs and the cropping programme were controlled centrally. There was an elaborate system of records and reports and accounts, in all of which Lord Iveagh himself took a keen and active interest.

The balance of the 23,000 acres of the whole estate in 1950 included 2000 acres more to be reclaimed for farming, 4000 acres of estate forests, 3000 acres leased to the Forestry Commission, 2000 acres leased to the Air Ministry, 1300 acres leased to tenants; the remaining 3500 acres were rough grazing and poor unproductive land. During the following twenty-five years, the acreage farmed was increased to 11,250 and of farms let to 1600; estate forestry was down to 2500 acres, and there were still 3500 acres of unreclaimed heath. Large numbers of cattle, pigs and sheep were still kept, and large areas still carried lucerne for cattle food and to increase land fertility.

Although an apology is due for quoting so many figures, they are revealing and help to justify devoting so much space to farming in a chapter on the forest. The activities of the Elveden estate and others in Breckland have profoundly changed the ancient landscape over vast areas interlocked with those that have been afforested by the Forestry Commission.

This huge estate is managed from an office in the estate village opposite Elveden church and the entrance to the heavily wooded park of Elveden Hall. A short run along the main road towards Newmarket shows us a fair cross-section of the work and landscapes of the 23,000 acres most of which lies between the Forestry Commission plantations of Thetford Forest on the north and of King's Forest on the south. Through the pine belts and the old twisted Scots pines along the roadside, we get glimpses of arable fields, cattle and sheep grazing, farm buildings and piggeries, and plantations which are part of the forestry enterprise. On either side, many miles of well-surfaced private roads give access to the fields and the farms. Two miles from the Elveden cross-roads stands the war memorial, surely one of the most impressive village memorials to be found anywhere. It is a column over 100 feet high and stands at the meeting point of the three parishes which contain the majority of the estate. The fluted column itself is of a whitish stone (Weldon, according to W. G. Clarke writing in 1925) and is of very similar design to The Monument in London, with tiny slit windows; the top is of Portland stone and is carved intricately and similarly to the top of Nelson's Column but is capped by a large stone urn instead of a statue. The square base has panels on three sides recording the names of estate people who lost their lives in two world wars, including in the second war an Arbon from a family who lost several members in the first, and Arthur, Viscount Elveden. The fourth side contains a little door, inside which 148 steps lead up to the square section and balcony just below the urn. What a wonderful view it must be across the neighbouring unreclaimed heaths—one of the largest and most interesting of such areas lies on both sides of the main road here but for how long is uncertain—to the background of Forestry Commission and estate woodlands, and no doubt over them to the distant chalk hills and the Fens.

The culmination of the changes of the past 150 years can be seen as a general picture by travelling across and round the area, but remembering that changes are still going on, and that the detail and beauty of the forest and the spaces between can be fully enjoyed and understood only by walking and looking and sitting and watching.

The road from Bury St Edmunds to Mildenhall runs down the Lark valley, and, as far as Lackford the river marks the boundary between the forest on one side and gently rolling arable on the other. At Hengrave, being still on the 'other' side, we are distracted by the beauty of the Park and the Hall, probably at their best in autumn. Walking in through a gap in the encircling wall and trees, past the quaint lodge, we come first to the churchyard among the parkland beech. The little church, in an almost too-good-to-be-true, idyllic setting, has a stocky round tower, 'probably Norman', but the nave and chancel date from the 1400s and 1500s. A small wrought-iron gate in the far corner of the churchyard leads through to the front of Hengrave Hall. This appears to be a magnificent grey stone house of the sixteenth century, an unusual thing in East Anglia, but a closer look reveals that the greater part of the front is of a greyish brick that is a perfect match for the stone of the cornices and turrets and ledges. The sun streams into the diamond-paned windows, and illuminates the colour in the ornate carved coats of arms over the front door. A few late house-martins sit basking in the autumn sun on the ledges over the upstairs windows, and occasionally circle over the forecourt and return. South-eastwards is a fine open prospect to the trees at the far end of the park. Great russet beeches overhang the lake near the main gate, and tower above the miniature avenue of pollarded limes.

Beyond Flempton we see on the rising ground across the river the dark pines of the King's Forest, and as we turn away from the river at Lackford and go along the Icknield Way to Cavenham and Tuddenham, we pass through country which has something of the look of the

Breckland, although there are not the vast open prospects of fifty years ago before afforestation and cultivation transformed thousands of acres from wild beauty to orderly profitability. On Cavenham and Tudden-ham Heaths, nearer the River Lark, large areas of old heathland, with scattered mixed woodlands, are protected as National Nature Reserves of great historical and botanical interest. They still have some of the atmosphere and mystery of the old Breckland, and are frequented by many interesting birds, including the stone curlew, now one of Britain's rarest breeding birds. This part of the valley with its peaty floor and scattered alders, willows and pines, illustrates how the Fen penetrates into the Breck. It has a peculiar fascination and variety, with a flood plain bordered on the north by pine forests whose edges are beautified by silver birch and young red oak, and on the south by ancient heaths and woods.

As we go west to Barton Mills, the meeting place of many roads, we see the new cut-off channel just north of its starting point on the Lark. Here the channel is only 40 feet wide, compared with 150–200 feet at the Denver Sluice end. It was completed in 1964 as the main feature in a great flood relief scheme for the eastern Fens. It runs north through Woodcock Covert and Victoria Plantation where no river ever ran before, and continues for 26 miles on its unnatural course along the eastern edge of the Fens, with sluices to take away when necessary the waters of the three rivers, the Lark, Little Ouse and Wissey that run from the heart of Suffolk and Norfolk through the forests into the Fen basin. North of Mildenhall, beyond the new plantations, the channel emerges into open country and is seen more obviously as a new dividing line between forest and fen. The older dividing line is the Eriswell to Lakenheath road along which is a line of old twisted Scots pines. Just as the fen penetrates up the valleys, remnants of the sandy breck lie out in the fens and are seen from Eriswell bridge as small scattered groups of pines growing on sandy patches over the peat. The mixed nature of the area is emphasized by the existence of Undley Common west of the cut-off channel, and Fenhouse Heath to the east, and is epitomized in a simple form just north of Lakenheath beside the Feltwell road, where one can see a field where the black fenland peat merges into the light sand of the breck. Lakenheath itself is one of the larger border villages, with a great variety of local building materials, brick, pantile, flint, chalkstone (clunch) but the overall effect has little of the beauty achieved by an apparently similar variety seen for example at Burnham Market in north Norfolk.

The Little Ouse, here broad and full, enters the Fens at Wilton Bridge, near Lakenheath Station (about two miles from the village), after flowing through the heaths and forests on the Suffolk-Norfolk border, and after passing under the cut-off channel which is normally quite low and shallow but with a tremendous capacity for taking flood water between its wide, high banks of chalky clay. From Hockwold westwards, a little road runs to Blackdyke Farm, where a bridge leads over the channel to a small, dark building perched at the top of the high, chalky bank. Its door carries a warning not to enter without breathing apparatus when the red light indicates the presence of chlorine fumes within. This is the pumping station from which a 100-inch tunnel takes water 12 miles south to Kennett and thence through the chalk hills into the upper reaches of the River Stour on the Essex border. In the chapter on the East Anglian Heights I have already described the Ely Ouse-Essex Water Scheme and the pumping station and control centre at Wixoe, about thirty miles from Hockwold.

Turning back towards Lakenheath, we notice again a low marshy area penetrating eastwards between heath and warren. This is Wangford Fen which is crossed by a new road that was made to take the place of an old road cut off east of Lakenheath when the airfield was constructed during the Second World War; at the same time the main road from Mildenhall to Brandon had to be diverted. The airfield destroyed a great deal of Lakenheath Warren, and much of what remains of the Warren has been altered by afforestation, neglect and the reduction in the rabbit population. Until the airfield came, the Warren stretched from Maidscross Hill, just east of Lakenheath village, for about three miles. It was probably the largest and the longest surviving rabbit warren, having been in the ownership of the Bishops of Ely from the 1200s to the late 1800s when it was taken over by Duleep Singh, and later by the Elveden estate. It was split into two by the airfield, leaving Maidscross Hill isolated from the major, eastern part of 1500 acres beyond the diverted main road. Rabbits flourished until about 1954 after which myxomatosis destroyed most of them in a very short time. As a result, pine seedlings, and some other trees and bushes, are spreading out from the neighbouring forest, and the old open heath landscape is disappearing, together with many specialized plants that normally grow in the short rabbit-cropped grass but not in thick, rough grass. Traces of boundary banks and old warreners' lodges remain, but the Warren is in the hands of a large estate with a well-deserved reputation for reclaiming even the poorest land for agriculture, and the policies of large scale economic farming seem unlikely to allow such a large area to remain unproductive indefinitely. Research by naturalists is permitted, but up to date no arrangements have been possible for any of the Warren to be protected and managed as an important historical and ecological relic of the Breckland.

The new road across Wangford Fen is on a low causeway, with lateral tracks running between the peaty fields. Forty years ago much of the Fen must have been rough marsh grazing. Now it is mostly cultivated but still has the feel of the fen about it as one walks on peaty tracks bordered by wet, reed-lined dykes. To the north and east in the hazy distance, the pine forests clothe the rising land.

Cawseyhorn Drove goes south to Pashford Poors Fen, belonging to the successors to an old charity, and now managed as a nature reserve by the Suffolk Trust for Nature Conservation. It has a fascinating variety of habitats, including dry breck with Scots pines, low pockets of fen, a spring and fen ditches, and mixed woodland with scrub. Consequently birds, insects, and plants are varied and numerous. It is strange to see reeds growing in among the oak, birch and pine on the slightly higher ground, but no doubt most of the reserve is usually very damp. Preservation of the right balance is a challenging job when conditions are changing so rapidly. Out on the fen side of Lakenheath, and beyond the cut-off channel, is a similar area, Lakenheath Poors Fen, where peaty and sandy conditions both occur.

From the east end of the new road, one sees the sad remains of the little church of Wangford standing close to the edge of the huge airfield. On the other side, hard by the great forest south of Brandon, is Wangford Warren, also managed by the Suffolk Trust for its special interest as a rare survival of a Breckland sand dune area still bare of vegetation in part and actively changing from day to day. It is a mixture of bare, light sand, in hollows and banks, and areas of fine hair grass, black and green mosses and grey lichens; the only remaining active area of a large sand blow-out which in 1668 overwhelmed the village of Santon Downham and partly blocked the Little Ouse. One can easily imagine the sand flying on a hot, windy day, the dunes on the move and the little sandy cliffs being eroded by wind and sand particles. At the west end, approaching the lower level of the neighbouring fen, bracken and reed grow together. This reserve is another interesting relic from which we can learn much of the history and changes in the Breckland scene, but the enjoyment of visitors is marred at times by the appalling noise of large jet aircraft circling and landing at Lakenheath Airfield; the end of the runway is little more than a quarter of a mile away. Lakenheath is one of a chain of military airfields on the Fen-Breck border which have affected the landscape and local conditions in many ways. Much of the remnants of Lakenheath Warren is now within the airfield boundary. The towns and villages and the country-side for miles around suffer from the awful, searing blasting noise of aircraft, and the roads are full of huge American cars. Comment is perhaps futile, but these are changes that arouse strong, mixed feelings.

Most of the aircraft approaching Lakenheath pass over the little town of Brandon, which is superficially rather dull. It is, however, at the heart of an area with a very long history of settlement from pre-glacial times to the present when the town is being expanded by an overspill scheme bringing people and industry from London. It has the distinction of having the oldest and newest of industries. Flint, mined in the area, was used for tools in the Stone Age, and flint knapping continued at Brandon well into the second half of the twentieth century; in fact in 1977 a flint knapper was cutting flints for the repair of stone and flint panels in Suffolk churches. Just across the river, in Norfolk, Brandon has a very large 'timber conversion depot' established by the Forestry Commission, to handle the products of the forest which go for pit props and other timber uses, and for conversion into paper pulp, hardboard and packaging materials. On the eastern edge of the town are two chalk pits; one is very old and now disused behind a dilapidated building that once housed a whiting factory, the other is still producing chalk for agricultural use on some of the excessively acid local fields.

The headquarters of Thetford Forest are at Santon Downham in the heart of the forest about two miles from Brandon. On the site of Home Farm, between the village and the Little Ouse River, are the buildings which house the administrative, estate and engineer's departments. In an attractive setting of old farm buildings and walls, the Forestry Commission have built themselves new offices in a boldly designed but pleasing building faced with timber. The entrance hall is laid out as an information centre with publications and displays illustrating the work of the Commission throughout Britain and especially in Thetford Forest. There are from time to time special features explaining research into populations of deer and red squirrels, and measures necessary to limit the numbers of deer both to ensure the survival and fitness of the species and to limit damage to trees.

A Forest Trail starts from here, and with the help of the Forestry Commission leaflet we can appreciate the beauty and history of the forest. From the Forest Centre we walk through a plantation of common deciduous trees planted in 1880 as a feature of the old village. This is now a modern forestry village set round a lovely green backed by the forest; the old church stands at its east end. It is hard now to believe the accounts of seventeenth- and eighteenth-century travellers of the vast sandy deserts which then lay round the village, and the terrifying sandstorms which handicapped coaches and horses and blocked the roads. Even as late as 1872, Skertchly wrote "from Thetford to the Fens, so barren is the land that one is often reminded of the deserts of Africa——hardly a drop of surface water——and for miles neither ditch, pond nor spring. Little cultivation is possible, but the loose sandy soil is occasionally tilled." Now, a hundred years later, on a fine autumn afternoon, with smoke rising from the cottage chimneys, and the little Norman church with its perpendicular tower, nestling in the woods at the end of the green, the village is as sheltered and peaceful as could be found anywhere in Britain.

The walk takes us past the church and down a forest road, by Jubilee Plantation, planted in 1969, with the help of local schools and councils and the United States Air Force, to commemorate the fiftieth anniversary of the Forestry Commission's establishment. A little beyond, and aptly illustrating the forestry cycle and its effect on the landscape, are 110 acres clear-felled about 1970 of Scots pine that had been planted in 1925. In 1971 the same area was planted with Corsican pines. On the slopes nearby is a plantation of Douglas fir, planted in 1926, and across the valley plantations of Scots pine planted in 1928. These are now large trees approaching maturity, having enjoyed for many years the additional light and air let in by earlier thinning out of younger trees.

Going back up the gentle slope from the valley we see, beside and through the twentieth-century plantations, low banks that were thrown up to divide areas of land under the Land Enclosure Act, 1805. Further historical features and evidence of the changing landscape can be seen from the road when we pause at Stop 4. A section of the road near this point is open on the north-east side, and one looks out over the clear-felled area across the valley of the Little Ouse. Hidden from view, but accessible from the Forest Trail, is a footbridge across the river close to the site of a stanch, one of a number that served much the same purpose as locks to aid navigation by barges until the early part of the twentieth century. On the far bank there is now a picnic place and the river is used only for fishing and canoeing. Also on the far side, the site of Santon House, which was an old moated dwelling, can be identified by a belt of beech trees. Another long belt of beeches farther away, marks the site of the beautiful picnic area near Two Mile Bottom on the Mundford road. The beeches stand out in all their fiery, autumn glory, in contrast with the surrounding dark forest of Scots and Corsican pines.

Along the road where we stand, is an avenue of old limes on a wide grass verge, backed by the dark pine plantations. The splendid but seriously ageing trees, nearly 100 years old, are about sixty feet high, dividing only six to eight feet above the ground into two or three main branches going up nearly vertically to create a fine 'upsoaring' effect. When we saw them in the autumn, each tall, grey old tree stood in a circular pool of its own golden leaves, but many leaves were still on the trees adding to their beauty against the dark pines. Parts of the avenue have been felled in stages during the past thirty years, and new limes planted to take the place of the old trees. Those that still remain are trimmed and lopped to prolong their life and beauty, but they will all have to be felled and replaced in the years ahead so as to perpetuate the avenue.

The open view across the valley will be lost in a few years when the young Corsican pines grow up. Thus we see the landscape changing quite rapidly as the cycle of felling and planting goes on, both for timber and for amenity. We see too the carefully planned efforts of the Forestry Commission to enhance and maintain the beauty of the roads through the plantations, and to help people to understand and enjoy the forest and its setting.

On the way back to the village, the trail takes us into the forest on the other side of the road. The trees here were planted in 1928 and the undergrowth of snowberry in the thinned areas is quite dense and gives cover for deer which may be seen occasionally bounding away between the trees. The trail rejoins the road near a small marl pit which was used, before the forests came, to enrich the poor, sandy land with a chalky clay found just below the surface. Such pits, now disused and usually overgrown with trees, may still be seen on many of the large fields around the fringe of the Breckland.

Evidence of much more ancient mineral workings can be seen at Grimes Graves about a mile north of the Little Ouse, not far from Santon Downham. This is one of Britain's most famous archaeological sites and dates from Neolithic times. We visited it for the first time on a late, fine autumn afternoon, and found it on a stretch of heathland now surrounded by dark pine forests. Our reading, and the aerial photographs we had seen, had led us to expect a bleak, open landscape of humps and hollows, something like the surface of the moon. Humps and hollows there were, but the overall effect had changed with growth in recent years of many seedling birch trees and scattered buckthorn and guelder rose, up to a height of five or six feet. The spaces between the trees and bushes were kept clear by rabbits and human feet, and in the short turf were many tiny plants typical of chalk grassland, including wild thyme, rock rose and harebell. The hollows, about fifteen feet across, were surrounded by low banks of excavated chalk and sand and had been refilled when mining ceased—it is thought about 3000 years ago. Recent research by the British Museum has clarified some of the mysteries that have for centuries surrounded the nature and purpose of these workings and has established, with the help of a computer-plotted contour map processed from overlapping aerial photographs, that there were over 500 pits in the area of 93 acres. Other scientific research suggests that the mining started about 4000 years ago.

Only Pit No. 1 is open to the public. It is capped now with a large concrete slab, supported by transverse beams, and one descends 30 feet by a vertical ladder from a narrow trapdoor to the floor of the pit. I had expected a bottle-shaped pit like the one under Royston High Street, with a narrow neck, opening out lower down, but Pit No. 1, apparently typical of those at Grimes Graves, was more beaker-shaped with vertical sides up to within a few feet of the ground level, then sloping outwards to the edge of the hollow on the surface. The shadows of people passing up and down through the trapdoor causes the light in the pit to fluctuate in an eerie fashion on the lumpy, chalky walls. At the base, the black 'floor-stone' can be seen at one or two points round the edge of the floor, and in the seven galleries which radiate from the pit and are dimly lit by rosy electric lamps. The galleries are only two or three feet high, and working conditions must have been horribly cramped and claustrophobic. The Norwich Castle Museum has a dramatic reconstruction of one of the pits and its galleries with naked Neolithic miners at work hacking the flints from the chalk walls, for use as axes and other tools and weapons. The digging was done with bone 'shovels' and antler 'picks', many of which have been found, together with rough chalk bowls thought to have served as lamps, and ritual objects including a small chalk figure of a woman. All these features and the history of Grimes Graves are described in the official guide, by R. Rainbird Clarke; both the text and the illustrations are fascinating and, to me, far more interesting than the average ancient monument guide.

A run of five or six miles through the forest takes us from Neolithic flint mining to London overspill at Thetford. On this brief journey we are reminded of other aspects of ancient and modern history. Now hidden in the forest is Thetford Warren Lodge, the roofless remains of what the notice board describes as "a small fifteenth-century stone house with defensive features, the principal chamber being on the first floor. Probably intended for the gamekeeper of the Prior of Thetford who enjoyed right of free warren". It has 3-feet thick walls of rough flints with limestone quoins and narrow slit windows. Inside the chimneys are lined with old red bricks, and the chimney breast protrudes outside for the full height of the wall. A photograph in W. G. Clarke's book of 1925 shows the Lodge with a hipped roof covered with thatch and with single-storey wings, also thatched, on either side; the longer wing had chimneys, doors and windows and looked like a pair of cottages. In 1935 the buildings were burnt out and later only the Lodge itself was restored, though not re-roofed, and there is now no obvious trace of the former wings. Although popularly referred to as a hunting lodge, it was associated with a rabbit warren, a common feature of Breckland up to the early twentieth century, and was used for drying rabbit skins, storing traps, nets and lanterns, and accommodating the warreners. It had its own well, over a hundred feet deep. Now the building stands in a little fenced-in glade surrounded by silver birch and pines.

Between the Lodge and the outskirts of Thetford is a very attractive golf course on which many seedling oaks have been allowed to grow naturally with numerous branches spreading out at ground level and looking like large, rounded bushes. The approach to the town passes new houses very pleasantly set beside Redcastle Furze, a small wood of oak and pine in which low banks and ditches are the only visible signs of a Norman castle. Near it was a ford which may have been an alternative crossing for the Icknield Way whose main crossing is generally assumed to have been where Nun's Bridges now span the Little Ouse and the Thet. A little east of the Red Castle stood a cathedral, the neglected remains of which can be seen in a rather poor setting next to a petrol filling station between the Brandon Road and the river. Thetford Priory, north of the river, has been severed from the centre of the town by a recent diversion of the A11 road, but it is still very pleasantly situated on the edge of the town and close to the green water meadows. We found it unexpectedly extensive, with the remains showing clearly the plan of a church, cloisters and other buildings of cathedral proportions. The stumps of the pillars consist mostly of the rough flint infilling, but a few still have some of their casing of 'imported' stone. Parts of the exterior were faced with finely cut black flints.

The Ancient House in White Hart Street was given to the town in 1921 by Prince Frederick Duleep Singh and opened as a local museum three years later. This seemingly small building, dating from the fifteenth century, is half-timbered and oversailing at the front and is most impressive inside with high carved-beamed ceilings on the ground floor. It contains most interesting displays connected with the local history, archaeology and natural history of Thetford and the Breckland. At the time of our visit in the autumn of 1977, there was a special exhibition illustrating the research by the British Museum into the history of Grimes Graves .

From the Ancient House, the street runs down past the parish church with its faced flints and tall tower in the centre of the old town. Just across the road is the Bell, another fine old timber-framed building full of interest inside and out. It has a Map Room hung with framed old maps of Norfolk, and in the entrance hall are photographs of the Inn and neighbouring streets in Victorian times. Where houses then stood between the Bell and the cast-iron river bridge of 1829, is the present car park enclosed by the modern extensions to the hotel. These have white rendered walls and black boarding and a flint panel, acknowledging local traditions, and on the whole are successful in spite of their large scale in relation to the original building. The outer side of the extensions faces over the Little Ouse, still crossed by the cast-iron bridge, and adjoins the delightful Riverside Walk shopping centre. A 'three-armed' footbridge spans the confluence of the Little Ouse and the Thet and gives access to a very pleasant tree-clad island. Riverside walks and grassy tree-shaded open spaces are notable in the middle of Thetford and they have been laid out and looked after so as not to appear too urbanized. The new riverside shopping centre is linked to the old shopping centre of King Street from which vehicles have been excluded in a pedestrianization scheme which was designed by an Ipswich architect, Peter Barefoot, and won a European Architectural Heritage Award in 1975.

At the foot of the street, opposite the old timber-framed part of the Bell and next to the parish church, stands the Town Hall with its fine red-brick Georgian façade. In front of it stands Thomas Paine, or rather his golden statue, vigorously sculpted by Charles Wheeler, President of the Royal Academy and dedicated on 7th June 1964. It was presented to the people of England by the Thomas Paine Foundation of New York. On the base of the statue Paine is described as World Citizen, Englishman by birth, French citizen by decree and American by adoption. Other panels bear quotations from his pronouncements on the rights and virtues of man, and a relief of the globe, supported by wings, bears the inscription "My Country is the World, My Religion is to do Good". He was born in Thetford in 1737 in a house in White Hart Street, which stood close to the present Thomas Paine Hotel but was demolished a few years ago to make way for the diversion of the main road away from the town centre. He was educated at Thetford School but spent much of the rest of his life in other parts of Britain, and in France and America where he died in 1809. He made a reputation for himself as a revolutionary thinker and writer, but his works—the main ones were *The Rights of Man* and *Age of Reason*—are probably seldom read today. Some of his pamphlets, contemporary portraits of him and a cast of his death mask are in the Ancient House museum.

From the Town Hall, King Street slopes gently up to St Cuthbert's Church, and it is a pleasure to wander along free of the dangers and noise of traffic and to see how well the new buildings have been designed in harmony with the old. The new buildings and alterations in the town centre have been necessary to serve the accelerated growth of population by overspill from London. In Thetford the exercise seems to have been rather more successful, economically and visually than in some other overspill towns. It has revived an old town which found itself after the war surrounded by forests and a large battle training area, and thus without the prosperity which most country towns derive from an agricultural hinterland and associated industry. Once the government, the London County Council, Thetford Borough Council and Norfolk County Council had reached agreement in 1956, growth proceeded rapidly, with the impetus being co-ordinated enthusiastically by Ellis Clarke, who was then Town Clerk. A good standard was set and held for the new development around the town and for the rebuilding and improvements within it. The best of the old remains, including the character of the old streets, and the riverside walks and meadows have been kept and improved sensitively. There is very little derelict property and the town is pleasantly busy, with its centre still on a humanly small scale. The new houses on the outskirts are set in or near the pine woods and many overlook heaths and commons.

Beyond the top of King Street one comes to the part of the town where the pattern of the streets, as in other towns with castles such as Bungay and Framlingham, follows the outline of the Norman castle's earthworks. The streets are narrow and are lined closely with old houses of faced flints with white brick quoins and black pantiles, or of large uncut flints and red brick; and with high flint garden walls with occasional little, low, narrow doors with pointed arches. Here and elsewhere in Thetford some of the houses and walls contain stones, some of them carved, that obviously came from old ecclesiastical buildings such as the priory and the cathedral when they were demolished. Some buildings and walls include lumps of brick and chalk-stone or clunch. In Thetford, especially around the Castle Hill, I noticed that many of the small cottages are faced with cut flints, whereas in most parts of East Anglia where flints are used, this refinement usually occurs only on larger houses and other buildings, notably churches. The cut flints used on these Thetford cottages are not as smoothly faced as those seen in the more elaborate churches of the region, but the work is of quite a high and pleasing standard.

Castle Hill is a mound of chalk 80 feet high with very steep sides. With its associated banks and ditches, it forms an attractive informal park with many huge beech, sycamore and ash trees. A line of tall trees stands along the road and enhances the view of the flint and brick cottages opposite. Paths up the steep slopes are eroded down to bare chalk, and lead up through the trees to the flattish top from which there is a splendid view over the flint walls and houses to open country, pine belts and dark forests; the tall trees in the castle grounds obscure the view of the centre of the town. On the lower side, curving, narrow streets that have a much more ancient feel than the age of the buildings warrants lead one to Nun's Bridges which span the Thet and the Little Ouse where the Icknield Way crosses them. They are small, narrow, two-arched bridges of white local brick now weathered to the colour of stone, and between them is a smaller, single-arched bridge across what I take to be the bypass channel of a former watermill. Here, near the site of the Nunnery, new, well-designed houses stand among old Scots pines and overlook the former water meadows by the Little Ouse. This is another example of the sensitive preservation and use of ancient beauty for the enjoyment of the present population and visitors. The meadows are fringed by large willows, horse chestnuts, aspen and sycamore, and one may walk from here along the river bank to the centre of the town by the cast-iron bridge. On reflection it may seem strange that such a small town had two castles, a cathedral and a large priory, but it was already of some importance in Saxon times, and by the date of Domesday it was comparable in size and status with Lincoln and Norwich. Today the town is a satisfying mixture of old and new, and repays study particularly of its street pattern and its variety of building materials, some of which I have already described. There are also some of lath and plaster and timber-framed, but the predominance of grey brick, cut flints, rough flints and pebbles, gives old Thetford the character of a stone town rather than one of brick and plaster; it seems in its older parts almost like one of the more attractive small north-country towns.

The road out of Thetford to the south is over Barnham Cross Common, now covered with long grass, gorse bushes and a few scattered pines. New houses and schools built for people moving from London look out over the Common down to the shallow valley of the Little Ouse. Between here and Elveden lies Thetford Heath which has escaped afforestation and agricultural reclamation and is managed as a nature reserve. Its surface reveals, in the pattern of heather and other vegetation, the existence of stone stripes, a relic of the Ice Age seen here and at several other places, notably Weeting Heath, in East Anglia.

On the other side of Thetford are other open areas at Brettenham and Bridgham Heaths. Parts of these are cultivated and parts held by the armed forces for training, but next to them is East Wretham Heath, a notable nature reserve belonging to the Norfolk Naturalists' Trust. It includes Ringmere and Langmere whose levels fluctuate from month to month and year to year, and has many unusual and lovely wild flowers and grasses, and a great variety of birds, animals and insects. Its 362 acres of heaths, woods and meres are extremely beautiful as well as being of outstanding interest and importance. On a hot sunny day, with a few white cumulus clouds in a clear blue sky, conditions are perfect for seeing, hearing and feeling something of the beauty and atmosphere of the former Breckland as described so vividly by W. G. Clarke.

East Wretham is just on the southern edge of what is now for other reasons one of the most mysterious and alluring parts of the Breckland. This is the Stanford Training Area of 20,000 acres held by the Ministry of Defence and classified as a prohibited area. It contains several military camps and is used for various forms of training exercises. The Nature Conservancy Council, in *A Nature Conservation Review* (of all the most important natural history sites in Britain) describe it as "the one remaining piece of Breckland large enough to give the essential character of the district as it was before twentieth-century reclamation began—large unenclosed tracts of gently undulating, untilled, sandy and flint-strewn prairie extending to the horizon and broken only by the occasional row of trees or larger wood". The Review published in 1977, goes on the explain that "because of the very recent character of many of the brecks, here, however, there is not the full range of biological interest, especially in terms of species representation, for which the district is famous". I cannot better that assessment, but it is worth mentioning the meres and the sheep, and the isolated churches and ruined farmhouses of the tiny villages whose inhabitants had to leave in the early part of the Second World War, thus adding to the already long list of deserted Breckland villages. Even those still occupied around the fringes of the Training Area have a strangely quiet and remote feeling and seem not to belong to the outside world. It is claimed by the Ministry of Defence that military occupation and the exclusion of the public have, in spite of training activities involving soldiers, tanks and guns, preserved and protected the character and wildlife of the area which is recognized by the Nature Conservancy Council as a 'key site' in their review. Under arrangements recommended in 1973 by the Defence Lands Committee, who reviewed defence land holdings throughout Britain, a local liaison committee has been set up representing military and nature conservation interests, to discuss and co-ordinate protection of the scientific interest of the Stanford Training Area.

In the autumn of 1972, I went to look again at the Hill of Health which I had first seen forty years earlier. Then, from the rising ground north of Culford, I had looked over miles of true Breckland heath towards the great war memorial, five miles away, on the Norwich road.

Now the Hill of Health is part of the garden of a new bungalow, but is evidently treated with respect. It is quite a high burial mound, about fifteen to twenty feet with five tall, crooked, Scots pines growing on it. The grass is kept short, apparently by man and not by rabbits as of old; and man, presumably, has planted the several small oak trees among the pines. The mound and the new bungalow are discreetly hidden by hedges and trees, and are almost invisible from the surrounding countryside. Not so the large modern house on the opposite side of the stony track. The yellowish bricks and bright red pantiles make some acknowledgement to local tradition, but the neighbouring estate cottages are all built of black, faced flints set in Suffolk white bricks and roofed with slates. This new house appeared grossly assertive in the corner of a large field. It was in a rectangle of un-relieved grass, surrounded by a line of small, spindly evergreens, which, even if they survive, will look like the boundary of a cemetery, and completely out of keeping with the arable and wooded landscape.

In the background was a glorious display of varied autumn colours in an old and obviously very mixed deciduous wood. The dry, sandy, flinty track climbed gently to the north with a thorn hedge and small trees on one side; it ran between arable fields that occupied all the land between the scattered woods. We saw sugar beet, mangolds, and winter corn, and a field of sheep. The soil was brown and stony, with big knobbly flints.

In broad daylight, it was hard to imagine the old heathland that stretched for miles to north and west. Now the western and northern background was of the dark pines of the King's Forest, and it seems unlikely that, even on a clearer day, one could see the distant column of the Elveden estate war memorial; but the dark edge of the forest ahead was relieved by the fiery colour of autumn beech. Indeed throughout the day that followed we were frequently impressed and delighted with the beauty of the deciduous trees, both old and new, along the edges of the forest plantations. Criticism of the monotony of the new forests planted in the 1920s and 1930s has persisted to the present, but in some cases more by habit, ignorance or imitation than by up-to-date personal observation. Many of the beech, oak, lime, silver birch and chestnut that line the roads in Thetford Forest must have been there long before the Forestry Commission started work in 1922. Since then the Commission have done much more to beautify the forest edges and especially the roadsides by planting more similar trees, and red oak and wild cherry, and by including some larch in the coniferous plantations. All these effectively relieve the monotony in all seasons, but are most striking and beautiful in the autumn.

Year by year the cycle of planting, thinning and felling goes on, so conditions are never static, but the general impression is that the forest and its wildlife increase in interest and variety, and more and more people enjoy sitting and walking in it. The acreage is, however, so vast that it is never difficult to get away from the summer weekend crowds in the picnic sites to remote and beautiful rides and riverside paths.

The remaining open land between the plantations has more or less settled into a pattern. Quite large areas of old heathland are protected as nature reserves, and the Stanford Training Area seems likely to be indefinitely prohibited to the general public and thus to serve the interests of nature conservation over its 20,000 acres. Farming continues on much of the rest and the scope for further reclamation—or afforestation—is now somewhat limited, but some vital sites such as the rest of Lakenheath Warren and the heaths near the Elveden monument remain vulnerable, and there is a continuing threat of further gravel workings in the Lark valley. Some sites at Lackford where gravel has been taken out and large lakes left are being in-

Thetford Church and Thomas Paine

Helmingham Hall

Anglesey Abbey

Snape Maltings—Music School, Concert Hall and old maltings

Helmingham Estate Cottages

Lode Mill, Cambridgeshire

A.B.M. Maltings and B.S.C. Sugar Factory, Bury St Edmunds

Gough's Maltings, Bury St Edmunds

Snape Maltings—roadside buildings

corporated into a large country park. This promises to be a well-planned, unobtrusive and very attractive park with lakes for fishing and boating, wildfowl reserves, and a car park and picnic site on a restored rubbish tip (which itself obliterated a disused sewage works) next to the reconstruction of timber and thatch huts on the site of an Anglo-Saxon settlement. All this is very close to Rampart Field, a small heathland area used by the public for some years and showing signs of wear and tear to the extent that cars have to be restricted to certain areas in rotation to avoid complete erosion of the turf on the dry, sandy soil.

From Lackford, the ford over the Lark, the Icknield Way goes north-east through the four-mile length of the King's Forest. At the far end a small monument commemorates the planting of the Forest—

> This Stone commemorates
> the Silver Jubilee of
> King George V
> The Forestry Commission
> began in 1935 to afforest
> The King's Forest
> and to plant with beeches
> Queen Mary's Avenue
> which follows the course of
> The Icknield Way

These forests have been with us long enough to be accepted and enjoyed as part of the natural scene, but the real spirit of the old Breckland, in spite of its inhospitality in storm and winter, has a more subtle and lasting appeal, which can, I think, be seen and felt at its best in the Lark valley below Lackford, with the heather and pines of Cavenham Heath and Icklingham Plains on either side of the rough water meadows with their willows and great, gnarled black poplars. The endless acres of the forest and the breck are perhaps not to everyone's taste, but as Olive Cook wrote in 1956, "Breckland begins to exercise an irresistible fascination. Like the fens of Cambridgeshire, which have no facile, obvious attractions, which have indeed a reputation for uncouthness, it richly rewards the effort to know and understand its strangeness."

11

Mansions and Maltings

IN travelling round the East Anglian coast and
countryside, I have concentrated mainly on the
landscape and its changing characteristics, and
have only briefly and incidentally described some of the typical
buildings of the region. There are many other books, covering smaller
areas—counties, towns and villages—and architectural histories, that
give details of most of the thousands of notable buildings, large and
small. For the most part I leave them to the specialist writer and
reader, but I felt that I could not conclude this book satisfactorily
without describing a small selection of mansions and maltings, important and interesting as such, but of considerable significance in
other ways. The mansions have contributed not only their architectural splendours, but their landscaped parks, and on large estates,
their farms, churches and cottages, and their profound influence on the
life and work of country people. The larger maltings have been
uniquely impressive in town and country, for their size and functional
design, and for the part they have played in the agricultural economy
of a barley growing region.

Mansions and maltings alike have declined in numbers. Some very
fine examples of both have disappeared, and a few are in a sad state of
dilapidation and uncertainty. I have restricted my descriptions to two
or three of each, but I have tried to place them in the wider context
of history and landscape, and have inevitably referred in brief to a
few other relevant examples.

Many of the finest brick mansions in England are in East Anglia,
especially in Norfolk and Suffolk. The fifteenth century produced the
splendid and well-known Norfolk examples at East Barsham Manor,
of ornate, moulded brickwork, and Oxburgh Hall with its moat and

magnificent gatehouse. The sixteenth century saw the building of Melford Hall in Suffolk, where, from the large village green, the gables, and turrets with ogee tops, can be seen above the high park wall. Blickling Hall, like Oxburgh and Melford, is now in the hands of the National Trust, and is a gem of the early seventeenth century, surpassing in beauty (I think) its architect's larger creation in similar style at Hatfield in Hertfordshire. There are many smaller, less well-known mansions, especially of the sixteenth and seventeenth centuries, but few more beautiful than Hemingstone Hall and Erwarton Hall, both within a few miles of Ipswich. Hemingstone, backed by wooded slopes, faces south over a little valley, and positively glows in the summer sunshine. Erwarton, in a quiet corner away from the main road to Shotley, is a modest Elizabethan house, with a very unusual gatehouse (which is not a house, but serves as an ornamental entrance from the road into the drive), 'tunnel-vaulted', and with nine pinnacles reflecting the chimneys of the Hall.

For a more detailed description, I have chosen a much larger house, also within ten miles of Ipswich. Helmingham Hall, successor to an earlier house, was built in the late fifteenth century, and enlarged considerably in the eighteenth and early nineteenth centuries. Its extended history is not readily apparent when we see it from the outer side of the wide moat that completely surrounds it and is crossed by two picturesque, cast-iron, brick-pinnacled bridges with short, working drawbridges between them and the house. The walls, crow-stepped gables, ornamental chimneys and pinnacles, are of a warm red brick, and the tiles are similar in colour, admirably setting off the beauty of the white-painted stone mullioned windows. The four sides are different in detail, but the overall effect is, as Pevsner says, "remarkably unified". It is also remarkably beautiful, whether seen closely, or looking from the churchyard in the south-east corner of the medieval deer park that surrounds the Hall. The origin of the park explains the fact that it is not formally landscaped, except for two avenues, one leading from the twin lodge houses to the front of the Hall, and one running half a mile west from the Hall to an eighteenth-century brick obelisk on a low, artificial mound. What we notice mainly in the park are the huge, scattered oaks, some of them now stag-headed, up to nearly thirty feet in girth, grotesque giants older than the oldest part of the house; and the belt of large trees, mainly oak and ash, interspersed with hawthorn around the boundary ditch. A tiny stream in a narrow, eroded gully lined with oak and ash, is undoubtedly the scene of Helmingham Dell, drawn and painted by John Constable when for a time he enjoyed being "quite alone amongst the oaks and solitude of the Park". In the shade of these same parkland oaks, on a summer's day, red and fallow deer and their calves graze, while the stags roam the park in groups, the red deer looking particularly impressive with their splendid antlers. Canada geese swim on the large fishponds near the church, and other ornamental wildfowl on smaller ponds near the Hall. There are beautiful gardens, enclosed by tall brick walls, with statues of eagles and the heads of winged horses on the pillars.

In recent years the gardens have been open to the public on Sunday afternoons in the summer, but the Hall is not open. It is in fact still occupied by Lord Tollemache whose family has been associated with Suffolk since the twelfth century and with Helmingham since the fifteenth. The estate grew over the centuries, by acquisition of land mainly in the neighbouring parishes of Ashbocking, Framsden, Pettaugh and Gosbeck, to the present total of 5700 acres. Apart from the park, the estate consists of seventeen farms let to tenant farmers; 1400 acres are 'in hand' and farmed by Lord Tollemache. While only about 120 acres of woodland remain of the original boulder-clay forests, there has not been the wholesale clearance of hedges seen in some areas bordering the estate, and there are very few fields over 30 acres. Even where hedges have been removed, the hedgerow trees, usually oaks, have been kept, and the lanes are bordered by trees and thick high hawthorn hedges. Much of the estate has a well wooded appearance, helped by the parkland 'core', and it is fortunate that oak, ash and thorn predominate rather than elm.

The farmhouses are mostly quite large and varied, several having pink- or cream-colour-washed walls, and red pantiles or plain tiles. Old Hall Farm, one of the largest and perhaps the most attractive, has a cream-washed front, with crow-stepped gables on the front porch and on the end walls. Valley Farm is of red brick, its gables bearing simple pointed brick finials, and its roof covered with plain tiles. Framsden Hall, the grandest of the estate farmhouses, has been the family dower house since its acquisition in 1520. It is pink-washed, with barge-boarded gables and dormers, but it stands discreetly behind the magnificent 200-foot long, timber-framed barn which has red brick infilling between the exposed timbers; the barn has been re-roofed with concrete pantiles, but they are appropriate in colour and profile. Throughout the estate, the farm buildings are mostly of local, traditional materials, red brick, pantiles and black weather-boarding; here and there are modern asbestos-clad buildings but they are mostly sited inconspicuously.

While the farmhouses and buildings are varied, they are seen to be part of a large estate, but an even more impressive sense of unity is provided by the farm cottages. There are well over a hundred of them, in small groups in each parish, and while they have a pleasing informal variety in design, they have common features, especially their red brick walls, steep pantiled roofs and wavy barge-boarded gables and dormers. Ninety-one of these cottages were built and fifty-two old cottages rebuilt by Lord (John) Tollemache between 1852 and 1881. They were well spaced out, usually in pairs, but there are a few blocks of three. Each cottage had a half-acre allotment on which the tenant could grow corn and vegetables and keep pigs. No doubt the bricks were made on the estate near North Park Farm, where there is no trace of the brickworks except that a couple of small cultivated fields are lower than the original ground level.

The school and school house, just within the Helmingham parish boundary, were built in 1853, in the estate style, with red brick and pantiles and wavy barge-boards; the family coat of arms is set in the wall of the south gable. Just across the valley, in Framsden, is the largest single group of cottages—seven pairs.

A few of the allotments are still cultivated by tenants in Framsden, but most of them here and in other parishes are now cultivated with adjoining arable fields. This is, of course, a sign of changing times, and inevitably some of the cottages are now occupied by retired estate workers and other people; only about sixty still house present estate employees. But the influence, social and visual, of the history and continued existence of the large estate, still gives the group of parishes an interesting unity that is, however, very different from the formal and compact estate villages of, for example, Houghton in Norfolk, Milton Abbas in Dorset and Harewood in Yorkshire.

The estate workshop at Helmingham continues in use. The smithy just across the road is, alas, disused but bears a little board with the name of 'J. C. Knights, R.S.S., Shoeing and General Smith', and still contains the bellows and many of the old tools and other relics of the trade.

Much of the history of farming in the nineteenth century on the Helmingham Estate is recounted by George Ewart Evans in *The Farm and the Village*. He describes in detail farming with hand tools and primitive horse-drawn implements, and the lives of the farm workers who lived in the cottages and cultivated their allotments; and of the schoolmaster whose job was made more difficult by the fairly frequent absence of many children when their help was required in the fields.

While it seems that the Tollemaches had a commendable regard for the welfare of their tenants and workers, it is interesting to reflect on their contrasting lives. There is a similar contrast between the churches of the two main estate parishes. At Helmingham, the church stands in a beautiful setting of tall trees in the corner of the Park, with views to the moated Hall a quarter of a mile away. It is a fine Perpendicular church, of stone and cut black flints, with flint flushwork in the tower and porch, and was extensively restored in Victorian times.

Inside, much can be learned of the Tollemache family, as their elaborate monuments fill most of the wall spaces between the windows. The finest, dated 1615, commemorates four successive Lionels whose statues occupy arched niches and are elaborately and beautifully painted and gilded. Much of the remaining space on the white walls and arches is taken up with biblical texts and admonitions painted in blue, red and black, a feature which, I think, detracts from the beauty of the church and must surely have distracted the congregation.

Framsden church stands at the end of a lane leading from the Otley road, past a group of estate cottages. It too is secluded, but its setting, its exterior and interior, are humbler than those of Helmingham. The walls inside the nave under the hammer-beam roof are plain, and the only texts seen by the congregation are "If ye love me keep my commandments" on the chancel arch, and "Watch and Pray" over the door as they leave the church.

About four miles north-east of Cambridge, stands Anglesey Abbey. Like Helmingham Hall, it has a long history, but its past and present are totally different from those of the red-brick, moated mansion on the boulder-clay of East Suffolk. I will cover the first 800 years of the life of Anglesey quite briefly, as the present character and appearance of the house and grounds are largely the work of the man who bought them in 1926 and bequeathed them to the National Trust in 1966.

In 1135, an Augustinian Priory was founded here, on flat ground on the edge of the Fens, near the head of a Roman canal—Bottisham Lode—one of several connecting the string of villages north-east of Cambridge with the River Cam. The Priory, with substantial re-building in 1236, consisted of the canons' living quarters, surviving as the oldest part of the present house; and a large cruciform church and cloisters to the south and west, most of which were demolished after the dissolution of the monasteries in the 1500s. About 1600, the Chapter House, with the former monks' parlour and dormitory, were converted into a domestic dwelling.

One of the first occupants was Thomas Hobson, a Cambridge carrier, whose consistent refusal to let out his horses except in their proper turn, originated the phrase 'Hobson's choice'. Anglesey Abbey, as it came to be called, then had a succession of owners, including Sir George Downing from whose estate Downing College, Cambridge, was founded in 1800, and the Rev. John Hailstone and his son Edward who wrote a history of the priory and the parish of Bottisham.

Until the nineteenth century, none of the ecclesiastical or secular owners appears to have done much to improve the setting of the priory or the house on its low, wet, open site. By 1900 there were narrow tree belts along the western, and part of the southern, boundaries, and some trees around the house, but the present seclusion and beauty were achieved during the forty years of the last private owner, Huttleston Broughton, better known as Lord Fairhaven, the title he acquired in 1929, when his father died. Huttleston and his brother Henry, are reputed to have bought Anglesey because it was conveniently near Newmarket and Bury St Edmunds where they owned the Barton Stud, and because it was 'good partridge country'. Although Lord Fairhaven maintained his sporting interests throughout his life, he devoted much of his time and considerable wealth to building up a truly remarkable and unusual collection of pictures and other works of art, and to the rare achievement in this century, of creating an extremely beautiful landscaped park about 100 acres in extent.

The neglected appearance of the house before Lord Fairhaven renovated it, altered the interior and built extensions, was no doubt partly due to the fact that the walls were built of 'clunch', hard chalk from Burwell quarries, but much softer than the Northampton and French stones used for the Cambridge colleges and the fenland churches. The south front, five bays in width, was, and is, seventeenth-century in appearance, with stone mullioned windows on the two main floors, and high dormers above. A library wing was added in 1937-8 on the west side, with a splendid mullioned bay window in the gabled end, which is discreetly set a little back and separate from the old front elevation. At the rear, a bridge from the former monks' dormitory, leads to a square, two-storeyed, stone art gallery designed by Sir Albert Richardson and built in 1955-56. Externally, this is a rather bulky, box-like building, and has not yet weathered sufficiently to disguise its newness; however it is well hidden behind the old buildings and screened by trees. It is not part of my brief to judge the merits of the alterations and additions, but some historians have criticized them for effectively destroying the traces and atmosphere of the old priory.

The interiors of both the thirteenth- and sixteenth-century parts of the Abbey are so immaculate that it is indeed difficult to believe in their antiquity, but the furnishings, pictures, tapestries and other works of art create, in the words of Robin Fedden in the National Trust guide, "a richly exotic atmosphere that it would be difficult to parallel in this country". Each visitor will study what interests him most, and in this book on East Anglia, I will confine myself, with one exception, to mentioning items particularly related to the region. The exception is an enormous collection of over 750 paintings, watercolours, drawings and prints of Windsor Castle, covering a period of 350 years; they are not all on view, but what we see is a most impressive and fascinating record.

In the living-room, formerly the Chapter House, the guide-book draws our attention to "one of Gainsborough's rare seascapes". The picture is labelled as *Mettingham Castle, Suffolk* and shows a picturesque ruin standing on a low cliff above a little seaside beach where fishermen are hauling in their net. Gainsborough must either have forgotten where the scene really was, or used extreme artistic licence, as the ruins of Mettingham Castle are over ten miles from the coast, and a mile from the River Waveney! Elsewhere in the house are several pictures of Cambridge colleges, including a large one of King's College from the Backs, painted by William Westall in the nineteenth century. Cambridge, with King's College Chapel, Trinity College and the University Library (then very new), appears also on a delightful tapestry panel of 1931. With Anglesey Abbey in the foreground, the tapestry shows a wide and fancifully arranged 'aerial panorama' stretching from St Ives across to Ely and Newmarket.

In the magnificent library, on the centre of the west wall, hangs John Constable's large oil painting showing the embarkation of George IV in the royal barge at Whitehall steps, in 1817, on his way to open the new Waterloo Bridge, the nine white arches of which stretch across the river, with the dome of St Paul's in the background. The elm wood shelves of Lord Fairhaven's new library were cut from the piles of that same bridge after its demolition in 1934. The Fairhaven collection of pictures includes two other Constables, one of Lamarsh Hall and one of Flatford, which were accepted on loan by the organizers of the bicentenary exhibition in 1976, although their authenticity as Constables had been in doubt in earlier years.

After seeing these, and the countless other treasures, it is refreshing to explore the gardens, as they are called, though they consist mostly of avenues, lawns and grassy glades in a delightful mixture of formal and 'romantic' patterns. Avenues and walks are punctuated and terminated discreetly but effectively, by urns, statues and busts, with here and there small, classical temples. East of the house is a long, lime avenue, interplanted with a variety of unusual coniferous and deciduous trees, leading north to the Quarry Pool, and the little white, vertically-boarded water-mill (restored in the late 1970s) spanning the Lode which forms the northern boundary of the Abbey grounds. A line of Lombardy poplars on the far bank, planted in 1887 to commemorate Queen Victoria's Golden Jubilee, are not now much taller than those planted east of the pool nearly fifty years later in honour of George V's Silver Jubilee. Indeed, while Lord Fairhaven's overall plans for the 'gardens' provided for a large degree of informal beauty, he made a habit of planting special features to commemorate notable anniversaries. A large stone urn on the line of the Daffodil Walk, was placed there for the 800th anniversary of the founding of the priory. In 1937, to commemorate the coronation of King George VI and Queen Elizabeth, an avenue of horse chestnuts was planted four deep in staggered rows on either side of a grassy ride over half a mile long. Forty years later this is a splendid sight, especially when the trees, now thirty to forty feet high, are in full flower. The coronation of Queen Elizabeth II was marked by the creation of the Circular Temple Lawn, now best approached by the northern branch of the chestnut avenue. From a ring of poplars one emerges on to the lawn where groups of different coloured trees form a beautiful setting for the centre-piece of the circular temple of ten Corinthian columns of Portland stone. The Queen's Silver Jubilee in 1977, was commemorated by the planting of an avenue of over one hundred hornbeams, under-planted with bluebells, to replace the Daffodil Walk's elms and daffodils, both lost by disease in recent years. Beside this new avenue is a ditch reminding us of the pattern of drainage ditches and narrow fish ponds which once surrounded the priory on the west, south and east. They can still be traced as long hollows in the green lawns, especially in the open south glade in front of the Abbey, and are normally dry; but after heavy rains they are again filled with water because of the high natural water table, and some of the paths become temporarily impassable as in the Winter Dell.

The National Trust in 1966 inherited not only the responsibility of maintaining the Abbey and its art treasures, but the continuous task of preserving and enhancing the beauty of the grounds. Most of the trees which Lord Fairhaven planted have many years to go before they will reach maturity, but a large area of elms south-east of the Abbey were dead or dying in Jubilee Year and will have to be felled and replaced with other trees. The Trust has planted many new trees elsewhere in the grounds and can be relied upon to follow a con-tinuous programme of maintenance and new planting, to perpetuate this remarkable and beautiful oasis between the flat, bleak fenland to the north, and the wide, open fields of the chalky slopes to the south.

We move on from mansions to maltings, and find ourselves on high ground on the north-eastern edge of Bury St Edmunds, within sight of the tree belts and rectangular paddocks of the Barton Stud. The industrial estate beside the railway is dominated by a malt factory, which was the largest of its kind when built in the 1960s. There are two main buildings, end to end, but so dissimilar that one could be forgiven for thinking there were two separate factories. The taller building, rising to over 100 feet, is rectangular and flat-roofed, with a higher tower at the east end where small side windows indicate the existence of twelve floors. This end has a façade of windows rising to the tenth floor, above which are the bold letters, A.B.M., the initials of Associated British Maltsters. The long sides have windows on the ground and top floors only, and are 'saw-edged' in plan, evidence that the building is a massive grain store divided internally into 138 hexagonal silos each 100 feet deep. This is a splendid example of functional architecture in reinforced concrete, and well deserved the award given by West Suffolk County Council. In contrast, the other, lower building—the malt factory—is disappointing in appearance. Above its low, yellow brick walls it has a huge pitched, asbestos-covered roof, with small, square metal cowls that do not bear comparison with the picturesque slate-roofed cowls of old maltings.

Nevertheless, the whole complex is most impressive for its sheer size, and extremely interesting as an example of the almost complete automation of the centuries-old processes of malting barley. This has always been an important industry in a region where the climate and soils are ideal for the growing of corn. A.B.M. chose the site at Bury St Edmunds for its central position in a barley-growing area and for its good rail and road connections with other parts of Britain and the East Anglian ports. Most of the barley arrives by road from local farms, but in the occasional years when the East Anglian crop is insufficient, barley is brought, mainly by rail, from Yorkshire and Scotland, and sometimes it is imported from Australia. As the barley grown in the region can be stored in farm silos until needed, the malting season for the factory now runs from harvest time until the following May, at least twice as long as in the old maltings which operated from harvest time until mid-winter.

Here at Bury, the grain arrives in huge lorries from which small samples are taken and examined by experienced eyes, and chemically in the laboratory. On acceptance, the grain is tipped into ground-level grills and is cleaned and dried mechanically in the tower at the east end of the silo block. Conveyor belts then take the grain along the ground floor, up inside the west end, and back along the top floor where it is fed through small steel trap-doors into the numbered silos below. As and when required it is released through hoppers at the bottom of the silos and passes along conveyor belts to the 'steep tanks' in the upper part of the other building. In these circular, hopper-bottomed tanks, twenty-four in number, the barley is soaked, or 'steeped', in water until it is ready to start germinating.

From the 'catwalks' below the ridge of the roof, we look down to the long, horizontal cylindrical germinating drums, which are fed by gravity from the steep tanks. Inside each drum the germinating grain lies on a perforated deck, and the temperature and humidity are automatically controlled. Occasional rotation of the drums prevents 'matting' of the growing roots. All these vital processes are in essence the same as those that were controlled and executed by human skill, with simple hand rakes and shovels, in the old traditional maltings.

When germination has reached the necessary stage, the grain is discharged from the drums and conveyed to the brick-lined kilns where the growth is stopped by heating and drying. As with all the other processes in this huge factory, the kilns are fully automated; since the factory was opened the oil-fired burners have been converted to use North Sea gas.

At each stage, samples are tested in the laboratory, and the finished product, looking virtually the same as when it arrived, is stored in the silo block, until it is ready for despatch by road and rail to brewers and distillers all over Britain and in many countries overseas. The whole establishment is controlled by a very small number of men, a few of whom worked in earlier years in local 'floor' maltings where human skill and experience were much more personal and intimate factors. As in other industries, it is interesting to study the contrasts between the processes, buildings and 'atmosphere' of new and old. We tend to be overawed by the complications of modern technology, but to the layman a factory like the one I have tried to describe, is very impressive in its size and orderliness, and is not without the subjective pleasures of sight, sound and smell. Unless we have had personal experience of old factories and methods, we romanticize what has disappeared, and forget that, for example in earlier maltings, nearly everything was done by sheer, hard, manual effort in what must have been very trying extremes of dust and dampness, heat and cold, dependent on the particular work in hand.

At Bury St Edmunds, there was, for many years until the early 1970s, a link between old and new malting methods, in that a local firm, Robert Boby's, manufactured machinery and equipment for maltings including the modern A.B.M. factory.

From the 100-foot high, flat roof of the silo block, we look down on the other factories and note the predominance of agricultural industries involved with farm machinery, animal foods, meat products, agricultural chemicals and fertilizers. Just across the railway is the sugar factory, one of the earliest in Britain, but now gradually losing its old buildings of the 1920s, as a major modernization scheme proceeds in the shadow of the massive cylindrical silos.

Looking west over the lower pitched roof of the malt factory, our eyes are drawn to the twin Jacobean-style brick towers at the east end of the railway station, which itself is worthy of closer inspection. A little nearer to our elevated viewpoint stand Taylor's red-brick maltings in a sad state of dereliction, just below the railway embankment. On the other side of the station, we see the higher roofs and cowls of Gough's Maltings which still operate by traditional methods, but with the modern advantages of a laboratory, mechanical grain handling, and automatic temperature controls.

The two main buildings, narrowly separated by a disused rail siding, were built in the 1890s. They are of red brick with white brick bands and 'trimmings', and red painted, circular wall plates bearing the name R. Boby, Bury St Edmunds. The small windows are barred and shuttered, and the roofs of slate are capped by square-section tapering cowls above the kiln floors. To one side are large asbestos-clad buildings added in the mid-twentieth century, for grain storage and drying. The interior of even these newer buildings is quite different from the concrete plainness of the A.B.M. silo block. Steep wooden steps and 'catwalks' take one up and along the narrow spaces between the cylindrical and square silos, from which grain is conveyed mechanically to the old granary building. At the top, just under the pitched roof, a barley 'dresser' with a vibrating screen, sifts out the chaff, dust, and any grain too small for malting. Small, square holes in the wooden floor lead into wooden chutes down which the barley passes to 'steeps' in the lower part of each of the two old buildings.

In the steep tanks, the grain is sprayed with water from above and aerated from below. When it is ready for germination, after about three days, it is transferred to the germination floors where it is spread to a depth of about six inches between the cast-iron pillars that support the low ceilings. Here we see and feel something of the atmosphere of old maltings, where in spite of mechanical aids, the process is still dependent on human skills. Men still move about in the dim light, and turn the grain on the germinating floors, to regulate aeration and temperature, and to prevent matting of the roots, but instead of using the wooden shovel and rake, they have power-assisted shovels and turners (the latter are similar to electric lawn-mowers). The small windows in the side walls are opened or closed to assist in the control of temperature, but there are also cold air ducts from a refrigeration plant to facilitate all-the-year-round working.

From the germination floors, the grain is transferred by elevators and conveyors to the kilns where it is spread on the floors. One kiln has the original floor of 'pot-tiles' of thick clay perforated with circular patterns of tiny holes; the other kiln has a modern, wedge-wire floor. The kilns are heated from below by gas burners which superseded the coal-burning 'ovens' whose black-painted, cast-iron fire doors, bearing Boby's name, can still be seen. On the kiln floor, the grain is turned by the 'paddles' of a mechanical turner running on rails along the side walls. The heat rises into the tall, tapering space above and is expelled by electric fans through the top cowls which are the distinctive feature of the outside of all old maltings. When the 'kilning' process is complete, the floors are cleared by men using power shovels, and the malt, as it now is, is 'screened' to remove the roots.

It then goes into store for eventual despatch, either in bulk or in sacks, to breweries all over Britain.

Although Gough's Maltings at Bury are not among the most handsome of such buildings, their continued use preserves them as a familiar feature in the local scene. All over East Anglia, town and village maltings have become redundant through the change-over to a few large modern malt factories, and many of the fine old, red brick buildings have been demolished. Others, notably at Ipswich and Manningtree, are doomed, while negotiations continue at Lowestoft and elsewhere to save at least parts of splendid buildings for which it is well-nigh impossible to find alternative uses. In a few outstanding cases it has proved possible to save old maltings, a very gratifying exercise for all concerned as the results not only provide buildings for public use and enjoyment but preserve a valuable part of our architectural heritage.

At Beccles, riverside maltings, close to the yacht station, were converted into flats, with boat moorings, and a public house and restaurant. The work was designed by Norwich architects, Feilden and Mawson, and resulted in very attractive and useful buildings at a point frequented by many people cruising on the Broadland rivers.

Ely Maltings stand by the River Ouse, which is also used by motor cruisers, and have been converted into a public hall. Here is a fine, massive and simple building, contrasting with the small-scale complexity of Beccles. Just a century after being built in 1868, the maltings became redundant, but the brewers were prepared to sell the building for a nominal sum to the local council who had been considering for some time the need for a new hall to replace the Corn Exchange, demolished a few years earlier. After a feasibility study by Arup Associates, the council appointed a local firm of architects, D. A. Adams, to design and supervise the work. The internal floors were removed to create a large concert hall, retaining the massive roof timbers of Baltic pine, and the three rows of small windows in the sand-blasted, mixed brickwork of the side walls. The end facing the river was adapted to provide a foyer on the ground floor and a conference room upstairs, with new, larger windows looking over the riverside walk. The stage, green room and changing rooms are at the opposite end under the pyramidal roof of what was the kiln. Seen from the quayside, the whole building is most impressive in its overall size and simplicity, but the detail is worthy of examination. The brickwork is greyish-red, with red and white bands and window surrounds. The narrow barge boards have a wavy profile, and the row of small dormers relieve the plainness of the large expanse of slated roof. The steep, slated roof of the kiln at the west end is capped by a small ornamental cowl.

The erection of the maltings in 1868 is recorded in the small stone tablet on the east gable end, while the generosity of the brewers and the architectural merit of the conversion are acknowledged on plaques in the foyer. Here also is a case containing a wooden malting shovel, and pictures of the interior of one of the old 'floors' with its low ceiling supported, as at Bury, by cast-iron pillars.

The few maltings that have been successfully converted to other uses, as at Beccles and Ely, were in the national limelight briefly when they received architectural awards and commendations, and then settled down quietly as local features serving local needs. Only Snape became and remained nationally and internationally famous.

Snape maltings were built on the south bank of the tidal River Alde immediately downstream of the lowest bridge. The bricks were made at the Snape brickworks about half a mile to the north. On land adjoining Laurel Cottage, a white-brick, Victorian house, we can still see old ponds and clay pits and two low red brick pantiled buildings which were part of the works. Dated tablets on the maltings indicate the progressive extensions in the second half of the nineteenth century. The keystone of the arch of one of the finest roadside buildings bears the date 1859 and the initials of Newson Garrett, the founder of the maltings, and incidentally father of the Aldeburgh family that included Elizabeth Garrett Anderson, the first woman doctor. Another enterprising branch of the Garretts, at Leiston, built up from small beginnings one of the country's largest farm machinery factories; the old factory was demolished in the 1970s but Garrett's still exist as engineers in newer buildings near the railway station.

The large group of maltings built at Snape concentrated the work, and improved the methods, of many former small village maltings in the area—an interesting fact when we remember circumstances a century later when large, automated malt factories superseded most of the remaining old maltings of the towns. The site was chosen deliberately at an existing small, tidal port from which barley and malt could be exported by sailing barges to London and the Continent. From 1859 to 1960 there was a branch railway line, 1 mile 32 chains in length, built specifically to serve the maltings. It can still be traced from its junction with the main line, across the peaty fields, to the river where four sawn-off bridge piers remain. A siding extended across the road into the maltings, where horses hauled the wagons to and from the various buildings on a network of lines in front of, through, and behind the buildings. The maltings ceased to operate as such in about 1965, but the storage of grain and processing of animal foodstuffs continued in the roadside buildings.

Soon after that date, work began on converting a building at the rear into what was to become one of Britain's finest concert halls. It was planned to serve as a main, permanent centre for the Aldeburgh Festival which was started in 1948 by Benjamin Britten, Peter Pears and others. Until 1967, the concerts and other events had been held in the Jubilee Hall and the parish church at Aldeburgh, and in other Suffolk churches as far afield as Blythburgh. The Maltings Concert Hall was opened by Her Majesty the Queen on the afternoon of Friday, 2nd June 1967. The inaugural concert was preceded by Benjamin Britten's own ceremonial arrangement of the National Anthem, and commenced with *The Building of The House* written specially for the occasion and, in his own words, reflecting "the excitement of planning and building the Maltings in a great hurry". Imogen Holst, one of the other artistic directors of the Festival, conducted her father's *St Paul's Suite*. Delius's *Summer Night on the River* evoked the peaceful beauty of Snape beside the reed beds and marshes of the Alde.

The conversion was universally praised as a superlative success, architecturally and acoustically. Before entering the hall, the Queen had said that from without it gave an admirable impression of strength, simplicity and skill. Her words unconsciously forecast those published by the Civic Trust in the 1968 list of awards for distinguished new buildings and schemes. Their assessor referred to "this masterly conversion . . . the whole building still has the robustness which is characteristic of the other buildings constituting the Maltings at Snape. The Suffolk vernacular has been wholly respected, even though new solutions have been found for new problems as, for instance, the ventilators on the roof. Where it has been appropriate to copy the past, this has been done uncompromisingly and forcefully. . . ." The conversion had been designed by Arup Associates, architects, and executed by the craftsmen of William C. Reade of Aldeburgh Ltd. The Civic Trust Award was well-deserved recognition of the imagination, skill and enthusiasm of everyone involved.

I am tempted now to describe the Maltings and their setting as I saw them on the day after the royal opening, but it is probably better to cover briefly the years following that event, and then to describe the Maltings as they are today.

After outstandingly successful Festival seasons in 1967 and 1968, the ceremonial presentation of the Civic Trust certificates and plaque was delayed by a disastrous fire which completely destroyed the interior and roof of the concert hall during the night of 7th June, a few hours after the opening concert of the 1969 Festival. With characteristic resource and determination, Benjamin Britten and his colleagues immediately arranged for the remaining events of the Festival to be held elsewhere, mostly in Blythburgh Church. The Maltings concert hall was rebuilt, with detailed improvements, within a year, and re-opened by the Queen on 5th June 1970 with a programme of *Music for a Royal Occasion*, ranging from Byrd in the sixteenth century to Britten's own *Gloriana*, which had been first produced at the Royal Opera House in 1953 as part of the Coronation celebrations. The 1970 opening was the climax of a year of tremendous effort by everyone concerned, after the awful experience of seeing the charred ruins of their first grand achievement.

Since 1970, the Aldeburgh Festival has continued as the main event, but there are concerts at other times of the year, and the Maltings are used for recording music. The new hall has proved to be as acoustically outstanding as the first, and to hear a concert there is a memorable experience. No one can fail to be impressed by the beauty of the setting and the sheer quality of the sound, whether it be harsh or sweet, loud or soft, produced by a large orchestra or a small group, or soloist. As Imogen Holst has said "there is magic in the way the walls and roof respond to the music!" There is magic, too, in the way in which people have responded to the inspiration and ideas of Benjamin Britten and his friends. Although he died in December, 1976, the Festival continues, and so do the Snape Maltings Training Orchestra, the Britten-Pears School for Advanced Musical Studies, and the Britten-Pears Library of music and books on music. The Library is accommodated in Britten's home, the Red House at Aldeburgh, but it is accessible only to scholars and research students by appointment.

It may seem strange that such a remarkable cultural centre has developed in this remote spot near the east coast, but it has been inspired by a little group of brilliant people with respect and feeling for the splendid buildings which they have saved and converted.

The entrance to the concert hall is by a plain door in the black-painted, north wall above which the steep, black roof soars to the four white-painted square ventilators. After the coldness of the entrance, we are warmed by the glowing red brick walls of the foyer and of the hall itself, in which the small side windows have been bricked up but can still be faintly seen. Above the side walls rises the unpainted timber-lined roof, supported by slender wooden struts and thin steel tie rods, in contrast with the massive roof timbers of Ely Maltings. On the tie rods hang the lights which illuminate the huge, full width stage without a proscenium arch. The rows of seats of unpainted, varnished wood with basketwork seats and backs, all in keeping with the functional beauty of the hall, rise like a huge wave towards the back of the auditorium.

In the upper part of the foyer are paintings by F. G. Cotman of Mr and Mrs Newson Garrett, and of a few of the men who worked in the maltings in Victorian times; and there are bronze heads of Benjamin Britten and Peter Pears. In the gallery on the other side of the hall are photographs of old craftsmen, and of the buildings before and after conversion.

Bob Ling, now caretaker of the concert hall, worked in the maltings before their conversion. He explained to me that the main hall had been the kiln building, evidenced by the roof cowls, and the restaurant across the east end had been the screening loft where the malt had been 'dressed' after kilning. The preceding processes of steeping and germination had taken place in the low buildings attached to the south side of the hall; the three-storey building beyond them was the granary. All these other buildings were being adapted in the late 1970s for use by the music school. The floor levels of the granary were having to be altered, and new, barrel-vaulted, red brick ceilings were being constructed. This and the neighbouring building provide practice and lecture rooms, and a lecture theatre-cum-rehearsal room capable of seating 150 people.

These further adaptations have, like the main concert hall, been designed so as to preserve the traditional character of the maltings and their incomparable setting. Any 'smartening up' of the surroundings would have detracted from the strong functional character of the buildings and their harmony with the landscape of marsh, river and distant heath, which has an austere and subtle beauty contrasting with the embowered lushness of Glyndebourne.

The concert hall and music school are hidden from the road by an almost continuous range of buildings still partly in commercial use. They are very conspicuous and varied, but impressively unified, of grey and red brick with white painted windows, external wooden steps and projecting weather-boarded granary hoists. Access to the rear is through arches, one of which took the rail siding under the gilded clock and roof-top bell cupola. Some of these roadside buildings were, in 1978, unoccupied and looking rather neglected, but proposals to convert them for houses, rural crafts and exhibitions and for art galleries will, it is hoped, result in sensitive restoration. Everything possible should be done to preserve Snape Maltings as a whole, for they are a truly wonderful group in a locality of exceptional interest and beauty, with an atmosphere and history which the work of Benjamin Britten has done so much to capture and enrich.

Epilogue

My research into the history of Snape Maltings has revealed a rich succession of events and changes in the fields of building, commerce, farming, culture and the landscape. It has also made me aware of my own blissful ignorance on the occasion of my first remembered visit. In May 1940, just before the evacuation of Dunkirk, I spent a week at Aldeburgh. The feeling that this could well be my final holiday in Suffolk, concentrated my enjoyment of the idyllic weather and the beauty of the coast and countryside. In a little dinghy borrowed from one of the Wards at Slaughden Quay, I sailed up the Alde estuary, between the woods and heaths on the north and the marshes on the south. Withies marked the narrow, winding channel between the shallow water that covered the wide mud flats as the tide rose. As I passed the little thatched church at Iken, on its low rise overlooking the river, the channel became narrower and more tortuous, until at the turn of the tide, I reached Snape Maltings beside the little, hump-backed bridge. Time and tide did not permit me to land, and I sailed back on the ebb to Aldeburgh. It had been a rare and memorable day and I had enjoyed every minute of it, soaking up the sun and the scenery, without realizing or caring that I had learned and understood very little of what was then so desperately threatened.

We must be thankful that the threat of invasion did not materialize, and that so much of East Anglia survives apparently unchanged and unspoilt. But, since 1940, Snape and the area around it have experienced many dramatic changes which remind us of what man has done to the region, and of the need for vigilance in the future if we are to prevent or mitigate further changes for the worse.

The future of the maltings (though not as such) seems assured, but the railway and the barges have disappeared, and the local brickworks, one of many that existed in East Anglia, has long been closed down. The Alde estuary and its shores are protected as part of the designated 'Area of outstanding natural beauty', and the coast has the additional status of a 'heritage coast'. But within sight of the maltings are the twin lines of huge pylons and wires carrying power from Sizewell 'A' Nuclear Generating Station which awaits the construction of Sizewell 'B' on land already cleared for the purpose. A few miles to the south, Orfordness has been cleared of the forest of masts of the short-lived radar establishment, but its buildings and earlier defence works remain; and for the future the government is still trying to decide whether its own coastal conservation policies should be sacrificed for another, much larger, nuclear power station. Between Orfordness and Woodbridge, several thousand acres of pine forests have obliterated the old, wild heaths, but now provide recreation for many people, and help to screen from view two huge military air bases.

Between Walberswick and Blythburgh, and at Westleton, Mins-mere and Havergate, large areas of heath and marsh are protected as nature reserves, and wildlife of all kinds flourishes. But at Snape, a new concrete sluice just above the bridge controls the flow of the river, and reduces the risk of tidal flooding upstream; already some of the old, peaty pastures are being cultivated. Church Common, east of Snape church, has been converted in recent years from heath to arable, up to the Priory cross-roads where only one of an ancient group of barrows remains as a small mound overgrown with gorse. It was here that the remains of a Saxon ship burial in the seventh century were unearthed in 1862, soon after Newson Garrett started to build the maltings down by the river.

In these final notes, by concentrating on what has happened in one small area in the last forty years, I have tried to show how much the speed and magnitude of change have increased in recent times. Some further changes, especially those connected with international defence, are probably beyond our control, but there is now a much greater awareness of what is happening. Official and voluntary bodies con-cerned with conservation are now much better informed and organized, and try to insist on undesirable developments by government agencies or others being fully investigated before final decisions are made. In general there has been an encouraging trend towards better under-standing and co-operation between bodies whose interests inevitably conflict to some degree.

So far, even the demands of NATO and continental trade, and the ravages of modern farming and Dutch elm disease, have left much of the peace and beauty of East Anglia unspoilt; indeed increased trade and prosperity have helped the survival and renovation of our historic market towns and villages. We have learnt much by the recent work of our archaeologists, and many large and vital areas for wild life have been taken over by organizations concerned with nature conservation. Planning authorities, local and national, have played an effective part in preventing many horrors, protecting the best of town and country, and providing facilities to help us to enjoy the countryside. Much good work has been done, but we cannot expect things to stand still, least of all in East Anglia at the end of the twentieth century. We can all play some part in influencing decisions which affect our environment and personal interests, whether we want to live in pleasant surroundings, to study birds at Blakeney and the Ouse Washes, or merely to sail blissfully up and down the Alde on a summer day.

Bibliography

General

The Landscape of Towns, Michael Aston and James Bond (Dent, 1976)
A Land, Jacquetta Hawkes (Penguin, 1959)
Local History in England, W. G. Hoskins (Longman, 1959)
Fieldwork in Local History, W. G. Hoskins (Faber, 1967)
The Sea Coast, J. A. Steers (Collins, 1969)
Annual Reports of the Forestry Commission, Nature Conservancy and
Countryside Commission

East Anglia
East Anglia, R. Rainbird Clarke (Thames and Hudson, 1960)
East Anglian Forests, Forestry Commission (H.M.S.O., 1972)
Nature in East Anglia, S. A. Manning (World's Work, 1976)
Constable—Paintings, Watercolours and Drawings, Leslie Parris, Ian
Fleming-Williams and Conal Shields (The Tate Gallery, 1976)
Annual Reports of the Great Ouse River Authority

Cambridgeshire
Cambridgeshire, E. A. R. Ennion (Hale, 1951)
Portrait of Cambridgeshire, S. A. Manning (Hale, 1978)
Fenland River, Rodney Tibbs (Terence Dalton, 1969)
The Cambridgeshire Landscape, Christopher Taylor (Hodder and
Stoughton, 1973)
The Cambridge Region, ed. J. A. Steers (British Association, 1965)
The Buildings of England—Cambridgeshire, Nikolaus Pevsner (Penguin,
1954)

The Great Ouse, Dorothy Summers (David & Charles, 1973)

Essex
The Buildings of England—Essex, Nikolaus Pevsner (Penguin, 1954)
Essex—A Shell Guide, Norman Scarfe (Faber, 1968)

Norfolk
In Breckland Wilds, W. G. Clarke (Scott, 1925)
The Buildings of England—North-East Norfolk and Norwich, Nikolaus
    Pevsner (Penguin, 1962)
The Buildings of England—North-West and South Norfolk, Nikolaus
    Pevsner (Penguin, 1962)
Norfolk—A Shell Guide, W. Harrod and C. L. S. Linnell (Faber, 1957)
Report on Broadland, Nature Conservancy, 1965
The Broads, E. A. Ellis (Collins, 1965)
Nature in Norfolk, Norfolk Naturalists' Trust (Jarrold, 1976)
Breckland, Olive Cook (Hale, 1956)
Portrait of Norfolk, David Yaxley (Hale, 1977)

Suffolk
The Suffolk Landscape, Norman Scarfe (Hodder & Stoughton, 1972)
The Buildings of England—Suffolk, Nikolaus Pevsner (Penguin, 1961)
Suffolk—A Shell Guide, Norman Scarfe (Faber, 1960)
Agricultural Survey of Suffolk, P. J. O. Trist (Royal Agricultural Society
    of England, 1972)
Suffolk Scene, Julian Tennyson (Blackie, 1939)
A Suffolk Garland for The Queen, ed. John Hadfield (East Suffolk
    County Council, 1961)

Index